From that flattest, muddiest, p(
To where the roaring cascades
Granite, limestone, grass and air(
You are England's mountains all.

CONTENTS

New Year's Day.

What to do with this brand new year? A germ of an idea had been planted when a friend told of his family's adventure of climbing Britain's three peaks (in three different trips) – Scafell Pike, Snowdon and, of course, Ben Nevis.

That sounded like fun, but it was only three walks (great in length, but few in number), I fancied something which would involve more walks and which we could do, as a family, over a number of months and, let's be realistic, years.

OK, so "let's walk up to the highest peak in every English county."
"It's been done."

Alright then, let's walk up to the highest peak in every English county – from the nearest pub!

"And go in the pub?"

If it's open yes.

"And have a meal?"

Well maybe, but that could get expensive.

It's agreed then, from the nearest pub to the highest summit of each of England's counties (and back) and have a drink/meal at the pub as time and finances allow.

But what constitutes a county? Good old Wikipedia lists 48 "Ceremonial Counties" showing peaks all the way from "The City of London" with High Holborn at a measly 22 metres above sea level, up to Cumbria's Majestic Scafell Pike at 978 metres.

So, 48, at an average of one per month – that makes four years. That's doable, definitely doable.

But let's start small and work our way up, after all we want to leave the best until last.

The walks were to progress up to the savage northern mountains, but first things first, let's slay the flatlands of the east.

A quick note....

The walks in this book are not in order of height (nor even in the strict order they were walked). They do, however, represent "more or less" the order in which they were done as we worked our way up.

The list of mountains at the beginning of each section does not, therefore, tally with the order in which they appear in the book. Instead these lists show the highest to the lowest in each region.

Walks were pre-researched by internet searching, OS maps and seeing what had been done before.

In "Climb Every Mountain" each county walk is accompanied by a hand-drawn map. All maps are north-oriented.

These maps are rough and ready and not to scale. It is always advisable to have some other means of wayfinding with you (GPS etc.), especially on the wilder jaunts.

This, combined with the description herein (telling you about conditions "on the ground" better than any map), should help you find your way. It is also advisable to take on the tricky routes during the warm months, giving you the longest hours of light and meaning that, should you become lost, you will at least not have the bitterest cold to contend with.

LEGEND

 A Point of interest

 Woodland

Road

P Parking

 Field Boundary

 Building

 Route

 Transmitter

 Railway Line

Peak

Other paths

River/Canal

Body of Water

Chapter 1 – The Flatlands of the East

Let's start at the very beginning, a very good place indeed. The low-lying counties, and build our way up. Get those calves tightened and the cardio-vascular on the go. Come on!

For the most part this means the east, and more generally the southern half of the east. Remembering the Tees-Exe line from school, think the Humber-Thames line and throw in Nottinghamshire and plucky little Rutland as well and you have eight of the lowest ten all together over that side. By way of convenience, the East Riding of Yorkshire has been included too, with apologies to the good people in the northern half of the county formerly known as Humberside.

Mainly sands and gravels and clay, with some sandstone thrown in, and even some chalk at the top end, the land, whilst geologically diverse, is largely shaped from the last ice age, well not shaped, littered, with the gloop and wash of the retreating ice-sheet. No "U"-shaped valleys here, no sculpting of the land, just a wash of deposit left over from the retreating tide and covered over with more alluvium. The Essex and Cambridgeshire peaks are on chalky bed-rock, although the Lowestoft Formation covers them with outwash sands and gravels, making the chalkiness almost academic. In this entire region (with the possible exception of East Riding), the landscape is determined by what the ice dumped there rather than what it did *to* it.

This region is 85 miles at its widest and twice as long at its maximum, with five North Sea counties and four in-landers taking up the slack.

It also incorporates the City County of London at a measly 22 metres above sea level, all the way up to East Riding's Bishop Wilton Wold at 246 metres:

East Riding	**246m**
Nottinghamshire	**205m**
Rutland	**197m**
Lincolnshire	**168m**
Essex	**147m**
Cambridgeshire	**146m**
Suffolk	**128m**
Norfolk	**103m**
City of London	**22m**

Suffolk

Great Wood Hill 128m (419ft)

Pub: Marquis Cornwallis The Street, Chedburgh, Bury Saint Edmunds

Suffolk IP29 4UH

Parking: Nearby Free

Walk: 3 miles

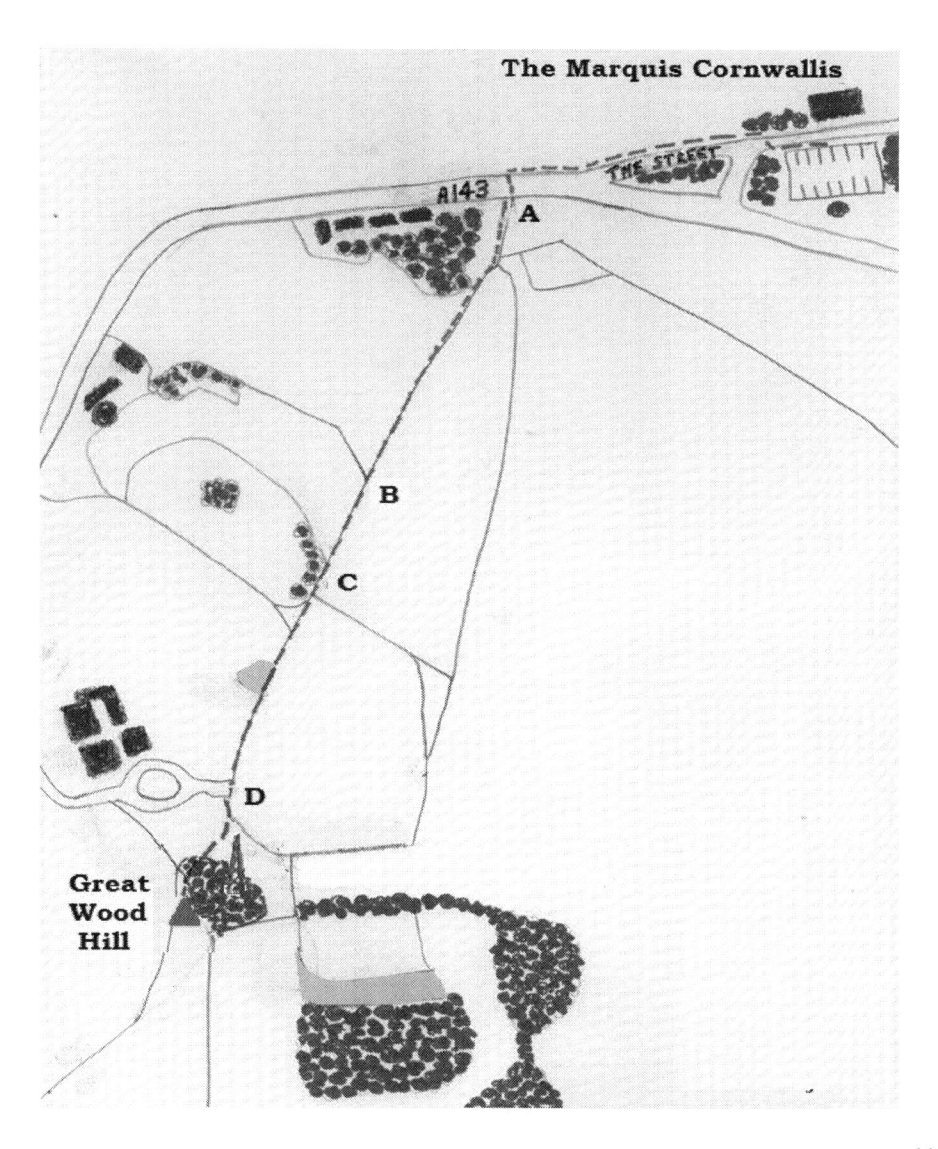

Where to start? Where indeed? The nearest to us, although in a different county is the "summit" of Suffolk, Great Wood Hill, a real titch of a "hill". Still, somebody has to be small to make somebody else look big, what would be the point of 48 Scafell Pikes?

On the positive, it's an easy in. All virtually flat and about three miles. I was always told average walking pace was three miles an hour – so that's not hard to work out.

It begins.......

What is more, the parking could not be more convenient. Just opposite the Marquis Cornwallis, to the west of the little village of Chedburgh, is a car park. Right next to, but apparently not associated with, the pub it is perfect for our purposes – close by, but with no obligation to dine or sup therein should those things not take your fancy.

Leaving the car park, you turn left down "The Street" and carry on that way for about 150 metres. You are now on to the A143 which is lightly trafficked but any cars which do pass by do so at speed – so be warned! You may wish to walk the field edge rather than the footway, but this part of the walk does not last long. Cross the road, when you see the first point of any interest (loosely speaking) which is an access with a gravelled mouth and double field gate (A).

The long path to the roof of Suffolk!

Having vaulted/found some way around the gate, you then need to proceed straight on for 50 metres on an unmade track. Now begins the longest part of your journey, three-quarters of a mile of uninterrupted concrete slab due south. Apart from a copse on the right for the beginning stretch, the aspect is very open, the next point of interest being a track coming in from the right 300 metres along (B), and the path goes on...

Ahead you will see a radio mast and the dark, but tiny, form of Great Wood Hill. Soon you will pass a tree lined lagoon (C), then another track (both right) and 250 metres on from this, a set-back area of hardstanding containing farm vehicles or equipment, or both, depending on the day and season. 150 metres more and another access from the right (D). Hereabouts, leave the path and head in the same direction you were walking, with the transmitter on your left and the "peak" on your right, just beyond the copse.

And that is pretty much that. However, there is some confusion as to exactly *where* the top is – these plateaux are most unhelpful and there is no trig point.

There are various versions ranging from "covered reservoir compound" to "a tussock just off the footpath", "on the footpath by the side of the reservoir", "somewhere near the woods" "In field just opposite entrance to transmitter compound."

However, the winner must surely be the Hill Bagger (they have their own website, by the way) who claimed, in August 2014, to have met the farmer who knew exactly where the trig point used to be as he had taken it out! The answer appears to be "On a bend in the lane, between the farm and mast, about 50 yards into a cultivated field."

Hmm, still not sure what *that* means, but the point is, surely, in the absence of a point (trig or any other physical feature) then the vicinity is enough.

Any way up, or should I say across, we're there, our first county top is bagged. Dizzy with success (rather than with altitude sickness at all of 128 metres) and faint with hunger, it's time to turn about and walk the long, concrete path to freedom. Over to your right (east) you might see glimpses of the village of Rede. Therein lies the pub of The Plough, but it was closed today. This is about the same distance as the Marquis of Cornwallis and actually the walk from there might have been a bit more rewarding with a definable incline and the woods as a backdrop. Never mind, the end is in sight.

The Marquis Cornwallis did us proud with pie, chips and pizza, standard fayre for a good old English pub and a game of pool afterwards, even if some of the locals wore sore heads from the new year celebrations and were a little, shall we say, sweary. The drive home was one of fulfilment, if anti-climax. It might be worth coming back here again though, and taking the path from Rede. 47 hills to go.

Next time - Norfolk.

Norfolk

Beacon Hill 103m (346ft)

Pub: The Roman Camp Inn, Holt Road, Aylmerton, Norfolk NR11 8QD 01263 83829

Parking: At pub – free if eating, £10 if not

Walk: 1 mile

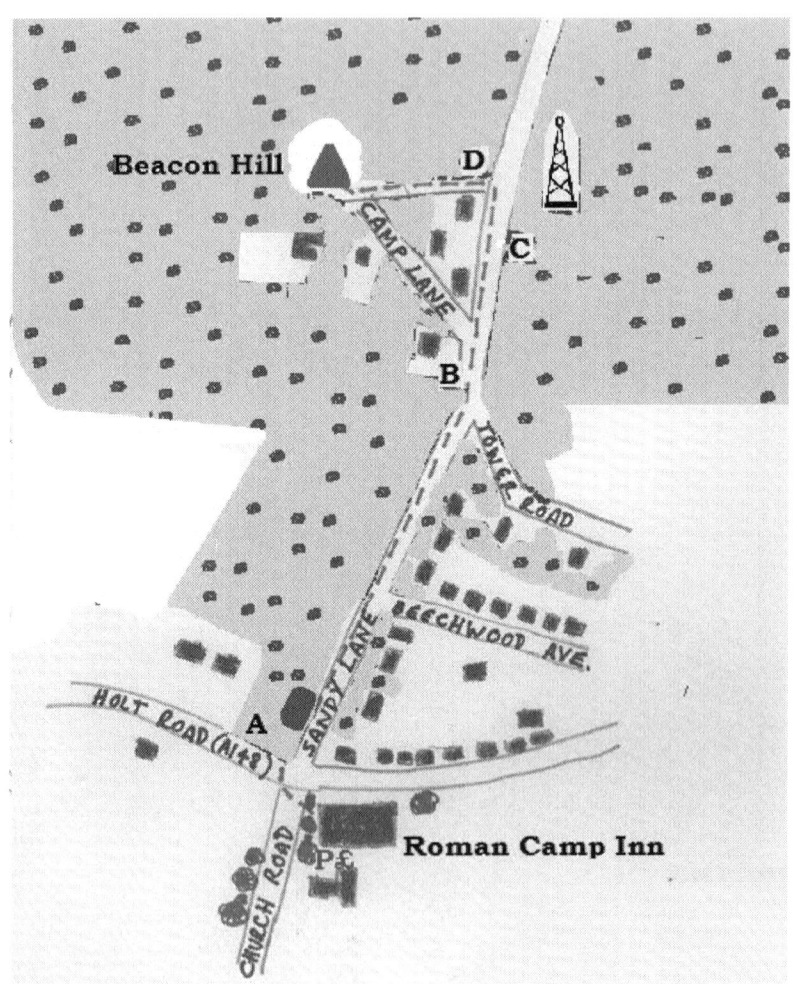

After the disappointment of Suffolk, its neighbouring county offers up a truly splendid and, yes, dead easy walk. Easier still because the air is a little less thin being 25 metres lower than

Great Wood Hill (!) and all the fresher for being so close to the sea.

Unlike many establishments carrying that name, the Roman Camp Inn is literally that (well, not a Roman Camp, but an Inn) and you can overnight if the mood takes you – don't do it on the basis of just this walk though, it really is too short for that.

You may park at the Inn, but you will have to pay £10 (at the time of writing), free if you are dining there. The Inn provides an excellent full lunch and dinner menu and, if you're early as we were, also coffee and muffins and we did eat our fill.

Slightly bloated and leaving the pub and Church Road behind you, cross the A148 Holt Road and then head down the leafy Sandy Lane (A) which is almost opposite the sign for the pub. It will be this little road which takes you most of the way there. There is a little bit of pavement to start with, but it's mainly verge and a lot of that isn't really usable as it covered in flowers - a riot of daffodils when we visited, so you will at times have to share the road with the traffic. It is 30mph and relatively safe.

All along are houses, well-spaced out with lovely deep gardens, most quite tasteful, but with the usual oddment of gated, stone-lioned "get orf moi land" newcomer-ness. Pass Beechwood Avenue (on your right) and carry on along and soon (about 500 metres from the start) you will arrive at a junction where you carry on in the same direction. You will see a brown sign indicating camping and caravans and you may well have one or two of these slumbering beasts of the road go past you; for the site (theirs and yours) is near.

Behind this, to your left, is a finger sign indicating West Runton. Follow this (it's still called Sandy Lane at this point, by the way) and soon you will see a pedestrian-friendly track forking off to the left (B) – ignore this, it leads to hell and the caravan site. Instead, plod your merry way along Sandy Lane which is now more wooded. A little way on you will come to an open area where you will be further enticed by promises of caravans with a sign on the right pointing you towards "The Camping and Caravanning Club" (C) ignore this. Instead, eyes left to the Roman Camp Caravan Park "Holiday homes for sale". Next to this, more importantly, is the National Trust sign for West Runton & Beeston Regis Heath. Take this (D) a little way, it goes by the name of Calves Well Lane, and you will be at the National Trust car park and, well, you are there.

(By the way, spoiler – Roman Camp is NOT repeat NOT Roman. According to Norfolktrails, and I quote "The surrounding woodland and heathland around the camp is dotted with shallow circular iron-working pits dating from about 850 to 1150AD.")

Due to trees and various folds in the land, the peak itself falls just short of giving views of the sea, which is a little over a mile to the north and visible from close by, but is superior to its Suffolk counterpart in terms of views and also in being able to pin-point Eldorado. Here is not a trig point, but a stumpy pillar built from local cob and brick, with concrete coping and a little collection slot, next to it a stake emblazoned with a National Trust badge. And just beyond that is a flag. There is nowhere higher in the whole of the county of Norfolk, now back to the pub!

Next – the twin peaks of Cambridgeshire and Essex!

Cambridgeshire and Essex

Cambridgeshire - Great Chishill - 146 metres (480 feet)

Essex - Chrishall Common – 147 metres (482 feet)

Pub – The Pheasant 24 Heydon Rd Great Chishill, Royston, Hertfordshire County SG8 8SR (note, despite the address, actually in Cambridgeshire) 01763 838 535

Parking – nearby, free

Walk – 5 miles

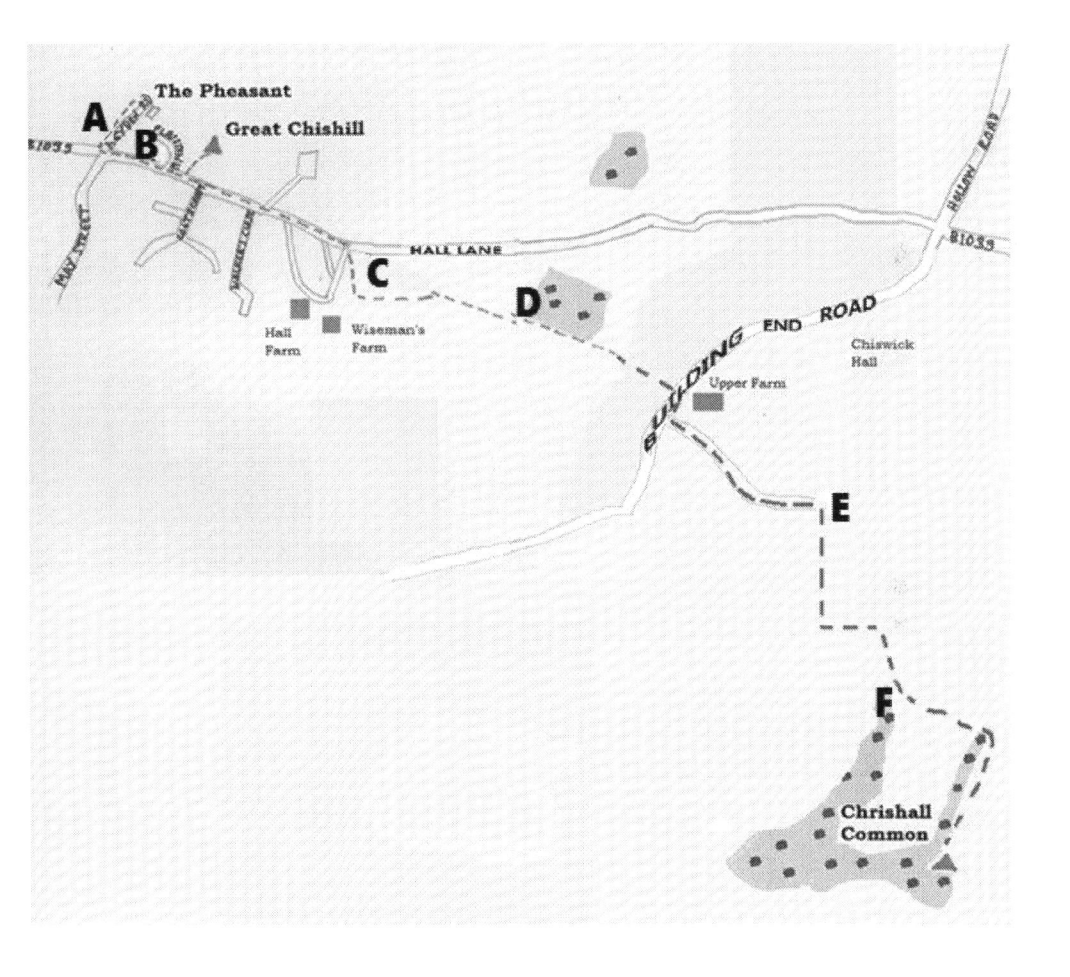

The first of the two-in-ones offers a chance to conquer the fourth and fifth lowest county tops in one fell swoop. Despite this less-than-ear-popping altitude, it combines a pleasant country walk with some pretty village streets and some undulation in these traditionally low-lying counties.

In the village of Great Chishill, With the cream rendered building of The Pheasant on your left, wend your way down Heydon Road past thatched and weather-boarded cottages and the splendid old red brick wall of Rectory Farmhouse will appear on your right. Carry on past a small park, a bus shelter and red telephone box on your left. Soon the knapped wall of Saint Swithin's Church (A), with its graveyard standing several feet above pavement level, can be seen on the right. This is the beginning of some quite lovely views over to that side. We're going left, but it's worth stepping over to the right briefly and having a look at the obelisk war memorial set in to a crescent within the flint wall, as well as taking in the view to the west, down Barley Road, past the thatched cottages and towards the green fields beyond.

That done, and only about 150 metres in to your walk, you turn back to your left and up Hall Lane, past Great Chishill's village sign and a multi-fingered post. The next bit of the walk is about 500 metres and is unspectacular, but is one of those bits that joins the good bits together.

Past the 1970s bungaloid cul-de-sac Plaistow Way ye go, then a few houses later the village peters out (on the left anyway) and you will have to use the right hand side path and, in places, highway verge, for the best part of about 250 metres. Shortly after you have passed the Great Chishill playing field (left) a beautiful white thatched cottage will appear and just beyond that a driveway (at the time we were there it was being guarded by a pair of stone lions!) Immediately next to this is a track-way off of the road (B), you need to take this.

Fifty metres or so along is a sub-station and if you follow the fence around a little way to the right, you are there or thereabouts. That's it, limited but pleasant views over to the east, across the Cambridgeshire/Essex countryside, a less than one kilometre walk and a peak bagged.

There are two main choices now. Turn back to The Pheasant and take on Essex' peak from its own nearby pub, or do a two-in-one. You are strongly advised to take the latter course, for reasons which will become clear later.

So, two peaks-in-one option it is then. Fresh from the conquest of Cambridgeshire, rejoin Hall Lane and turn left, following this for about 200 metres. Soon the road kinks left, but watch out for a footpath on the right (C). Follow this, first under tree cover, then breaking out and after about 150 metres take the path to the left, between two farmed fields, for about 500 metres towards a wood. Keep the wood (D) on your left and, soon half way along it, you will stumble in to Essex which looks, of course, no different to lovely Cambridgeshire.

350 metres after clearing the wood you will meet the ridiculously-named Building End Road. From here the point is about a mile due south and you do have choices. The best is to turn right down said strangely-named road, then first left (same name) and it sweeps around left (where it becomes Bilden End Road – seeming to be the way that word might be pronounced in these parts) to a field corner (E). This field you keep to your left as you march south for 400 metres, then turning left and east for

another 250 metres. Now turn right (south) towards a fringe of trees (F), having passed by these you come to a second, smaller, fringe and if you keep these trees to your right and walk at the edge of the small field, about 200 metres along you are at Essex's highest point. No trig, no pack-drill, just a footpath sign tells you, sort of, that you are there.

Well, there you are, you've done it. 2 ½ miles (plus the return journey, of course) for two peaks, a pretty good return.

Now for the pub. The pub, the pub indeed, oh the pub! On this day of victual disappointment, only on arriving did we realise, for some reason (and this may be to your liking, but caused difficulties for us – having two members of the party who fell in to this category) that The Pheasant refuses entry to anyone aged under 14 – no family dining here then! To be fair, they do have children's dining and play areas *outside* – however, that is weather permitting and we were there in winter. So no!

We did think up ways of locking the kids in the car with their sandwiches whilst we pondered whether we should sample the delights of the crayfish Caesar salad or confit of duck at The Plough. Of course we didn't do that.

Instead we decided to go to the pub nearest to Chrishall Common, but oh dear oh very dear.

Do NOT attempt to find a pub near to Chrishall Common, not unless you are very organised, have a lot of time on your hands and have phoned ahead and booked. We discovered that the pub that we "thought" was in Chrishall, didn't seem to be there any more (remember – phone ahead to check!). Those that were open were a fair distance away, were packed to the rafters/didn't do food – and one was run by Jamie Oliver's father, so was booked up hours ahead.

So, the two comparatively short walks, accompanied by a nice meal in one pub and a quick drink in the other did not come to fruition. Meanwhile the mood was becoming fractious through hunger. Bugger it.

In the end it was a rather unsavoury cold pie from a garage near Duxford which kept the wolves from the door.
Oh well, the sweeter taste was that the flattest of the flatlands of the east were conquered.

East Anglia had fallen, now for the lowest peak of all – the City of London.

City of London
High Holborn – 22m (72ft)

Pub: The Princess Louise, 208 High Holborn, London WC1V 7EP

(0207) 405 8816

Walk: 1/8 mile

Parking: Forget it

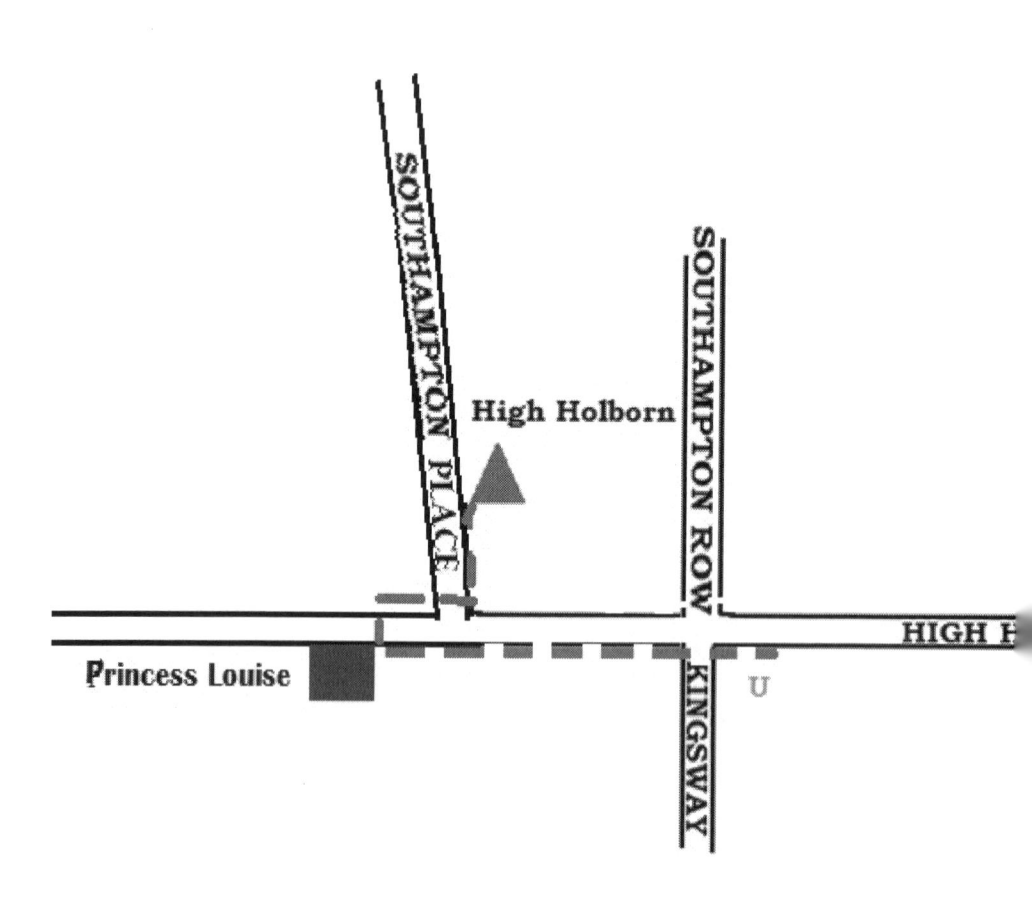

Ok, not *really* a county. However, along with Bristol it makes up the offering of "city counties" which are included amongst the ceremonial 48. The walk itself is as brief as the tiny county in which it abides.

This is as urban as it gets and is only realistically accessed by public transport. It is the only walk whose beginning is not car-bound.

Whichever way you are coming in to central London (presuming you don't live there), you need to alight at Holborn underground station (on the Central Line). It's actually the walk from here to the pub (a colossal 150 metres or so) which takes up most of the legwork.

Once above ground, cross Kingsway and the pub is then about 100 metres down on your left. You now need to cross High Holborn (there is a crossing virtually outside) and then head right and almost immediately, just past a bank, turn left up Southampton Place.

As is often the way with such unpronounced "high points" it is difficult to know where exactly "it" is, just *where* you would be at your safest should London flood. Many of the maps seem to indicate it is on or near this corner.

The "peak" itself appears to be just over the road and somewhere towards the far end of the first building (next to the cycle hire parking).
In a fair wind (or rather with favourable traffic lights) you could possibly do this pub-to-peak in less than a minute.
The walk is of course the most urban of all of the 48, you may see half a dozen trees at the far end of Southampton Place, but you

may not see the sun for the towering edifices on either side of High Holborn. All is very built, very city.

Once you have regained your breath from your mammoth journey, turn-about and make good your return to The Princess Louise. This is a real ale and pub grub kind of a place and has a beautifully preserved late-Victorian interior. If you crane your neck from within it, you *might* just be able to espy the recently conquered point. A pint of Guinness here and all was set fair for the evening's entertainment – Willy Wonka's Chocolate Factory.

They won't all come this easy!

Next – northwards and on to little Rutland.

Rutland

Cold Overton Hill – 197m (646ft)

Pub: The Old Plough, 2 Church Street, Braunston-in-Rutland LE15 8QT

(01572) 722714

Parking: Nearby, free

Walk: 3 miles

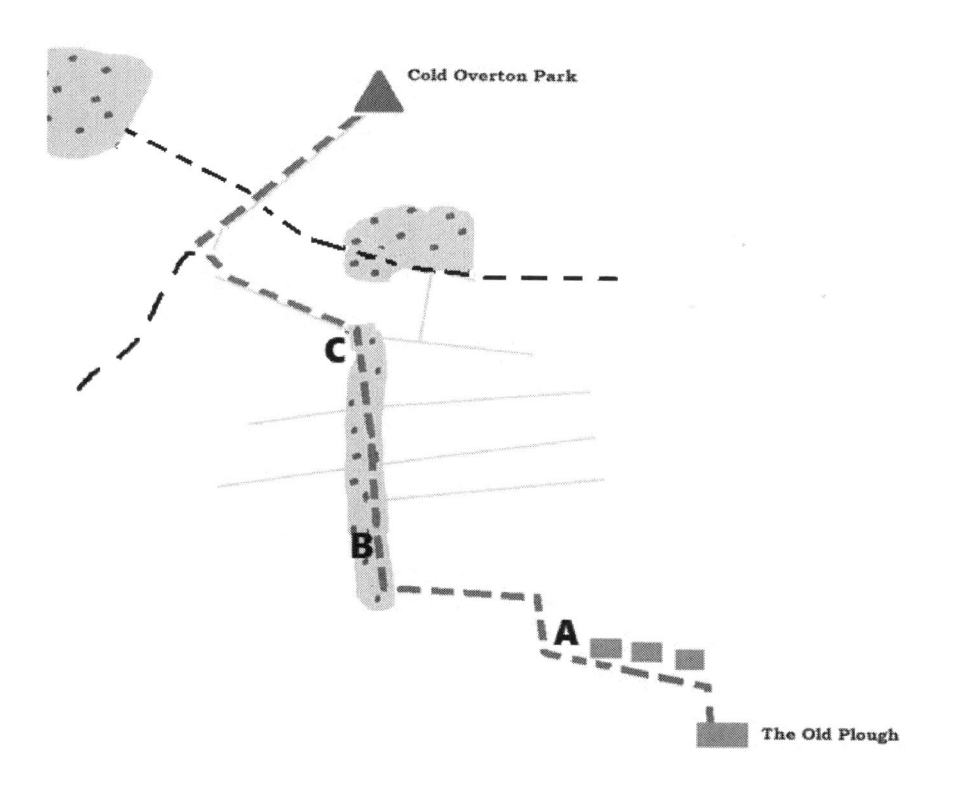

Rutland is one of the historic ceremonial counties of England and, if you exclude the oddity of the "city counties" (London and Bristol) it is the smallest. It still manages to pack a lot in though, the UK's biggest man-made reservoir, a small town and several villages. OK, it doesn't pack a lot in then, but it is quite unspoilt and mostly undulating, which is its charm.

Near to the town (and "capital") Oakham is the pretty little village of Braunston-in-Rutland. This is a quiet place and a charming little collection of stone buildings.

Our starting off point is The Old Plough at the eastern end of the village. This is a lovely old building, made mostly of local stone, but with some odd red brick interventions in the first floor gables.

Architecture over with, turn left from the pub's car park (if that is where you have parked) and leave Oakham Road, then turning in to Church Street itself, which you then cross. Stick to the left hand side of the Oakham Road or High Street as it has now become, for a very short distance (100 metres). You can either take the thin path next to the road or an elevated track the other side of a four rail wooden fence – the latter is preferable – then cross the High Street to access a bridleway (A) which appears between a hedged garden and a red brick wall with a chevron sign on it.

The track heads north very briefly, then turns west (left) for another couple of hundred yards with high hedges on either side. Now turn north again (B) and things open up a bit, with views of the rolling countryside, bare fields and fairy trees. Where the fourth line of hedging (i.e. the hedgelines which run east to west) hits you at right angles, you need to go through a field gate and turn leftish (west) on to the footpath (C). From (B) to (C) is about half a mile and is lightly treed – about which more later.

From this point a variety of possibilities opens up, but you could do worse than to proceed for a short while to a small group of trees and then head north (right) along a loosely worn path which has the hedge to its right, then breaking in to the next field by another gate. When the crops are in full bloom you may have to take the field edges.

In this field there may or may not be cows (none when we were there, but the Hill Baggers website has several accounts and they are clearly visible on Google Earth).

The sun sets on a chilly Rutland day

With a thick hedge on your left, you're nearly there, and by the time you have gone in to the next field and walked another few yards you may see what you are looking for on the left (over your hedge and on the right hand side next to another hedge). Go through the gate and proceed cautiously (this is private land) and you're there!

The views, whilst not breathtaking, are very pleasant, a softly rolling landscape over towards the metropolis of Oakham and Rutland Water beyond that. On this day the land was coated in powdery white – yes it had snowed! This was the only peak out of the 48 where we had it falling around us (having judiciously chosen the warmer months for most of our walks, especially the savage mountains of the north).

The walk back was uneventful apart from having our hats stolen by the grasping branch of a naughty tree that we had tried to duck underneath on that "lightly treed" path, how we did laugh. Oh, and the Old Plough was closed, due to the weather I believe. The car park was like an ice-rink

Oh well, north we go and on to Notts!

Nottinghamshire

Newtonwood Lane 205m (673ft) and Silverhill Wood 204.3m (670ft)

Pubs: For Newtonwood Lane - The Woodend, Chesterfield Road, Huthwaite, Sutton in Ashfield NG17 2QJ (01773) 872231

For Silver Hill Wood - The Carnarvon Country Pub and Restaurant, Teversal, Nottinghamshire NG17 3 (01623) 559676

Parking: For Newtonwood Lane, at The Woodend
For Silver Hill Wood, nr Carnarvon Arms.
Walk: 5 miles combined or 1 mile for Newtonwood Lane, 1 mile for Silverhill Wood

This county is unique in having two entries for the simple reason that the fake highest peak is so much more inspiring than the real one and it would be a shame to miss it out; it would also be breaking the rules to miss out the real one! The latter qualifies as an unremarkable, could be anywhere, bog standard bit of field near a road, the very essence of the eastern flat-land; the former an example of a good thing that man can do (which is itself a memorial to other good things, see below).

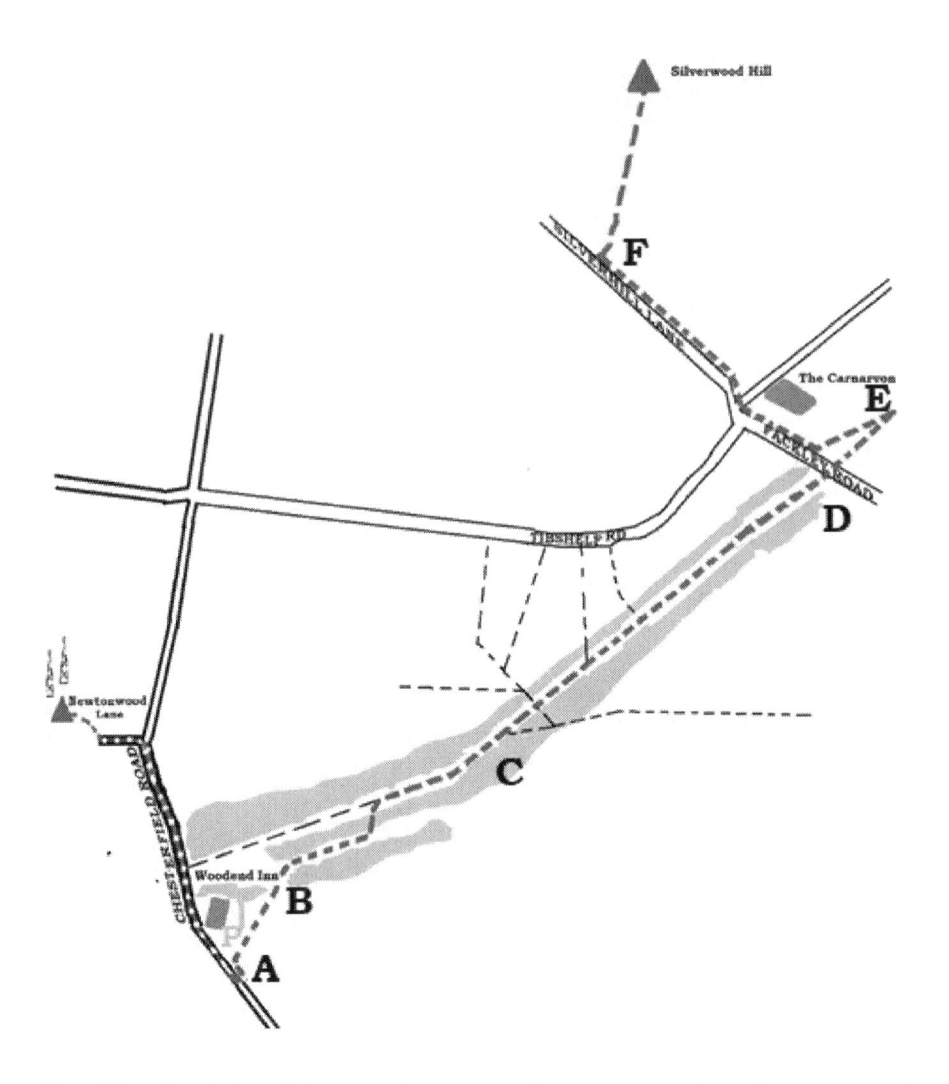

The Woodend itself has quite a spacious car park. Once parked there and with the pub on your right, proceed north-northwest up Chesterfield Road for about ¼ mile.

Up the narrow, tree-lined and fast-moving Chesterfield Road, there is at least a path. Very early on (50 metres) as the road winds itself over to the left then right you will cross over a railway bridge, but on looking down from it you will see that the railway line has gone and is replaced by a very charming little path, this is an option to take us to Silver Hill later.

Soon on the right you will see a turning which leads to a gated drive, go past this.

Very soon, before your pores have even considered opening up to allow out any sort of a sweat, Newtonwood Lane and the tell-tale transmitters (yes, those again) can be seen to the left.

Pick the place of your own choosing to cross the roads and carry on up the right hand side of Newtonwood Lane (unfortunately no path) before finding a break in the hedge where there is a fairly new metal kissing gate and you're off.

Then a crossing of little more than 100 metres across the field (around it if in crop) and you are at an uninspiring spiky-fenced enclosure which surrounds a chapel-like black brick, red tiled building and Nottinghamshire's highest (natural) point, which is picked out neither by trig nor sign, but GPS.

Job done. Well, half done.

We now have two choices – back to the car and drive to the next peak (the fake one, the nice one) or walk to it. Both involve heading back down the Chesterfield Road towards the Woodend Inn, which means chips. Chips and a glass of lemonade.

The Woodend has a full menu and a conservatory to sample it in, but today was a pleasant outsidey day and what better way to enjoy it than sitting outside by the children's play area eating sliced, fried potatoes and drinking sugar and water flavoured with lemon?

If driving to the next destination you find yourself driving back up the Chesterfield Road and then right up the Tibshelf Road (B6014) signposted for Stanton Hill, Sutton-in-Ashfield and Mansfield. This goes for just over a mile, snaking left and taking you to the village of Teversal.

Twin Peaks - Newtonwood Lane and Silverhill Wood

If you are walking, then good for you. After you've bloated (and, ideally, relieved) yourself carry on the way you were going and about 50 metres along on the left is a bus stop (A). Near to this is an opening and an ill-defined north-north-eastwards public footpath, seeming to head back-ish towards the pub (incidentally, there is a minor access point down a steep embankment off of the Chesterfield Road, but this would curtail chips). This goes on for about 120 metres before finding a gap between the trees at the corner of the field (B), then striking right.

You are now in a long grassy ride between two lines of trees and are parallel (to your left) with the Silverhill Trail. Look for any opening on the left and you will finally join the trail proper and so the enjoyment of walking along the old railway can begin.

This lasts for approximately one mile. About a third of the way along you will see a fork in the path (C), keep to the left (the right hand path is called Brierley Forest Link and takes you not to Silverhill, but a place called Stanton Hill). About half a mile on from here, should you wish to break with the lovely, but constant rail-walk, you could head up one of several paths on the left and join the Tibshelf Road. Anyone of these might shave a couple of hundred metres or so off of the journey, but the narrow Tibshelf Road with fast moving traffic is not a match for the Silverhill Trail.

Keeping with the trail means you will experience the joy of walking over a rail-bridge (D) which straddles Fackley Road. Having done that you need to find an exit to its left and turn about yourself (E), refinding Fackley Road, rather than hovering above it, turn right and within just over a hundred metres, there on the right is the pub.

The first thing you are struck by here is the odd village sign – a mosaic with, as its centre piece, an Egyptian pharaoh. Why? The reason becomes clear when you look at the pub – the Carnarvon "Country Pub and Kitchen" as it styles itself. It was of, course, the Earl of Carnarvon who assisted with the discovery of the tomb of Tutankhamun and met his end with the "mummy's curse" in Cairo in 1921. Nearby, although not on our walk, is Teversal Manor, home to the Carnarvons and also to the fictional Lady Chatterley.

There is plenty of parking at the Carnarvon, but if you aren't intending to dine there you could pull up somewhere on the nearby Pleasey Road or Silverhill Lane – both unrestricted, but with a possibility of causing nuisance if parked inconsiderately. Or you could even park up near the peak itself. Presuming you haven't done that, having left the pub behind you on the right, walk past the aforementioned village sign and then up the aforementioned Silverhill Lane (basically a continuation of Fackley Road) – this will take you there.

About 300 metres up the leafy, sparsely-housed, lane and opposite a caravan and camping park, is a break in the fence (F) and a green gate which, once squeezed through, takes you up a light coloured path of crushed aggregate and towards your goal. This is Silverhill Wood and already you are just 600 metres from the summit.

Just a little way along the cinder path pause a moment at the bench of a young man who died tragically young and, quite soon, peeking above the horizon to the left is the thing we have come for.

Set upon a huge piece of granite, there he is in bronze, the miner complete with helmet and light and the all-important davy lamp. "Testing for Gas" by Dufort is in memory of those who have come and gone in the mining industry hereabouts. On one side is a memorial plaque, as if to the dead, remembering 65 collieries from Annesley to Wollaton lasting from 1809 to 2011 (Wellbeck being shown as "open", but having closed since the statue was erected). Also on the summit is an orientation plaque showing the whereabouts of nearby points of interest.

Silver Hill is the site of an old mine spoil heap, then banked up by an extra five metres to give it the "county top" title. However, even then they got it wrong – a survey in 2010 found it to be 204.3 metres above sea level – as opposed to Newtonwood Lane's 205 metres! Ow! and after all that effort. Still, if one includes the statue then Silver Hill wins it. No matter, the views around are pleasant enough, including the obligatory Lincoln Cathedral some thirty miles east over this fairly flat countryside.

But it is not the countryside that you will remember as you make your brief descent towards the Carnarvon either to your car or to a right turn up the Tibshelf Road and thence the Silver Hill Trail, it is the wonderful feat of man to make a hill, actually *make* a hill of such size and cap it off with that splendid statue, even if it isn't quite the highest point in Notts.

Now east (and north) to Lincolnshire.

Lincolnshire

Normanby Top 168m (551ft)

Pub: Hope Tavern, Caistor Rd, Holton-le-Moor, Market Rasen, Lincolnshire LN7 6AH

(01673) 828 217

Parking: At/Near pub

Walk: 4 ½ miles

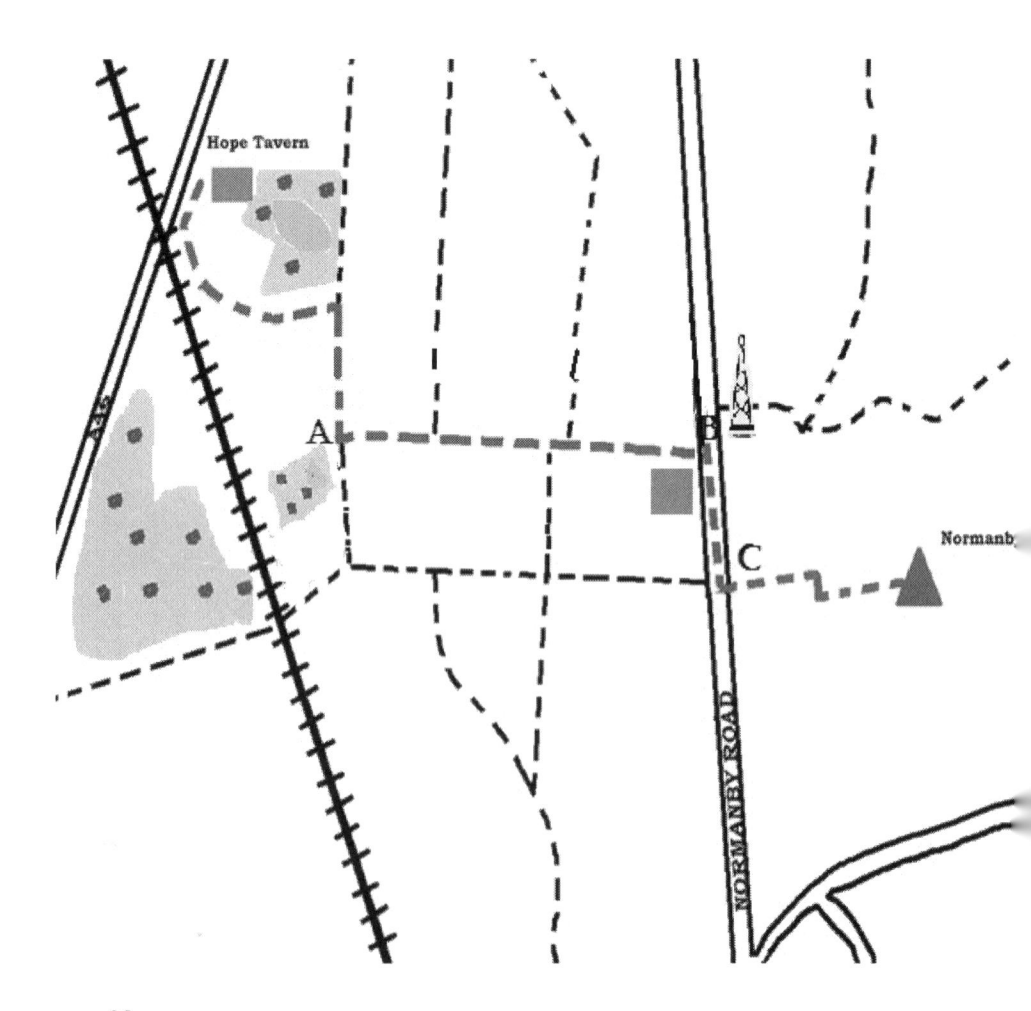

Lincolnshire's peak is notionally one of the lowest, however the shape of the land and its relative prominence is such that it gives surprisingly rewarding views of both Lincoln Cathedral and the Humber Bridge - the first real "wow" of the odyssey.

The pub is interesting too, located next to a level crossing and it is here that our journey begins. The Hope Tavern in little Holton-le-Moor has a large parking area to the left of it. If this is not convenient then there are one or two other gravelled or grassed areas nearby to the left (provided you don't block any accesses).

With the pub on your left, proceed south towards the railway line and where you see the sign for Holton-le-Moor, take the path between the railway and the pub garden. Trainspotters will enjoy the first part of the walk where the track is your companion for about 250 metres, but all good things come to an end as you then veer left and east, away from the iron road.

Now follow the field boundary south for about another 250 metres before it meets the edge of a copse and veers off left (east). This carries on for about a kilometre-and-a-half and in front of you is the rise of land which contains the "Tops" (Normanby and Nettleton).

500 metres along this path, the land begins to climb from about 50 metres to about 150 metres above sea level in a reasonably short space of time, the path kinking slightly right then left as it reaches a plateau and heads towards the road. The last couple of hundred metres appear to be private and you should strictly get the owner's permission first. The alternative (using the defined Public Rights of Way) is a rather circuitous route south then back north – this shortcut saves the best part of a mile either way.

This path takes you to the left of a group of farm buildings and, via a field gate (B), opposite a transmitter, out on to the narrow Normanby Road, at this point bearing the title of the "Viking Way." Head right along this road for about 500 metres, passing the farmhouse (Acre House) on your right and a green profiled metal agricultural barn on your left. To the left, ahead, on slightly more elevated land (obviously) is the giant golf ball of the Claxby radar station known locally as, well "The Golf Ball" (such imagination). By way of orientation, that is 1.2 kilometres away - twice as far as our destination.

After being clear of the farm and its buildings, look for the second field boundary on the left. At the time of writing, this was opposite a solitary tree and was marked by a double field gate (C). Turn left and vault/open this gate (closing it again, of course) and join the field and walk its edge; the hedge (to begin with, at least) on your right.

Now noticeably climbing again, you are looking for the third field on the right, i.e. the point after two field boundaries. Currently you are on the wrong side of the hedge for the trig, so find your gaps in the hedges where you can and proceed two fields up with the trig just a little way to the right (about 100 metres or so down) and there is the sacred obelisk.

As mentioned, the views for such a little hill are very rewarding, all the more so for having specific reference points – the cathedral which, apparently, can be seen from a clutch of summits – now at least from within its own county – and that bridge which failed to unite two counties immediately in the opposite direction – a bridge we will be crossing soon to cap off our lowland walks. Not bad for an elevation of a couple of hundred metres.

There are more interesting ways to find the peak, we took a longer route on one occasion which gave more scenic reward along the way. However, that bends the rules – it's a there and back from the watering hole.

The Hope Tavern has it all, good ale and pub nosh and, if you're there at the right time, good music, including *The Blooz!* Now north, over that blessed Humber Bridge and on to the East Riding of Yorkshire!

East Riding

Bishop Wilton Wold 246m (807ft)

Pub: Fleece Inn, 47 Main St, Bishop Wilton, York, North Yorkshire YO42 1RU

(01759) 368251

Parking: Near pub, free

Walk: 4 miles

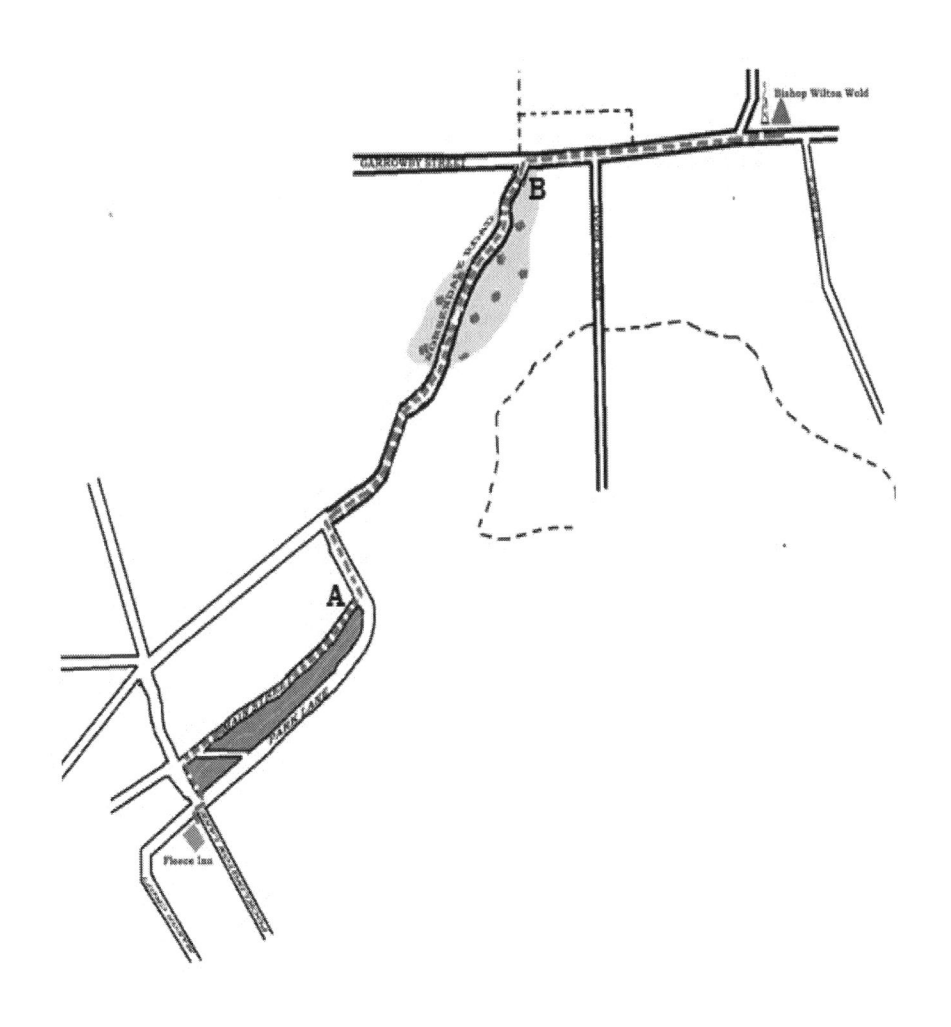

"Flatlands of the East? What do you *mean*? How can you even compare us to Norfolk or, or *Essex*? And how can you have *us* as a flatland and not your pesky Isle of Wight or even yer toffee nosed 'Greater London?' They're smaller than us. We're Yorkshire we are, Yorkshire and proud. Flatlands of the East my Aunt Fanny.

Sorry the East Riding of Yorkshire, but it is in this section that you belong. You are in the bottom third of peaks and although there are others who are a little shorter than you, they are just in the wrong place (I'm looking at *you* Merseyside). You aren't moorland, you aren't savage (well.....no) you aren't made of chalk (yes, alright, you are on the Burnham Chalk Formation, but that isn't *southern* chalk you see), and you're in the east – now in the interests of contrived geographical continuity - get over yourself.

East Riding, a county once again having recovered from its brief and traumatic coupling with part of northern Lincolnshire to make "Humberside." This walk takes place in and around the charming village of Bishop Wilton.

The walk is entirely on the road. There is a footpath sort of nearby, part of the way along, which might help to an extent, but it doesn't really get you where you want to go.

With our thirst slaked by an as yet not well-deserved lemonade at the Fleece Inn, we leave the pub behind us on our right, cross Pocklington Lane and walk along Main Street – a charming way which has buildings on one side and grass on the other and a tiny stream running through it. You are heading towards a steeple. Carry on for about 300 metres, then at the end of the green, fork left (A) still on Main Street and go past the Bishop Wilton CoE Primary School. Follow this, with buildings on the left, grassy slopes on the right.

At the top of this road turn right up Worsendale Road. Slowly uphill, a hardened path is on the right (to start with, at least) and a grass bank on the left. Later, this gives way to just grass banks. Follow this for a mile and about two-thirds of the way along a transmitter will appear on the right – which can only mean one thing.

When Worsendale Road ends it runs into Garrowby Street (A166) and you need to turn right here (B) and cross over to the other side of the A166 whenever it is safe and walk the verge, which, on that side, is wide enough to give you space. There ahead, on the left, is that transmitter getting closer by your every step. Eventually you come to a small path which takes you to the forbidden enclosure, denying you access to the very spot. However, you can get within a couple of feet of it by climbing a field fence and doing a lap of the enclosure (if the overgrown vegetation allows you to). Allegedly the trig is hidden somewhere therein, but we couldn't locate it.

As with most transmitter peaks, and especially those with little prominence, there is a sense of underwhelmed-ness.

However, turn about the way you have just come and have your reward. There is the Vale of York all laid out before you. Actually, despite its diminutiveness in the list, the comparative elevation to all around it does give it a surprisingly lofty feel, a broad, open vista not quite in the top ten, but not far off. Everything is a joy to behold with only the distant chimneys of Doncaster a slight deviation from perfection.

East Riding, the forgotten county reborn. And that, my friends, is the last of the eastern flatlands.

Now let's go and find some good old *southern* chalk.

Chapter 2 – The Chalklands of the South

Chalk, that lovely white stuff that year-round snow that gladdens the heart and, through its reflected light, also seems to brighten the sky.

From The White Cliffs of you know where, to The Needles, to the rolling Chilterns and Cotswolds it is a joy to behold.

These hills were formed in the Late Cretaceous period (Cretaceous coming from the Latin word for chalk) between 66 and 100 million years ago. The chalk is made from the calcium deposits of the armour-like plates of trillions of dead plankton or algae called cocolithophores from when all this was sea.

As to why this should be lying in a ridge, you can blame that on Africa which came slamming into Europe, causing all sorts of chaos (like the Alps) about 60 million years ago. Much of what was then exposed has eroded, leaving what you see today.

Whilst there are odd pockets of the stuff in the far north, it is generally restricted to a curl beginning in Kent and incorporating much of southern England west thereof up to Salisbury Plain, before swirling eastwards, wrapping itself around London and hitting The Wash – avoiding the far east of East Anglia and also the greater Thames Estuary.

The chalk does cross the wash toward northern Lincolnshire and the East Riding, but enough said about that.

The height of all of the baker's dozen is remarkably similar - from St. Boniface Down at 241 metres to 297 metres at Walbury Hill in Berkshire (see list, over). A difference of just over 50 metres across a spread of counties that covers an area 150 miles x 100 miles, which is a sign that all of these are the same age and have been subjected to the same forces of nature.

Berkshire	**297m**
Surrey	**295m**
Wiltshire	**294m**
Hampshire	**286m**
West Sussex	**280m**
Buckinghamshire	**267m**
Oxfordshire	**261m**
Kent	**251m**
East Sussex	**248m**
Greater London	**245m**
Hertfordshire	**244m**
Bedfordshire	**243m**
Isle of Wight	**241m**

Hertfordshire & Buckinghamshire

Hertfordshire: Hastoe Hill – 244m (800ft)

Buckinghamshire: Haddington Hill – 267m (876ft)

Pub: The Castle Inn, Park Rd, Tring HP23 6BN

Tel: (01442) 823552

Parking: Nearby, free

Walk: 8 miles

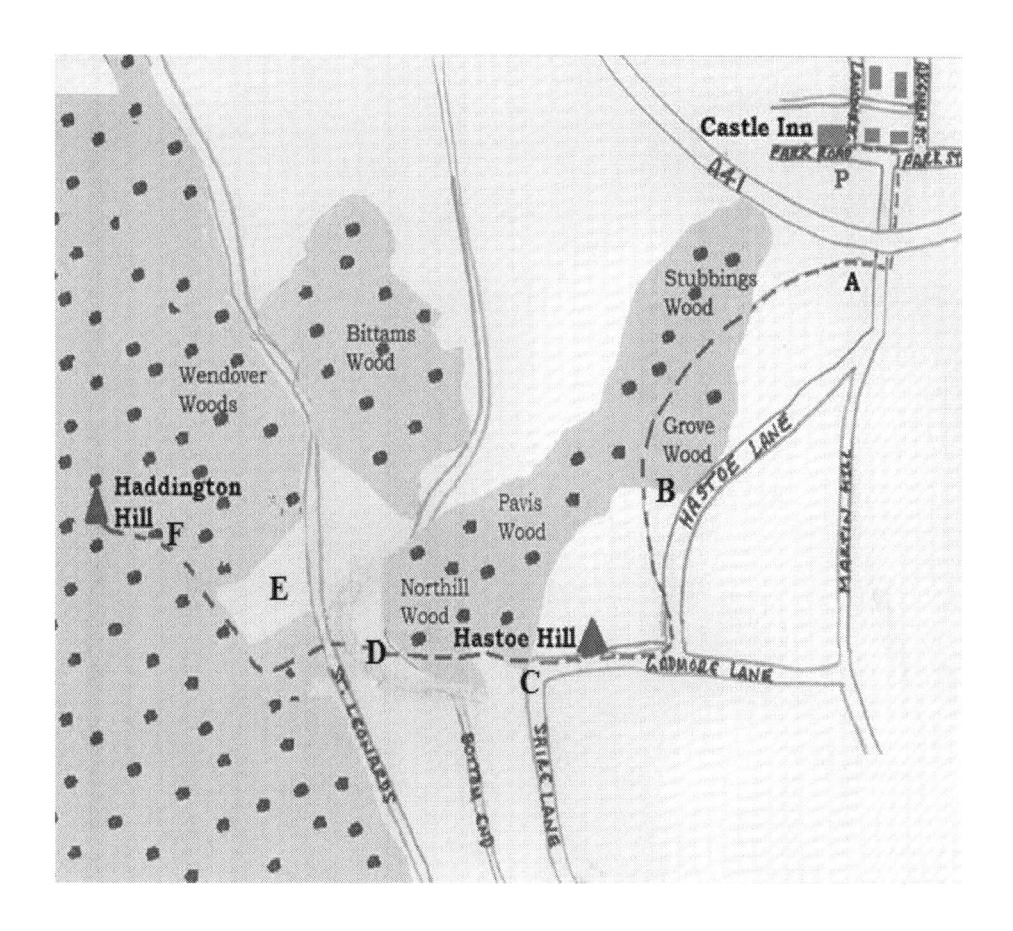

Herts, Beds and Bucks: three small counties in so many ways; counties who often like to throw in their lot together (take Three Counties Radio for example). So too can the three peaks be treated together, two of them being close enough to do in one hit. We had a weekend away (staying at the illustrious sounding "Premier Inn, Hemel Hempstead") and began our three counties mission as the weather reached its finest and the hours of daylight neared their fullest extent.

This was the first of the chalk hills, which dominate much of the south-eastern corner of England and the difference between this and the far-Eastern counties was immediately obvious with white flecks on every hillside, and mud coated by a fine snowy dust, interspersed with flint, truly a visual delight.

Our walk began in the telephone-sounding town of Tring in the Borough of Dacorum, parked opposite "The Castle" which is on the corner of Park Street and Langdon Street. Tring in general, and this road especially, are pleasing on the eye with its little row of white and pastille-rendered houses, mixed in with red brick ones, The Castle itself sitting higher than the others on the corner. Opposite are fields, and that is the way we are headed.

First though, stick to the same side as The Castle and walk past many splendid dwellings for a couple of hundred yards passing late 19th and early 20th century three-storey art decos until you come to a set of mock-Tudor houses, white-rendered and set back from the main street.

A beautiful way to end your time on Park Road as you now cross it and turn right, up Hastoe Lane. Here is a finger post showing you Aylesbury 7 miles, town centre ¼ mile. Pointing straight ahead though, is the sign for Cholesbury 2 ¾ miles, Hastoe 1 ¼ miles. That is the way to go.

There is a diminishing grass verge on the right, so you will need to take the single file tarmac path on the left and pass a bench dedicated to the late Brian Page. Carry on for about a quarter of a mile and under the A41, in a square under pass, the only visual detraction on this lovely walk.

Very soon after the under pass on the right is a public footpath finger-post and stile next to a steepish-sloping concrete farm road

(A). You could just carry along on Hastoe Lane, slightly longer but with hardened pavements – but where is the fun in that? Nip through the kissing gate next to the finger post and take Permissive footpath 26 "Stubbings Wood" and now the real enjoyment begins.

Soon the concrete path gives way to an unmade track which wends its way upwards and soon breaks out into an open field. Then swing left following the field edge with a post and five bar fence to your right, and a thin line of trees behind it (behind which a further, smaller, field backs on to a small woodland – Stubbings Wood). Now follow on the same line into the next field. As you reach the crest, and indeed on your way up, stop and turn around to have a look back where you've come from. Look north and north-eastwards. There is lovely Tring, and beyond it Ivinghoe Beacon and the Chiltern Hills, that long chalky ridge stretching for fifty miles over four counties in middle England, where we will be headed on our next walk in search of Dunstable Downs.

Our thirst slaked, we carry on up the slope as it eases off and takes us to the woodland edge. Really at this point you can either carry on along the field edge, or why not nip into the woods? This is the Stubbings Wood Special Area of Conservation (SAC) where the woodland floor was blessed with a carpet of bluebells.

Carrying on in a generally south/south-westerly direction, the name of the woods changes to first Deacon's Hill Wood, and then Grove Wood to the east. Soon we leave the latter near a barn and a wooden sign indicating Grove Farm (B). Now there is a sign saying "Tring via the Downs" and we are back on Hastoe Lane (remember Hastoe Lane?).

Carry on the way you were walking, down the lane, then in a hundred yards turn right down Gadmore Lane and soon you're there, wherever there is. It's pretty ill-defined, close to Pavis Woods, close to the border with Bucks. Because the land here is all of a pretty similar height (in fact, Wikipedia has its relative height, i.e. the amount by which it is higher than surrounding land, as 0 metres!) then the defining moment is taken away, and it could be any of a number of spots along Gadmore Lane. However, the height chosen on Wikipedia is SP914091, so let's stick with that. No trig, no nothing. If you were minded to, this could be the time to return and off to the pub. However, given that you're already in Buckinghamshire, and with the other peak *reasonably* close, why not push on and knock that off the list?

Carry on the way you were going and when Gadmore Lane swings around to the left (becoming Shire Lane), you leave it and take the dusty footpath on the right (C). A few yards in is a field gate and a kissing gate to its right. Through you go.

Here or hereabouts, no higher land is there in all of Hertfordshire

The path hugs and occasionally breaks free from the forest edge, finally emerging near a pylon and with Bottom End to your left, carry on straight ahead in roughly the same direction you were travelling, down a private track and pass about half a dozen houses (all on your right), this is the hamlet of Chivery and the last of the buildings is Chivery Hall Farm which sprawls both sides of the track (D).

Emerging from this lane, you are now on St. Leonards (no "Road" or "Hill", just St. Leonards) and just across it are Wendover Woods, which will be with you for the rest of the outward bound walk, less than a mile now.

Cut straight across and take the woodland path where you will be on your own for a short while (50 metres) before emerging and turning left on to a metalled road which you may have to share with the occasional car as you head west for about 300 metres, in the middle of which is a small stretch with a green gate which may occasionally be closed off (to cars at least).

Soon the road spins around to the right (north) and you with it. You will see the odd footpath which does look tempting as an alternative, but none of them look like they want to get you there any time soon, so you may as well take the tarmac and let the road rise with you.

Now to your right you will note that, although you are still amongst the trees, it is a close run thing, with just one line of trees separating you from an open field. This is a "bite" out of the woods (E) which stretches for about 200 metres before you are back in the thick of it. Just over 500 metres to go now.

Then, as your path twists around to the left, a sea of shiny metal creatures can be seen. The visitors' car park for Wendover Woods, for those who used four wheels. Cars are parked here and there and pretty much everywhere in this part of the woods.

The second path on the right will take you to the café (F). Even if you are not peckish, this pyramid-roofed wooden building is a good landmark from which to wayfare the final steps.

The café is open from 9 to 5 weekdays (9 to 6 weekends) and offers a variety of freshly produced food. Back to that in a moment though, because nearby a finger post indicates our target is near "Chiltern Hills Highest Point" it says. And so it ends with a cinder path, some wood-carvings and some alpacas. Yes, alpacas.

Taking the path involves the "Hilltop Trail", a sanitised, wooden edged affair which makes it all so easy. Some way along there are logs carved to look like woodland creatures, but these can only hold our attention for so long as, inexorably, we arrive at a slab of rock proclaiming itself a cairn, erected to commemorate the Queen's Silver Jubilee in 1977, with an inlaid copper plaque exclaiming "The Chiltern Summit. This cairn at a height of 876ft (267m) marks the highest mount on the Chiltern Hills.." and so on and so forth, by the parishes of Aston Clinton and Halton.

The views, it has to be said, are disappointing. This is a quite wide plateau and within a wood to boot. Elsewhere, nearby, there are better vistas, but from here, the only real views out are across a post and rail/barbed wire fence and onto a field of, well, alpacas. An incongruous element, these South American camelid beasts were only metres from the peak and blissfully unaware that they are, for most of the time, the highest up living things in this south midlands county.

And next door to this was a field of alpacas. Yes, alpacas.

Well, is it the midlands? The border with Hertfordshire is only a mile-and-a-half away and Hertfordshire is unmistakably in the eastern region. They get Anglia TV around here, so isn't this the east as well? Topographically, this is, believe it or not, a very western peak. Its parent peak is said to be, wait for it, Cleeve Hill in lovely Gloucestershire some sixty odd miles away and that just thirty miles from the Welsh border. Is that amazing? Or is it just that England is very slender?

However, no matter. The café in the woods is nearby. If you want to skip lunch at the pub you could always scoff here instead.   There is a choice of spuds in jackets, paninis, baguettes and so on, plus a kids' menu. Café or pub, café or pub? Why not do both? There's no pud by the looks of it, so Hot chocolate with cream & sprinkles here, proper food at the pub later, back to front, that's a possibility Too much cake though meant that little room was left for the main course.

For the kids there is also the "Adventurous Play Area" nearby, with much in the way of tree climbing or, for the more stout-hearted child, Go Ape's "amazing high wire adventure."
When all is done, the walk back needs to be undertaken and proper food consumed.

Remember the way back. Be on the metalled road and have the café on your left then just follow the road away from the car park. Eventually you will reach the "bite out of the woods" (E) now on your left, of course and the path will swing around to the left and cross St. Leonards. If you unwittingly kept with the road for that last little bit (instead of taking the path) then you will have to cut back 50 metres to the right to find the private track signposted for Chivery Hall Farm and the 600 metres which take you past those six dwellings (on the left) and on to Bottom End. Remember the path that hugs and flirts with Pavis Wood. Over the gate and soon back at the Shire Lane/Gadmore Lane bend where you head straight on (i.e. east - the left-hand choice, *not* right). Soon enough you will remember that you are on that plateau which denies Hertfordshire a true peak and as you pass into that county and break out in to the open again, now is the time to savour the lovely Chilterns again, only this time you're facing the right way and can look at them the whole time.

Now look upon that work of nature, remember the Cretaceous period and that crash between Africa and Europe?
Geology over with, remember at Gadmore Lane's end (about 400 metres along) to go left, down Hastoe Lane and the rest should be

a doddle. The target is in view and it's a choice of whether to stick with Hastoe Lane the whole way or to dart in to the woods at Grove Farm and dodge amongst the barns, taking a parallel route. Either way, we make our final descent and emerge the other side of the A41 and the last 250 metres of Hastoe Lane takes us down to Park Road, where a left turn brings us back to the car and the pub.

This is a bit of a locals' pub, not to say it isn't welcoming. And on the day we were there, the local team Watford were live on TV, so all eyes were on that. Due to all the tubby nosh at the Café in The Woods I have to confess to still having little appetite when we arrived back at The Castle. I therefore ordered a coffee. They didn't have a machine, so it was instant only, but gladly made for just a quid.

Two of the three counties had been done in one day – tomorrow Bedfordshire would complete the set.

Bedfordshire

Dunstable Downs – 243m (797ft)

Pub: The Pheasant Inn, 208 West Street, Dunstable LU6 1NX

(01582) 662706

3 miles

Parking: Nearby (free)

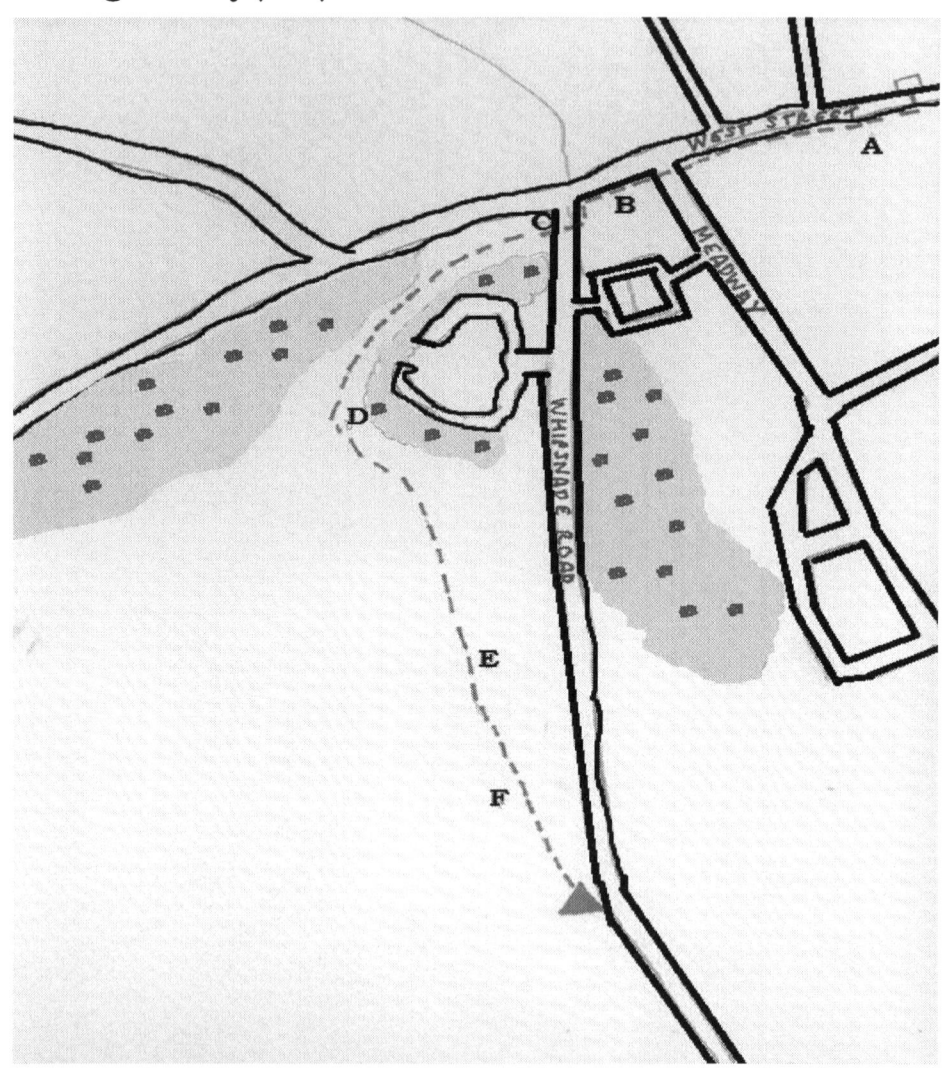

What a perfect peach of a peak this one is. There is a bit of town walking first, but then it's up from the foot to the top in very short measure, much reward for little effort – the way we like it.

Park outside the Pheasant (chasteningly next to a funeral parlour) and, with it on your right, cross over West Street towards a park and turn right. You soon sweep through a crescent, followed by Dunstable cemetery (A) complete with a decapitated bust. On, past Catchacre, and a group of flats, then you cross Meadway and come to a little parade of shops (B) – a good place to stock up on toffee crisps and Ribena – then on past the brown tourist sign for the zoo (Whipsnade).

500 metres from the start, you will arrive at the junction of Whipsnade Road. Cross here and turn left on to the grassy area. Just as you arrive at the grass, pass to the left of a large oak tree by the roadside (C) and head for the gap at about 9 o' clock, between two groups of trees. This grassy ride rises slowly up for about 200 metres and comprises the main "climb" (D). Although there is a little up and down a bit later, most of it is ridge walking.

The marvellous thing about this walk is that the peak and its ridge are so pronounced in comparison with their surroundings. Therefore, for every metre you climb you *will* get an extra bit of good view, there *are* no intervening hills or even trees to ruin things – maximum return on little investment.

As you break out in to the open you will see chalk where the grass has been worn away by feet and then you will pass through a kissing gate. There are several paths to choose from, but if you stay left you will be on the Icknield Way Trail. The views are glorious. As you rise still further, ahead you may see an outcrop of land which had been visible from the approach to Hastoe Hill (Hertfordshire) this is Ivinghoe Beacon and, beyond this, the Tring of yesterday.

To your right is the largely flat (and therefore this ridge is very distinct) Bedfordshire/Buckinghamshire countryside, the Vale of Aylesbury and all; to the left, glimpsed, is the B4541 carrying light traffic between Dunstable and Whipsnade and beyond. From here it is really very simple and there's even a nice visitor centre when you get there.

About half a mile along the ridge, the path braids, but it doesn't matter which you take (the left hand track is the more trodden path, though it does take you closer to the road, across which you may espy the Dunstable Downs Golf Club) about 300 metres on from that you pass a small parking area, then another 100 metres on another, larger, car park announcing "Dunstable Downs" (E). This is only 400 metres from the peak. However, save your contempt for the next car park along, whose nearest point is only 40 metres from the trig! I mean, really!

Soon enough you are at the Dunstable Downs visitor centre (F), an impressive building of about 700m2. However, stay your coffee lust a moment as you pass this and cross the entrance road to it, to a grassed area (well, all is grassed around here, but a *specific* area of grass, surrounded by a ditch) to the white trig point, a fitting colour for this chalky realm.

Job done, what spoils are there? The views described above are not uninterrupted (and not by tree or hillock) for in your purview here and there are people taking advantage of the thermals which such a ridge enjoys, hang-gliders. These wayfarers of the sky are to be admired, because surely one false move and.....but anyway, they do come close at times and you can almost see the whites of their eyes. Vying for airspace, and generally a bit higher, are the light aircraft launched into the air by winch down in the valley and any space left over is taken by the kites (both avian and textile) as well as other manner of birdlife. But there is still quite enough sky for everyone to look at and through to the distant fields.

You can enjoy all this whilst sipping a coffee and nibbling a freshly-baked scone bought at the Gateway Centre (the name given to the luscious curve of built form which sits atop the hillside. There is even a shop to buy out-doorsy stuff, including kites, should this take your fancy). There is a variety of kids' games (giant outdoor connect-4, hula-hoops, space-hoppers and so on). Beyond is a bit of education with a bizarrely-shaped wind-catcher. This structure is about 12-feet high and catches fresh air to send in to the visitor centre to cool it in summer and (somehow) warm it in winter.

This does go down as one of, if not *the* most interesting peaks in terms of "stuff to do" once there, and is a stark contrast to some of the more remote peaks. It's not everyone's cup of tea, but you pays your money...

The return walk is no less rewarding, with spectacular views out towards Leighton Buzzard and beyond and a chance to do a bit of (unofficial) on yer heels chalk hill ski-ing over to the left hand side. Now down the grassy ride between the lines of trees, left after crossing Whipsnade Road, and right down West Road. Soon enough you are back at The Pheasant Inn and for the second day in a row, the tea and cakes had filled us up.

Damn shame – on the day we were there – they were offering free curries on a Sunday! Next we head south, to the Downs and the Isle of Wight, via Kent – and Greater London!

Greater London and Kent

Greater London: Westerham Heights – 245m (804ft)

Kent: Betsom's Hill – 251m (823ft)

Pub: The Aperfield Inn, 331 Main Road, Biggin Hill, Westerham TN16 2HN

(01959) 54256

Parking: At pub, or nearby (free)

Walk: 2 miles

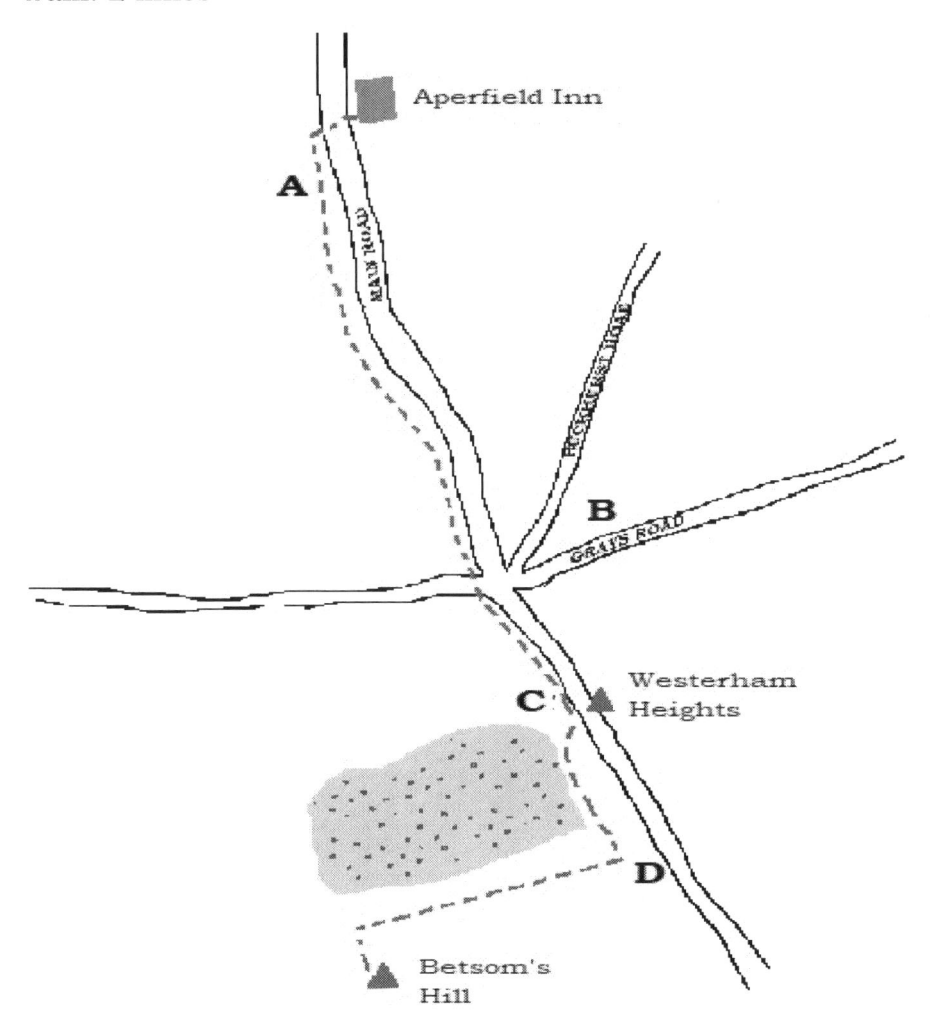

Two county tops just 200 metres apart? What could be easier? Answer – if just visiting the tops, little; but, if incorporating a pub, a few more things (but still not many). This is an odd little walk which seldom makes you feel that you are in "the country" not until the very end at least where *near* to the second peak a vista of the North Downs is its own reward.

It is a short walk, and would have been even shorter had the promised "Spinning Wheel" pub at Hawley Corner on the Greater London/Kent border still been as hoped, but no, 'tis now the Shampan Indian restaurant (which, when arriving to check whether it might still *really* be a pub, gave all manner of enticing aromas). As such it was disqualified as the nearest pub-to-peak in favour of the – annoyingly ¾ mile away – Aperfield Inn (annoying because we were tight on time and hadn't banked on a delay!).

The Aperfield was once the called the "Fox and Hounds" so called because the Surrey hunt used to meet here and still its country credentials are writ large with a promise of rustic and rural delights with every mouthful. With the Inn on your left, head south straight on along Main Road, Westerham. This is pretty much the only road you will go on and it will take you more or less to both peaks, well alright, not peaks, *places*.

Past a little row of shops on your right ye go, these are all run by the same outfit, the "Saddlery and Gun-Room", also offering "horse-ware" reminding us of the Aperfield's former name and purpose.

The next bit of the walk is pleasant enough, though hardly "rural" feeling, houses and houses, most very decent with nice deep gardens to give a green tinge to your ambulations, predominantly (but not solely) hedged to the left and open to the right, giving way eventually to trees on both sides, but still punctuated by buildings. Points of interest, if they can be so described, are the Great South Street Farm on the right which, if its gates are open, gives a view of the rolling countryside to the west and soon on from this, on the same side, the lovely "Old Farmhouse" B&B with its cockerel sign. Later still is the politely-designed (but clearly 20th century) Westerham Baptist Church (A).

Trees on the left, houses on the right, trees left and right, now things open up a little, but are still fairly sylvan. Soon the Indian restaurant with all its mouth-watering enchantment (it would be an infidelity to eat there instead of the Aperfield, a betrayal...we'd brought sarnies anyway) appears on the left (B), dominated by an odd "round-house" approach (albeit two-storey) with a thatched roof and an oversigned entrance to a garden centre on the right. You will see in front of you, on the corner of Grays Road, a county sign for Kent. Don't be confused though, you still haven't reached London's peak, you are now in Kent, but you will need to just nip across the road a little way down, back in to the smoke.

At this point the footway all but disappears and the verge is a nullity – *it's almost as if they don't want you to walk here*, so the best you can do is keep right and use what little grass exists next to the Westerham Heights Garden Centre. Matters improve slightly at the ranch-fenced Heights Stables, before getting worse (and perhaps a little dangerous) if briefly. But don't worry too much, it's nearly all over. As the built form returns, a little group of buildings emerges on the right. This is Westerham Heights Farm (C). Yes, this multi-elemented pile with its Kentish hanging tiles tells you that here or hereabouts, you are at the highest point in Greater London (just opposite, actually). Yes, the reach of Sadiq Khan extends even this far, though it is hard to reconcile it with Brixton or Hammersmith.

To the right - the highest point in all of London!

That's another one off the list, but victory is fleeting as you press on ever southwards in search of more spoils. Now looking left you will see some promise of country opening up before you. However, on the right and to save your skin, you may be able to find a place to poke through to do a bit of field walking as opposed to the traffic dodging which is on offer. Go past the oddly-named Graham Hall Coachworks bus-stop (D) and take the first turn on the right, up an un-named track and go past one bungalow and on to the second. And here (just a teensy way inside the garden) is the highest point in the garden of England. The chalk is beneath your feet here, but hidden by a deposit of clay and flint. The view is uninspiring, but look to the east (straight ahead) as you leave, cross the road (carefully) and take the farm track and enjoy the view of the North Downs and think of the peaks to come which lie therein and beyond, Ditchling Beacon, Blackdown, St. Boniface Down. This is the very beginning of the big chalk country.

The walk back is as simple as on the outward drag and does not require re-telling. Once back at the Aperfield (presuming you haven't given in to the lure of the Shampan) the menu is sumptuous, with belly of pork being a particular favourite. Enjoy your nosh, or just have an orange juice as I did, knowing that you have ticked two off of your list, with very little effort and think of better and higher things to come. Besides, there was no time to hang around – we had a boat to catch, off to the lovely Isle of Wight.

Isle of Wight

St. Boniface Down – 241m (791ft)

Pub: The Blenheim, 9 High St, Ventnor PO38 1RY

(01983) 855569

OR – The Crab and Lobster Tap, Grove Road, Ventnor PO38 1TH

(01983) 852311

Parking: Nearby, free

Walk: 2 miles

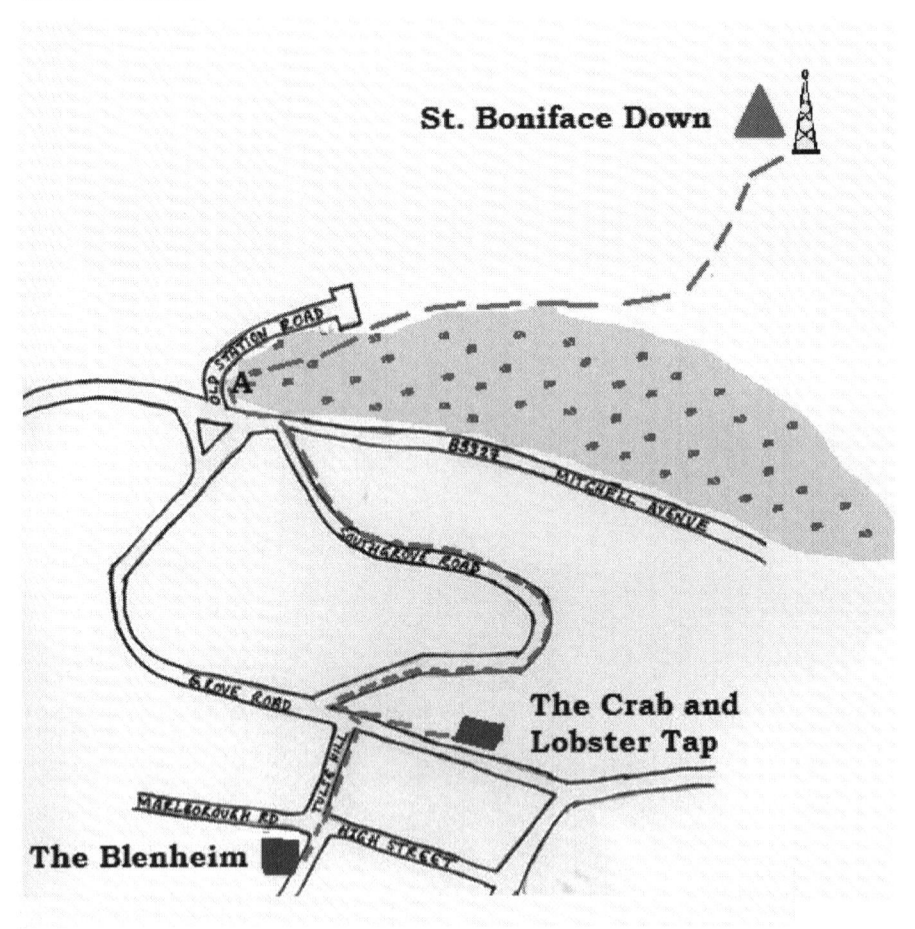

Before you even begin the walk, you can luxuriate in the prettiest of all the county top names....

On arriving at Ventnor, you are immediately struck by the "cliffiness" of the situation. Roads running around the edge of the land they have been cut in to. These have to be traversed and tramped as you tack your way up and up to where you need to go.

Parking is an event, depending on the time of year you will find the tiny streets parked out and may have to end up paying. However, there's every chance you may find a free berth and are good to go.

But then is the question of which pub to use as your beginning and end. There are two such which are almost exactly the same distance as each other from the peak. The Blenheim is a younger, thrusting, Sky TV, Karaoke and Kronenbourg joint, whilst the Crab and Lobster is a very traditional venue, claiming to be the island's first inn and boasting origins as far back as Charles I. The latter is probably a few metres nearer to the summit, but once you have found somewhere to park, the matter does appear somewhat academic.

Wherever you end up parked, you need to thread your way left and right and up until you arrive at Mitchell Avenue. This is easy to identify as it is the last road on the ascent, its bay-windowed town houses squeezed against the wooded cliffs behind. Just as the buildings have almost run out, opposite Grove Road and slightly to the left, is an inauspicious turning into Old Station Road with its prosaic industrial estate – a dry cleaners and garage door company on the left, and prettier if formulaic housing on the right. Just opposite the second industrial building (brown brick with symmetrical white windows and blue curtain walling), and just where the residential properties run out, is an uninviting footpath cut-through (A) which runs alongside an old stone wall, with a footpath sign telling you that Luccombe Down is one mile away, but that St, Boniface Down is a fraction of that.

Concrete steps now take you quickly upwards and soon you are out in the open and a National Trust sign greets you, stating "St, Boniface Down" and telling you that you are in Coombe Bottom. The sign explains how the south face has been colonised by the Mediterranean invader the Holm Oak, a seeming boast about the warm micro-climate. But read on....those lousy foreigners are not welcome here, oh no! They produce shade you see and under this dense canopy the natural chalk wildlife cannot survive.

To solve this problem, the Trust has introduced feral goats and cattle and these chomp the leaf and bark away and open up areas of scrub and all is well with the natural order of things. For this reason, it's dogs on leads please and close any gates which you may have opened.

The rest of this walk couldn't be more straightforward. Your footpath hems woods to the right (south) and open chalky heath to the left (north). You will notice the well-trodden path veers away to the left after a small group of trees and then runs parallel with its original direction, ducking in and out of tree cover.

Not for the only time on this odyssey, you will note that the highest point has been blighted. Being the highest point it is the best place for receipt and transmission of whichever form of broadcast is required and consequently here, as elsewhere, there is a clutter of equipment – on this occasion for the WightGreenLine Radar Station.

Still, at least it is useful for wayfinding and a turn to the left will take you there. The area is fenced off by mesh and concrete posts (the ones that lean out so you can't shin up them) and a minor act of trespass is required. Don't worry though, someone has got there before you and ripped part of the fence away, so on you stroll.

There are two main transmitters, what looks like a sub-station and various other concrete placements, which give this place a feel of the cold war. You can actually go inside of some of the abandoned places and truly feel like you should wish to leave quite quickly.

But what of the view? Lovely of course, rolling pasture to the north and the sea to the south. This was the first peak (Norfolk came so close) where the sea was actually visible. Also, due to the English Channel's proximity you get a true feeling of the absolute height from sea level to summit and it seems a long way. Extraordinary then that this is the thirteenth *lowest* peak of the 48, making you realise how much the land has already risen before you start on some of these walks.

There is a trig, just a little way from the proper peak, just next to, and I can hardly bring myself to say it, a car park actually **at** the summit. Not even a walk required to get there – well really!

The return gives you a chance to look out to sea for long minutes before disappearing into the woods, industrial estate and knot of tiny streets, ready for some fizzy lager or traditional ale depending on venue and a satisfying glow that for an hour's exertion another peak is ticked off.

Next – the boat back to the mainland (via a trip to the HMS Victory) and the South Downs peaks of Sussex await.

West Sussex

Blackdown – 280m (918ft)

Pub: The Red Lion, The Green, *Fernhurst*, Haslemere, Surrey GU27 3HY (01428) 643112

Parking: 500 metres (Paid)

Walk: 4 miles

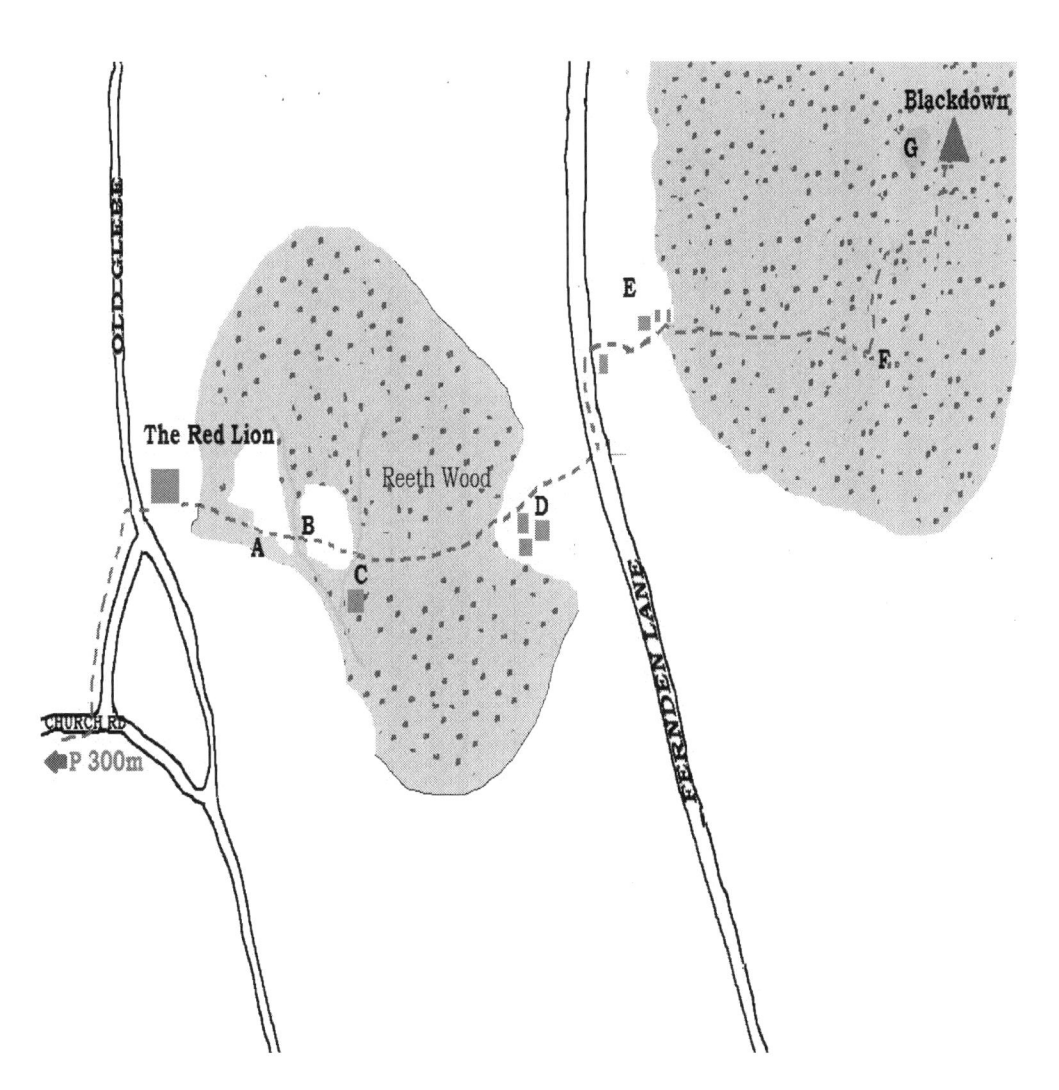

Have you ever wondered what it would be like to climb up a river? Well, for part of this walk we found out. We happened upon West Sussex's highest on a day when the heavens had opened and woodland streams were raging torrents.

Despite the postal address, little Fernhurst is in West Sussex and parking near to the pub is difficult. There are half a dozen spaces at the front, soon used up, and parking on the green is not an option. Therefore it is to the main village you go.

Coming from the south on the A286 (Haslemere Road) turn left on to Vann Road, then left again on to Crossfield and a pay and display car park. With its brutally flat roofed tower blocks, some tile hung half way down the walls, this is not the best introduction to an otherwise pleasant settlement as one makes one's way through the recycling bins. However, it soon gets better. Take a cut through the north-eastern corner of the car park between a red-brick garage block and a breeze block wall topped by a fence and you will soon be back out on to Vann Road opposite a small parade of shops. At the crossroads (and in the direction sign-posted "St. Margaret's Church" cross straight over and go down Church Road, with the churchyard soon visible on your right. Pass by several delightful old stone buildings and the Crossfield car park is soon a distant memory. Eventually on the left is the church itself, with the war memorial set in to the wall and this really is a pretty village which reaches its climax 350 metres on as you finally emerge on to a good old English green, with cricket pitch and all. Across the green, in a leftish direction is the Red Lion.

Now the walk proper begins. Between the pub and a tile-hung house to its right is a concrete finger post, showing you the way. Having passed a couple of houses and slowly ascending, you will note tennis courts through the gaps in the trees to the right (A). Then a small bridge crosses over a little stream (B) - thankfully this, at least, was flowing slowly and beneath us (rather than over our feet); and the path carries on within a thin belt of trees with open land on either side. Where the tree cover thickens you are now in Reeth Wood. Stick with the same path and soon you will come to the black weather-boarded Tanyard's Cottage (C). At this point the path strikes left (north-north-east), then right (east-north-east) next to, and in our case amongst, a stream which became a muddy torrent. Follow/swim this for about 500 metres then, at a junction of paths, turn neither right nor left, but take the one in the middle (eastwards) and within a couple of hundred metres you will come out in to the open and a group of buildings carrying the name "Reeth" (D).

Keeping these on your right, check left (north) and follow the path in an arc around to the right for about 300 metres before coming out on to the narrow Ferndean Lane where you turn left. Follow this for 150 metres, with farm buildings on your right, then hang right up the first public footpath which takes you on to a joint vehicular/pedestrian track. Stay with this for about 300 metres, passing just one house on the left at the very beginning, then arriving at the sumptuously barn-converted Cotchet Farm (E) which is also on your left at the very end.

At this point the peak is only about 500 metres away (as the crow flies), but there is not a simple trail to take you straight there. In fact, there is a variety of different, indirect ones. The simplest to recount is as follows: When you reach the last but one building at Crotchet Farm (a three-storey, stone affair), instead of carrying on up that track (which would lead you eventually to the peak also) go through the field gate to your right. This gentle pasture climbs slowly towards the goal and if you follow the central valley of these fields for about 450 metres you will come to a junction of paths. Take the left-hand path, this is called the Serpent Trail (F). Follow it for about 100 metres before another path appears on the right. At this point the peak is only about 150 metres away and you could try just tramping off-path and going straight for it (if you can see it, which you can't), but the area is quite marshy so it is best to stick to the paths as much as possible.

So take that right-hand path for about 100 metres until you are level with a pond some 40 metres away on your left. Turn and walk towards the pond (G), keeping it to your left, once you are past it the trig is nigh, roughly 20 metres away. It is well hidden though, as if ashamed. It needn't be, it's higher than its Eastern brother in Ditchling.

The views hereabout, if not *exactly* from the trig (which is within woodland and swamp) are amazing, particularly over to the west where the trees are fewer. This area is, strictly speaking, sandstone, part of the Hythe Formation, which does give it a less chalky feel (and although it might feel like you're "in the South Downs" you are actually in the Weald on the Greensand Ridge). In addition, the plateau nature of the summit and the bogginess all around does almost give it a feel of one of the higher peaty peaks. Whilst no monster, at just shy of a thousand feet, this is the first peak we reached which was in the top half (racing in at number 23!). On this day it was not a good idea to hang around as the heavens spilled their load, and soon it was time to gladly take the downhill and back to the Red Lion.

Next – Ditchling Beacon and a hope of sunnier times!

East Sussex

Ditchling Beacon – 248m (813ft)

Pub: The White Horse Inn, 16 West Street, Ditchling, West Sussex

BN6 8TS

01273 842006

Parking: Nearby (free)

Walk: 3 miles

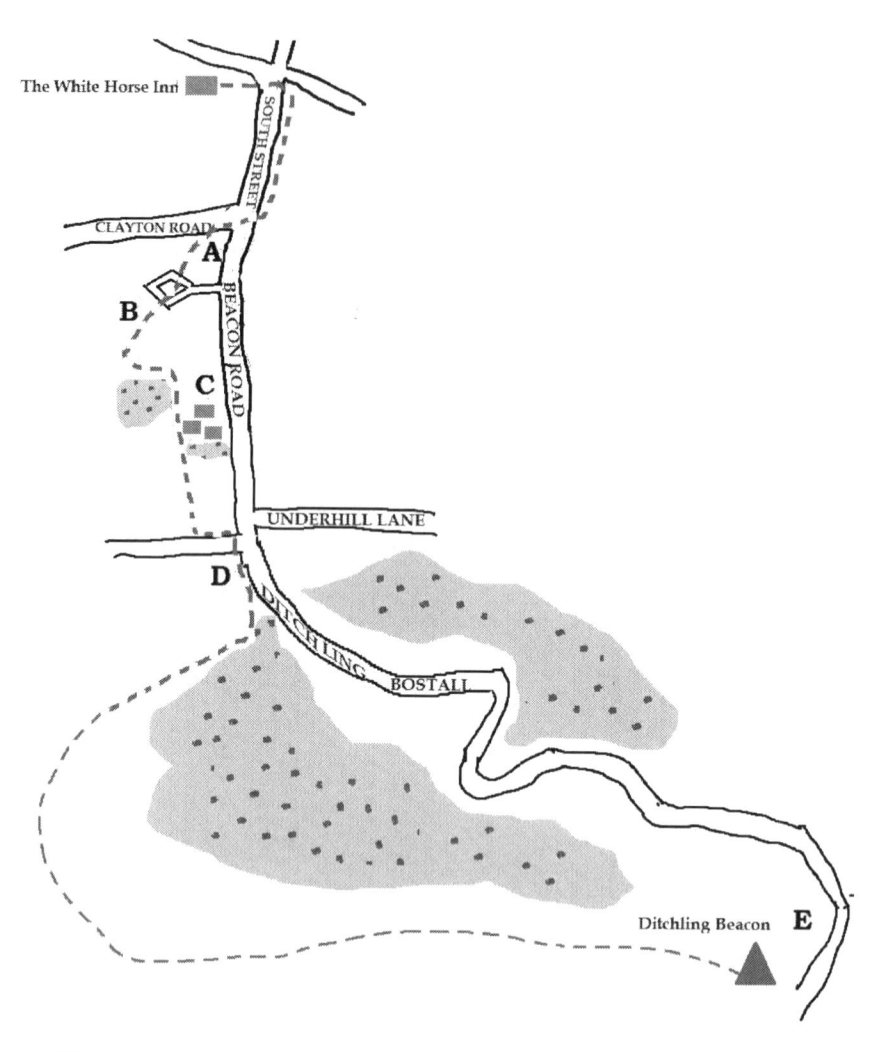

This really is a lovely little walk entirely within the South Downs National Park. It is split in to three chunks of village, flat pasture and steep climb up the chalky ridge of the South Downs.

You may be lucky enough to find somewhere near the White Horse Inn on West Street itself to park (presuming you are not staying at the inn itself). Failing that there are other options nearby.

Turn right down South Street for about 150 metres, crossing to the left as the path runs out on the right. You then come to a small green on the corner of South Street, Clayton Road and Beacon Road with a white finger post pointing left to Ditchling and right to Brighton. There is also a white post and rail fence around a planted area. Just behind this is a bench and just to the left of that is a narrow cut-through footpath, which is easily missed if the grass is high (A).

This nips between gardens and passes tennis courts on the left, trees on the right and finally breaks out by The Villa Bungalows (1930s, red brick) onto a grass roundabout with a Narnia lamppost. This last item helpfully contains a fingerpost sign pointing you over right to "Public Footpath to The Downs." Follow this direction and find a tiny path between two front gardens next to a sign for "Neville Flats 21-24."

This is quite a poky footpath, but worry not because within 30 metres it broadens and breaks out briefly in to woodland, passing under power lines and now into open grassy pasture which covers the sands and gravels (B).

The path goes out right-ish (south-westwards) for about 100 metres before hitting a field boundary and moving slightly left to go due south for 150 metres in the open, brushing woodland for 100 metres then continuing south for 250 metres more to a group of farm buildings at Park Barn Farm (C). Still south for another 250-odd metres you will eventually arrive at a road – Underhill Lane.

Really at this point your choices are several, and certainly the destination is there in front of you as broad as day – the South Downs, a simple chalk ridge rising out of the mudstone and running more or less east to west, right to left across three counties.

You could slowly and surely meander up the oddly-named Ditchling Bostall which begins about 150 metres to your left, or you could cut straight across to the footpath which climbs the ridge and joins the South Downs Way.

We did a mixture of the two, first turning left for 150 metres and then, near a grass triangle (signposted) just before Ditchling Bostall, on the right, crossing a gravelled car park area (D) and joining a footpath just off of it. This runs parallel with, and to the right of, Ditchling Bostall briefly before edging away to the right (west) on and up and around and through a woodland. Now you really begin to climb up the ridge, mixing pasture, woodland and chalky outcrops. Having climbed for about 500 metres you are now out in the open and a lot of the way up.

The path hugs the southern side of the woodland before wrapping around out in to the open, still climbing and to the east where eventually another path joins it from the right. At this point you will see to your right, about 80 metres away, a wider path – this is the South Downs Way which extends for 100 miles between Eastbourne and Winchester. You could rush to join this and then follow it leftwards all the way to your destination, but it makes more sense to stay with the smaller path for just another 250 metres before it joins it anyway.

It is at this point that your attention needs to be drawn to the right. Fifty metres, there in front of you, on the far side of the field, is the trig point.

The views which you have been enjoying on your way up can now be savoured for all their worth. To the south, towards Brighton, the city itself could not quite be seen, nor could the seven-mile distant sea, though others have claimed it to be visible, but we could just about make out Brighton & Hove Albion's new stadium at Falmer. To the north, back over Ditchling, towards Burgess Hill is the high Weald.

Having enjoyed the views, it's worth pushing on just a couple of hundred metres more, and I'll tell you why – ice-creams. It cannot be guaranteed, but during normal office hours (and, let's face it, depending on the time of year) there is often to be seen a little van chugging away with its coolants in full throttle. Take the edge off your racing pulse and let things drop a few degrees as you suck on a mini-milk or whatever takes your fancy.

Your face wiped clear of the guilty pleasures, it's time to turn back. Walking east-west along the ridge you get a different perspective, the South Downs Way spooling off towards

Winchester. Down the hill towards that gravelled car park, then left along Underhill Road for those 200 metres and then right across that field to Park Barn Farm. Onwards, right and under those power lines and then through that little footpath which takes you by Neville Flats and across that Narnia lamp-posted green to Villa Bungalows and by those tennis courts and out on to the green at the corner of South Street, Clayton Road and Beacon Road, heading back up South Road before finally turning left back on to West Street and the White Horse Inn.

This white building itself is Norman (12th century) in origin and is an active inn (seven rooms). Downstairs the pub offering is comely, with a fireplace and a walled courtyard garden. It has, by the looks of it, recently been refurbished and is very clean whilst retaining a traditional feel to it. The menu is a bit on the expensive side and is largely traditional fayre and the inn also boasts a range of local beers.

That, then, is the South Downs and the highest peak in East Sussex. The most southern and the chalkiest of all the chalks are, well, chalked off, but it isn't over yet.

Next – Surrey.

Surrey

Leith Hill

Height: 294 m (965 ft)

Pub: The Plough Inn, Coldharbour, Dorking, Surrey RH5 6HD

(01306) 711793

Parking: Nearby (free, but limited)

Walk: 2 miles

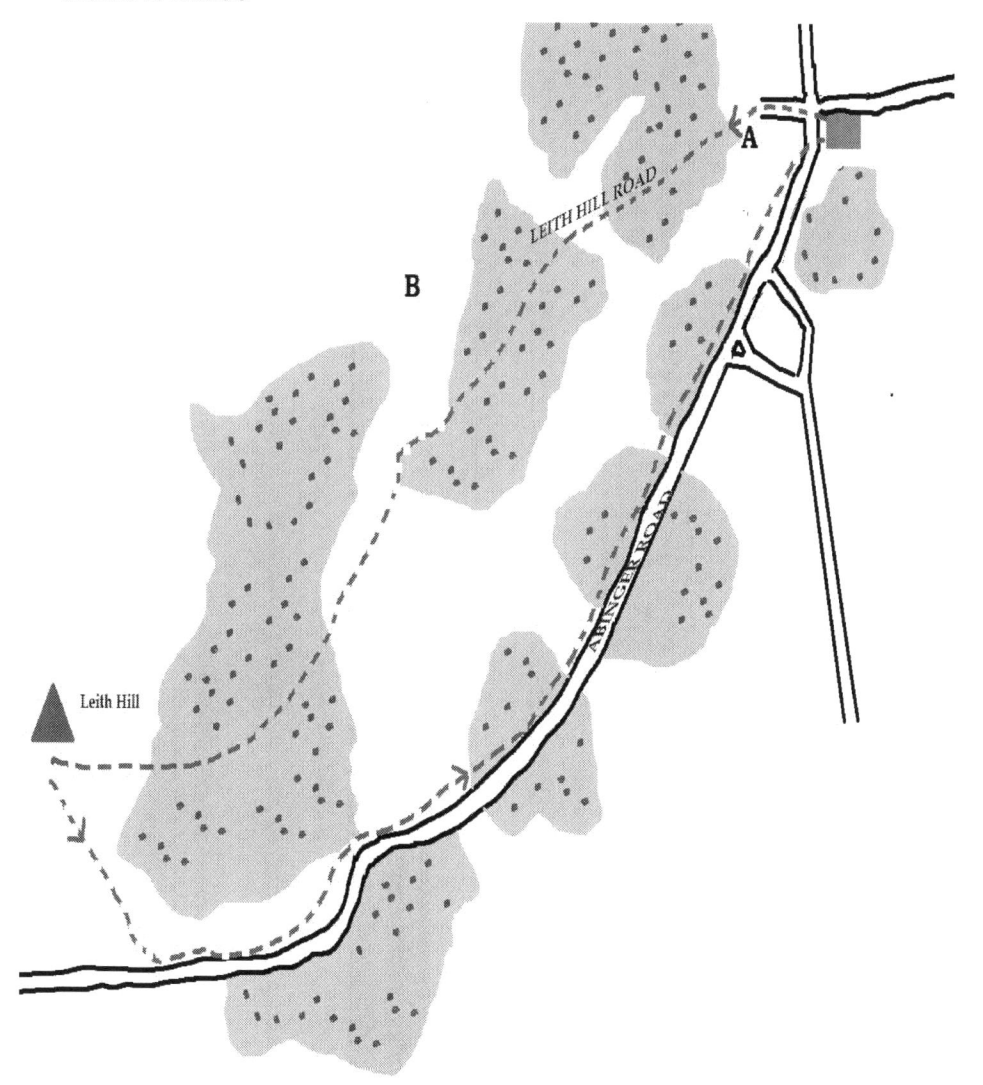

Leith Hill and Coldharbour are set amongst the Surrey Hills Area of Outstanding Natural Beauty and are possibly at their most glorious in the early autumn with the leaves beginning to red and brown.

The area is part of the Greensand Ridge, which forces its way between the white chalk to the north and the mudstone to the south. The Greensand was laid down in the Cretaceous period at the same time as the chalklands, but with silicates rather than calciates. However, by the expedient of where it is – it's going in the Southern Chalklands section and there's an end to it.

With the cream rendered (and, it has to be said, very popular) pub building on your left, proceed towards a little green area which has an old red telephone box (A) and go to the right of this up a little lane (Leith Hill Road, whose name should be a clue and which starts as a road and then becomes something less) with a village notice board, benches, finger-post and post box on the right, and a set of charming slate-roofed houses on the left.

The route from here, just over a mile, is remarkably simple. Just follow the path up and around slightly left for about 450 metres until it breaks out of the woodland and the path widens for about 100 metres, with Coldharbour Cricket Club on your right (B). As the path reaches the wood again, take the slightly diverted path around to the right onto open ground, into a copse then into the open again swinging left (south-westwards) for about 500 metres before re-entering the wood. It's actually quite difficult to lose your way as you edge on to ever higher ground because of the landmark Leith Tower.

As the woods clear again, you will see the tower in front of you, up a last hillock and you're there, the highest point on the Greensand Ridge and the second highest county top in south east England (slipping in between the next door neighbours Walbury Hill and Pilot Hill of Berkshire and Hampshire) at 294 metres or 965 feet. The fine gothic tower itself was built by Richard Hull in the late 18th century in a bid to reach over 1,000 feet above sea level (which he exceeded by a good 30-odd feet).

Views from it are said to be amazing (I say "said to be" because on this day a great storm was brewing, and so the tower had - just! - closed early, so we were denied this extra elevation) with London, the English Channel and 13 counties visible, supposedly. The tower is now owned and run by the National Trust – and it does splendid ice-creams, that at least was open.

It is believed that, on the summit of Leith Hill in 851, Æthelwulf of Wessex, (Alfred the Great's father), met the Danes who, having sacked Canterbury and London, were heading for Winchester and he sent them packing.

As you also prepare for home, you can either go the way you came, or, for some variety you could head downhill and south-eastwards towards the National Trust car park at "Windy Gap" (not sure whether that's windy as in twisty-turny, or in relation to the howling gale) until you meet the road (Abinger Road) at the bottom and turn left along about a mile of pleasant, but generally not earth-shattering, sylvan residential road. Either way will, inevitably, lead you to lovely Coldharbour and The Plough.

A 17th Century coaching house, on the menu is home-cooked food, home brewed ale and also four-star bed and breakfast accommodation. Or, just a glass of lemonade.

With the storm clouds gathering and the trees beginning to whisper, it was off to our Premier Inn in Camberley and, if the weather permitted, the twin peaks of Berkshire and Hampshire.

The Plough and Leith Hill Tower - 1,000ft above sea level!

Hampshire and Berkshire

Hampshire: Pilot Hill – 286 metres (938 feet)

Berkshire: Walbury Hill - 297 metres (974 feet)

Pub – Swan Inn, Craven Road, Inkpen, Hungerford RG17 9DX

(01488) 668326

Walk - 7 miles

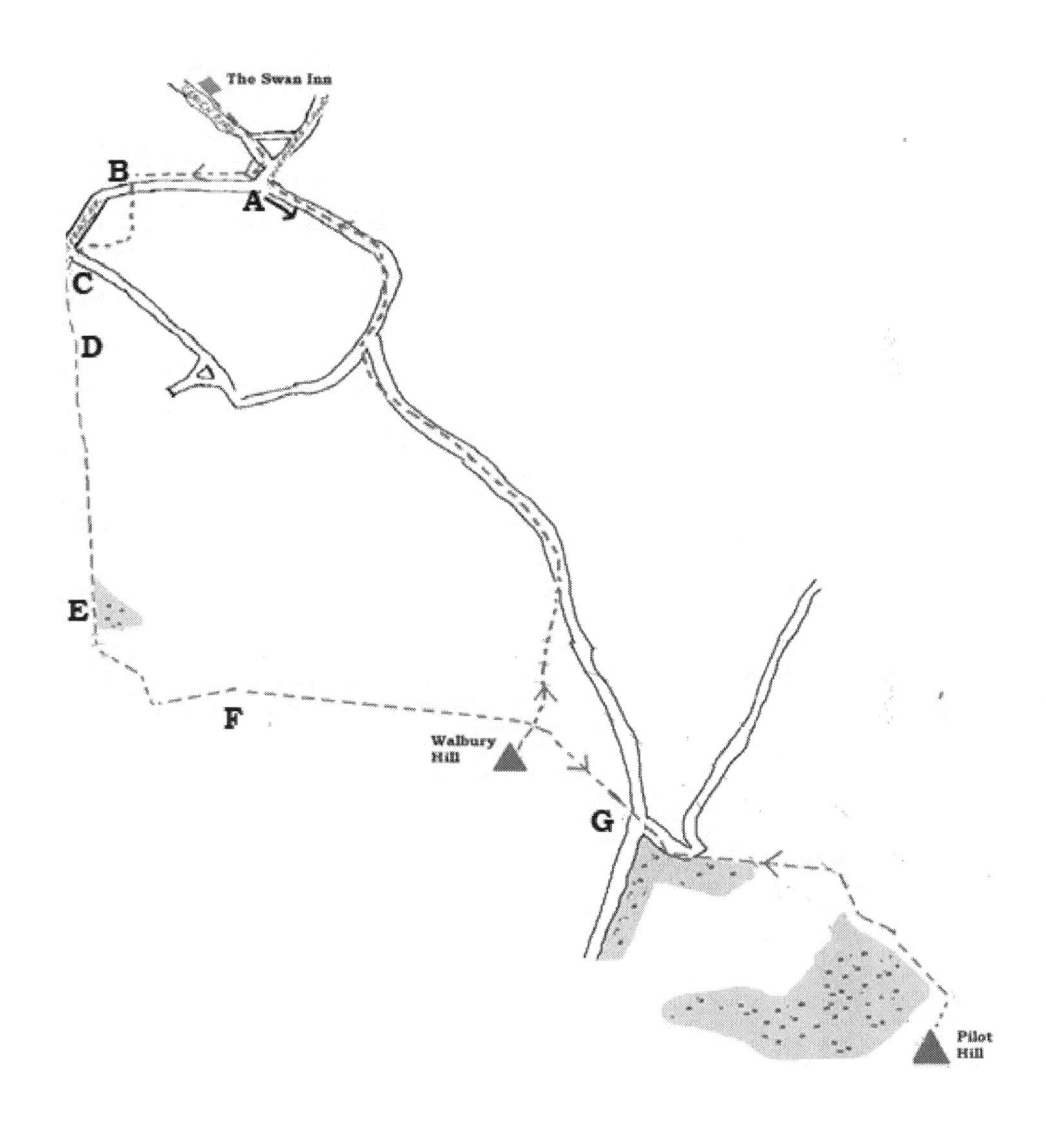

The progress from Surrey to these peaks had been delayed by a day for a surprise visit to Legoland. So it was from the not very far away Newbury-Thatcham (thanks again Premier Inn) that we progressed to the village of Inkpen.

Whilst it would be possible to take a different pub and a different walk from the south to take in Hampshire on its own, it would be a criminal act to deny yourself one of the most rewarding walks in southern England. It is so often the case that a hill range or ridge defined the boundary between two warring kingdoms, and in more recent times, counties (not warring, mind you) and so it is that two county peaks appear side by side (think of Kent and Greater London or Essex and Cambridgeshire, already done or, Cheshire and Staffordshire, West Yorkshire and Greater Manchester to come) so it is with these two and the chalky ridge of the Hampshire Downs.

Park up at or near the Swan Inn (it was closed at the time, but the landlord, bless him, said we could use his car park, you may not be so lucky so it could be pot luck somewhere in the village). Of course, if you're staying there (they have rooms and are accredited four stars by the AA) then parking won't be a problem.

With the pub on your left (why is it usually the left?) proceed south-westwards down the Road for about 150 metres until it forks slightly to the right and fifty metres on from that sweeps right (westwards) instead of carrying on west you could take the junction on the left (A) as indicated by the arrow and follow the road south, a more direct route but all road (we can pick that up on the way back anyway). Instead, if you do carry on west you will meet a footpath on the left (B) about 100 metres along after some very fine houses.

This footpath goes across open fields for about 150 metres, then right (west) in a lightly-treed area which then arrives at a junction of several small roads (C). Turn left here (not left and back on yourself, but the second left, signposted Ham, 2 miles) this pleasant country lane is Spray Road which you follow for about 200 metres. Now take a gated farm track on the left (D) and follow it for 200 metres before it jolts slightly to the right and then corrects itself again. You carry on walking at the field's edge, almost due south for about one kilometre and the ridge in front of you contains not one but two county tops.

The path strikes leftish around a lightly wooded area (E), then up and up Inkpen Hill, contours coming thick and fast. Once at the ridge, you are now on the Test Way. You need east (left) and then an early point of interest will be the ghoulish Coombe Gibbet (F), a slight detour at SU360620. No need to direct you to it, it's bloody massive. The gibbet, by the way, was only ever used for the hanging of the adulterous pair George Broomham and Dorothy Newman, for whom it was erected (if you'll pardon the expression) in 1676 after they murdered the former's wife and son who had discovered them *in flagrante*.

Walbury Hill itself is about one kilometre on from here, but although you will pass within 200 metres of the peak, resist the temptation and walk past it rather than taking the detour, we'll come back to it later, it is the pinnacle of this walk and must tantalise us a little longer. Instead, stroll on ever eastwards to Hampshire and Pilot Hill (a round trip of nearly four miles). At this point, the path is called the Wayfarers Walk, which runs 70 miles from Walbury to Emsworth east to west.

Continue along Wayfarer's along a chalky path which, 300 metres from the Walbury Hill turn off, then merges with a road. Carry on in the same direction until the road bends around to the right. At this point, take the turning on the left (G). After 20 metres, though, take the footpath right, next to a tiny copse and carry on along the ridge dropping slightly downwards. Go on with this path which now climbs again and takes you in to woodland. As you reach open land, there is a fence to the right and at the point where it ends (H) a gate will take you in to the field (right). This is the final field and, depending on the time of year (we were there in October when the crops had been harvested) you will find the trig at SU398601 about 150 metres south-east of the place where you entered the field. It is bang in the middle of this field and, of course, if the crops are in full swing it might not be a bright idea to trample them! Be reminded also that this last bit of the walk is private land with no public right of way, so tread lightly if at all. The views are not impressive due to the low fall of land and surrounding features which block long views, but better things are to come.

Retrace your steps the 1.9 miles along Wayfarers until the point at which a path off to the left takes you off of the main route and to your goal. This does require going over a wooden fence and on to private land again. But there it is 200 metres on, the pinnacle of the walk and the highest point in south-east England, eleven metres higher than Pilot Hill, but so much more rewarding with long views across the Hampshire Downs, North Downs and various other ups and downs.

Now for the walk home, and halfway between Walbury Hill and the gibbet, why not take a short-cut and go down that road? This is about 1.2 miles and as you reach Lower Green a sign will show you the way to the Swan Inn. There's only one road in, follow this then take the right at the first junction, then left and the pub is on your right 100 metres along.

Now for some food (if the pub is open – it wasn't for us on this Sunday), and the choice is not difficult, the pub boasts that it was "Joint 2nd in the national "Bangers and Mash" competition"! Hmm.....

Next – the land of the white horses: Oxfordshire and Wiltshire.

Oxfordshire

White Horse Hill 261m (856ft)

Pub: The White Horse, Marsh Way, Woolstone, Faringdon, Oxfordshire SN7 7QL

(01367) 820726

Parking: Free, near pub

Walk: 4 miles

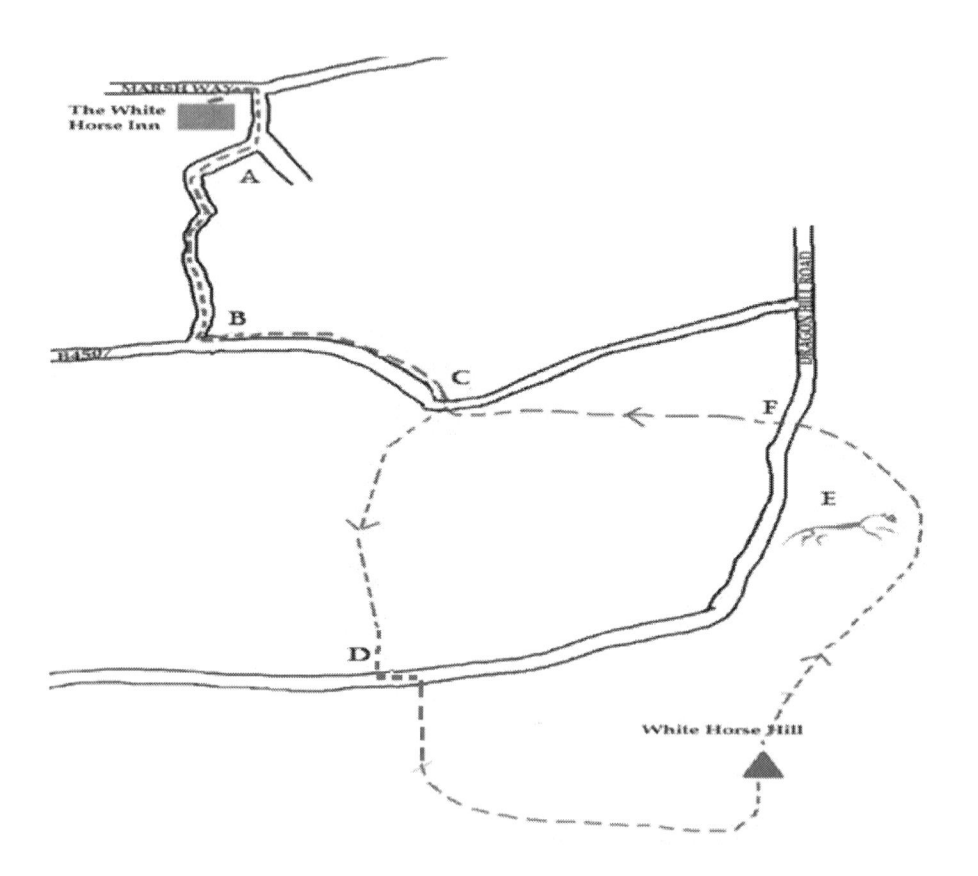

This is a little gem of a walk which gives much considering its relative lowness. It begins in a charming little village and produces a landmark of some repute.

We begin with a drink at the White Horse, a quaint thatched pub near to similar buildings in a sleepy corner of Woolstone. There is plenty of parking just to the north in its extended car park.

Drink drunk and with the pub behind you on your right, follow the signpost to "Ashbury" and "White Horse Hill" and proceed south down the tiny road past some stylish buildings. About 100 metres along is a fork which, if you took the left prong (A), would cut a bit off the journey. However, although this is publicly accessible to begin with it leads to private property. Instead, huffily turn right and notice the sign which says White Horse Hill 1 ½ miles – don't worry, it isn't that far, we can take shortcuts that motorists can't.

This long and winding (and, seemingly, nameless) road is very narrow and vergeless to begin with, although these do appear later as the road widens a little. Here and there you will catch glimpses, and on occasions full views through gaps in the hedges of our quarry, and pass by just one house on each side (opposite each other). After 500 metres you arrive at the junction of the B4507 (B) and need to ignore the brown tourist sign for "Uffington White Horse and Waylands Smithy" which is there to usher on motorists to do it the easy way and park nearby – for shame.

Instead, turn left and follow the sign for Uffington/Kingston Isle/Wantage for about 250 metres, taking the left hand side verge which is a little wider than its opposite number (which also banks up to become unusable a little way along). Do this for about 250 metres then cross the road and enter the field via a stile to the right of a field gate (C). Here is a National Trust sign telling you this is White Horse Hill and advising dog walkers that sheep are grazing here. Behind you is the Greensand (the same stuff from Leith Hill) and ahead of you all is chalk. The first bit is quite flat, but with the ridge laid out all before you just ahead, you get a feeling of the effect of Africa slamming in to Europe even at this great distance, causing the land to fold in long lines, but leaving other areas less altered. The flatter area is known as "The Manger" as if it were the place where chalky horse comes to feed.

Now you have choices. The trig is, naturally at the highest point slightly to the left of due south, but reached just as easily by going left or right, especially as you will want to see the horse as well. There is a third route, straight up through the middle, which is a trodden, if not well-trodden, path, but this does seem to link through to other paths anyway. To be honest, cross words had been exchanged in the car, this was the latest of so many walks all in the same year and was perhaps the journey too far in what I would refer to (to the annoyance of my family) as the "ill-fated whole in the middle tour" where the remaining peaks in this part of the world were mopped up and one or two things went a bit wrong. It was best, therefore, that we trod our own paths and had our own thoughts until we reached the horsey, then things would be alright again.

For the maximum enjoyment and a circular route, it is advised to go around to the right. You can aim for the edge of the ridge by keeping the fence on your right. Now find your way up to the road (Dragon Hill Road). This is about 500 metres as the crow flies, not much longer as the crow...walks.

There are various paths around the top and you may happen upon a parking area (D) which takes about ten cars, but wherever you hit the road you need to turn left. You will see the land still rising to the right, that, obviously, is where we are going.

150 metres on from the parking area is a meeting of paths and this is as good a place as any to leave Dragon Hill Road and head right, up a stony path just opposite a gate and orientation board. 150 metres up that and you are at the summit plateau, the roof of Oxfordshire.

This is an iron age hill-fort, a Scheduled Ancient Monument which is somewhat grandiosely and misleadingly called "Uffington Castle" covering some 30,000 square feet and if you walk across (around) this, you will find, at its far (eastern) edge, the point you are looking for – trig and all.

Whilst the views are as amazing as you might expect, you'll probably want to save your sarnies just a while longer as you head 250 metres south (i.e. in the vague direction back towards the pub) to the main attraction.

The Uffington White Horse (E), one of several such features in the south of England, dates from between about 1,300 to 500 BC and maintains its whiteness by being "scoured" every so often, where volunteers participate in "chalking days."

You can get right up to the horse (no touchy touchy) and get an idea of its scale from that. Looking over its long head and body down the Oxfordshire hills and there beyond whilst gnawing a cheese sandwich – surrounded by your loved ones - is one of the more pleasurable ways to spend an afternoon.

Heading back to base, keep the stallion to your left as you make your way downhill from head to tail and eventually you will swing around left and rediscover Dragon Hill Road. As a point of interest, there is a little hillock further along (F) reaching 197 metres in height, but really after the main show, why bother?

Generally track down and left, left and down towards The Manger and soon you are back at that gate, the circle complete and the small matter of the B4507 to contend with.

What a lovely walk, everything was alright again and everyone was ready for a bit more chalky fun as we headed to our final white hill – in Wiltshire.

Wiltshire

Milk Hill 294m (965ft)

Pub: The Barge Inn Honey Street, Pewsey SN9 5PS

(01672) 851705

Parking: Near pub, free

Walk: 5 miles

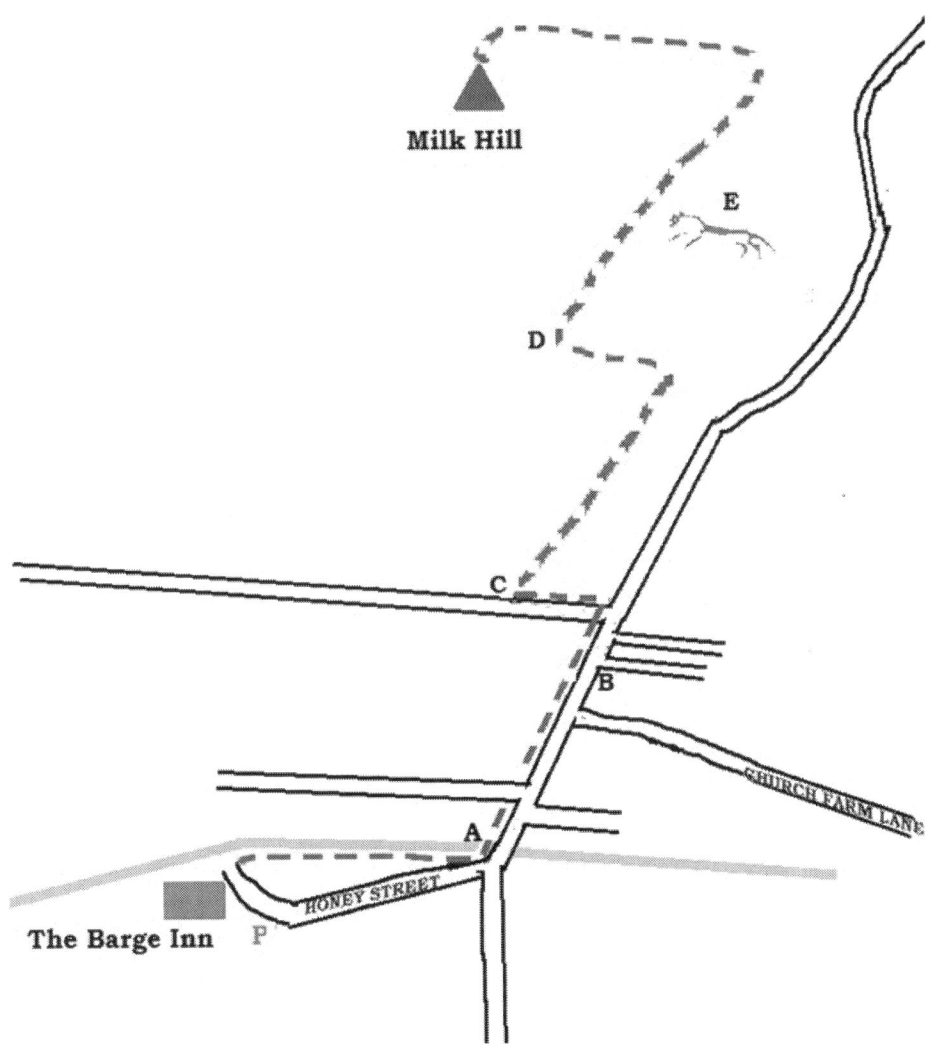

What a charming stroll! Lovely chalkland scenery, *another* white horse (two in one day!) and a canal-side beginning and end, with barges and all.

A quick drink at the pub (for us it was a Sunday and it was closing early). From the pub itself, already over-left you can see the very white horse which tells you the peak is just beyond. There is parking here and there very close to the pub.
Once parked up and supped up go to the canal, turn right and walk past the barges. Climb up some steps to join Honey Street and go over the bridge (A). There is no verge for the first part, so you will have to go carefully, crossing a small, nameless, road on your left.

Keeping left, you will have to cross front lawns and driveways to stay out of the traffic (the verge on the right is too thin) now the limited settlement of Honey Street runs out and a sign tells you that you are in Alton Barnes.

Now past a field gate on the left, and another 100 metres on to another and still carry on. Now Alton Barnes proper is on your right, with its few houses, near the end of these is a pair of brick, thatched cottages (B) and 100 metres on from these, with horsey in full view, is a turning to the left – with a sign for Devizes, Stanton St. Bernard and All Cannings.

Walk verge-side (as much as possible) for about 150 metres until a rough area appears on the right, (C), this is a field boundary which you take and the way ahead is clear, it points towards the white horse and the fold between two hills. The plateau peak is over-left and beyond view.

For the next kilometre follow the field boundary straight ahead towards the horse (north), on the day we visited, the grass was long and we disturbed (unwittingly) some red deer and were given a wonderful show of their agility as they fled in (unjustified) terror – sorry deer!

On reaching the edge of the field and the hill bottom, hang left (west), with the horse now on your right for about 200 metres. Now turn right where you will see a hedge and path and the climb begins (D). Be warned, there are barbed wire fences and at this point I did snare my midriff, saved from disaster only by the thickness of my braid. The climb goes on for about 300 metres up and slightly to the right (east). Now you will reach a junction of paths with the horse itself 150 metres to the right for a quick visit (E). Do not let the fact that this is a fraud from 1812 bother you!

Back to the junction and you are just 500 metres from the top, although the walk will be a bit longer to avoid tramping across a planted field.

Remember at the junction to use the right-hand path (from the horse, or just carry straight on if you didn't bother) and after 100 metres more a path comes in from your left. 100 metres more and you are at the field's edge (on your left). Keep this to your left and trace its eastern edge for about 350 metres before turning left with it and hemming its northern limits until a point about 200 metres along and then about 50 metres south in to the field (crops depending) and, well, that is it.

In truth, it was a bit difficult to find and locate exactly, so one is left with a "hereabouts" feeling.

As usual, a plateau does mean the view is a little diluted, but still impressive, over towards northern Wiltshire, with hang-gliders floating hereabouts.

Arriving back at the pub, dusk was just descending and the twinkling lights of the barges beckoning us. This was perfect and perhaps the loveliest welcome backs of all. The pub was closed, as we knew it would be, but we had already partaken.
That then, was the end of our chalkland adventure, 13 peaks of similar height and age and with varying degrees of whiteness, all slain.

Overall, it was 22 down and almost halfway there. Ahead of us awaited different types of terrain: moorland, peaty peaks and rugged beasts. But first was the little matter of mopping up all sorts of bits and pieces in the middle.

And it began with Warwickshire.

Chapter 3 – The Bit in the Middle

This little collection of peaks defies categorisation, it encompasses urban pimples of land, a majestic Welsh-border beast, gentle meadow and any number of other descriptions. It goes from little Bristol at 160 metres, to Herefordshire's giant Black Mountain at 703 metres. These peaks are a bunch of left-overs, they have nothing in common, other than the fact that they are in the middle and so can be thrown together.

Between them, these land-locked (apart from the Severn estuary in Gloucestershire) counties provide a sample of all that England has to offer and all within a fairly limited geographical spread. See list hereunder.

Herefordshire	**703 metres**
Shropshire	**540 metres**
Worcestershire	**425 metres**
Gloucestershire	**330 metres**
Leicestershire	**278 metres**
West Midlands	**271 metres**
Warwickshire	**261 metres**
Northamptonshire	**225 metres**
Bristol	**160 metres**

Warwickshire

Ebrington Hill

Height: 261m (856ft)

Pub: Red Lion, Front Street, Ilmington, Shipston-on-Stour CV36 4LX

(01608) 682089

Parking: Nearby (free)

Walk: 3 ½ miles

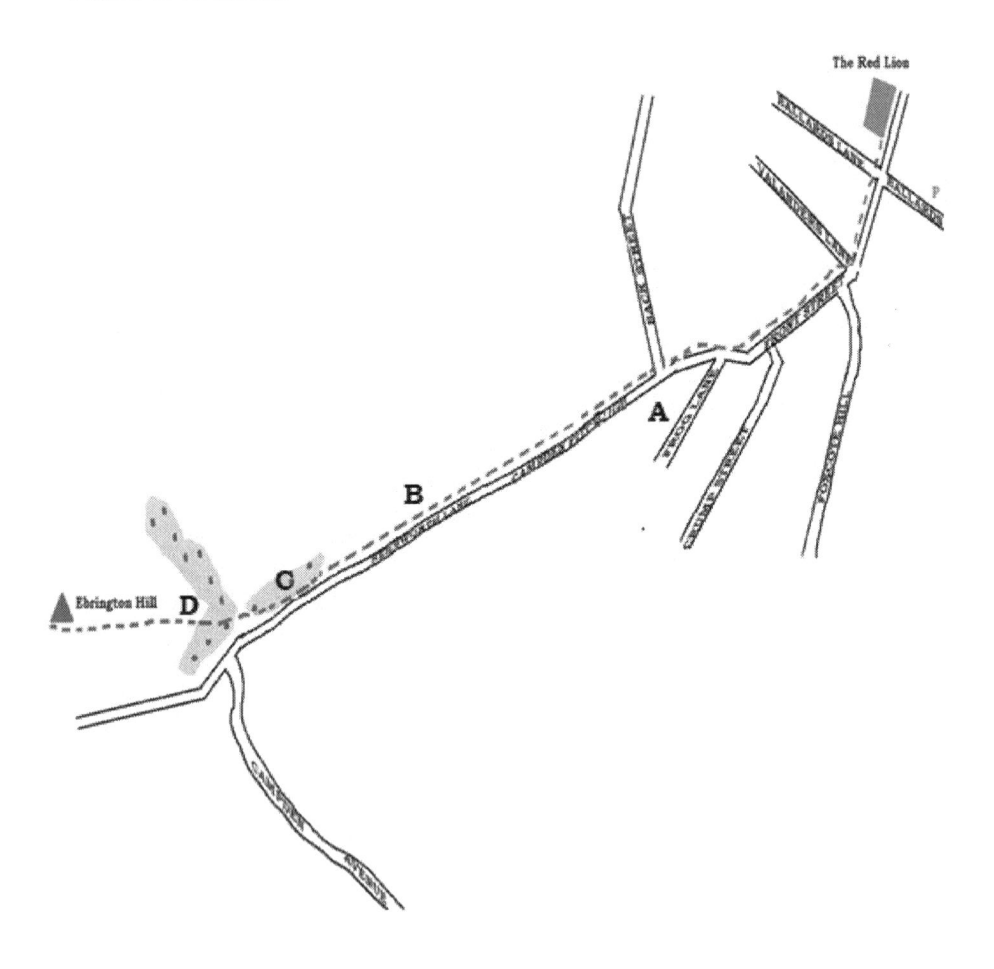

With no disrespect to the county of the Bard, apart from a visit to lovely Stratford-Upon-Avon, what would be the reason for coming to this county? There is nothing wrong with it, in fact it is very lovely (Kenilworth Castle, for example), but if you had to list ten counties you wished to visit, would you include Warwickshire? Along with Northamptonshire and perhaps a few others, it is one of those anonymous, in the middle, forgotten places. It is why pursuing an "every county" mission (highest point or otherwise) is so important to knowing your England – you would be missing out on so much.

Our visit here came the day after the two white horses and it would have been difficult to match that. The walk, however, was joyful enough – to start with.

Ilmington offers many opportunities for parking and there is ample space opposite the Red Lion pub, down Ballards Lane. From here, head back towards the pub and turn left along Front Street (incidentally, this is quite handy for orientation if you get lost –parallel to it and about 300 metres behind it is Back Street and, in case that isn't enough, in between is – you've guessed it – Middle Street).

There are footpath alternatives, but none of these are particularly convenient unless you want a much longer walk and if you are not in a hurry (which, on this day, we were – we had another peak to reach), so it's quite a bit of road/verge walking – actually a fair bit of the former, so not so bad all in all. Proceed along Front Street for about 150 metres and keep with it as it sweeps around to the right (Foxcote Hill on your left), carry on for about 80 metres and the thin end of a green becomes visible. Note and laugh at "Grump Street" (and remember yesterday!) to the left, but do not take it, stay faithful to Front Street. 120 metres on, the road swings around to the left and leaves the green behind. Carry on. 80 metres, Back Street on your right, follow Front Street still (A) and now it becomes Campden Hill, soon changing to Campden Pitch and later Nebsworth Lane.

About 400 metres on from where you passed Back Street, the buildings run out and you are in open country. There is just under a mile of road/verge walking, with things being generally safer on the right with a wider sward and facing the traffic, there are odd places where you might poke through the hedge and commit an act of trespass, all the while making sure you can find your way out again.

Two-thirds of the way along you will see, on the right (B), a ranch-style fence and gate (serving a house which is well set back) and 300 metres along from this your time on the road comes to an end as you turn right and climb a field gate (C) which is between two groups of trees and you are now ready to head in a slightly more westerly direction than the south-westerly road had been taking you.

Carry on for the moment (about 100 metres) in the same direction you had been going along Campden Pitch/ Nebsworth Lane as you pass amongst trees, now veering slightly away from being parallel with the road and distancing yourself gradually from it. Your path will break cover with the trees here and there, but finally after about 400 metres you are out in the open (D). At this point you are also on a recognised footpath for the rest of the walk.

From here, the summit is just about 300 metres and one field away, marked out by a transmitter.

If this is not clear enough, ensure that the field edge you walk on has trees to the right and that the cropped field is to the left. When the field and trees diverge, carry straight on ahead (west) towards the transmitter and soon enough, just metres from the Gloucestershire border, you are there.

The point itself is somewhere over to the right, up a muddy path and slightly in to the next field. Views are not brilliant, they are bucolic and rolling and do give some indication of distant places and a sense of elevation, although the whole matter is slightly undermined by the brutal yellow brick structures, antennae and "Danger!" signs.

We did struggle finding the exact spot (and did, in fact, end up in the wrong place and at the wrong transmitter and as we cast around searching for the promised land, the mood turned a little sour as Eldest had holes in his walking boots and this did not make for a pleasant time as the mud and goo (for these were muddy, muddy fields) found their way in and between his toes). For the aggravation of it all, the 'peak' was a little disappointing, pleasant though the rolling fields of Warwickshire (and indeed neighbouring Gloucestershire) were.

Job done, time to return and change footwear and a drink in the Red Lion, a cosy and friendly pub which specialises in Hook

Norton beer and, if you are there at weekends, you may enjoy live music.

We, however, had to drink up and move on – that other anonymous county, Northamptonshire, was waiting for us.

Northamptonshire

Arbury Hill – 225m (738ft)

Pub - The Windmill Inn, Main Street, Badby, Northants NN11 3AN
(01327) 311070

Parking: Free, nearby
Walk: 2 miles

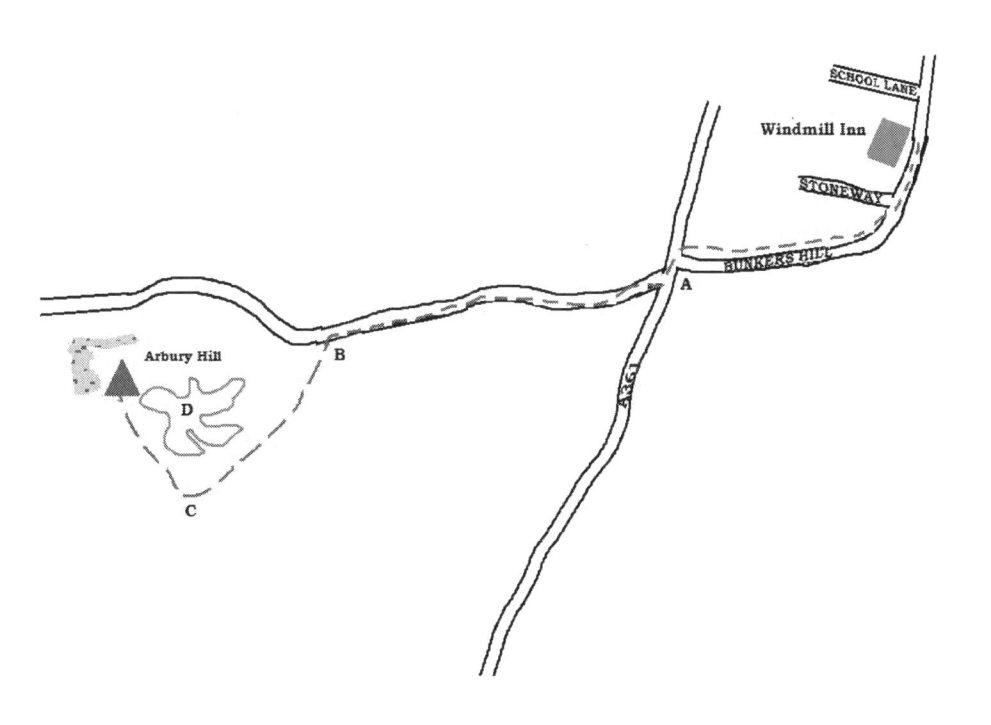

Northamptonshire, Northamptonshire, Northamptonshire, that other anonymous, stuck in the middle county (go on, name a famous person from Northamptonshire – well, alright, Diana Princess of Wales and the writer and poet laureate John Dryden, but I had to look that up, after those it's a bit disappointing).

The hill itself is a bit anonymous too, only missing out of the bottom ten by dint of the City of London. It is, however, a most pleasant stroll, especially in the dark, crisp latter months of the year and also if you don't mind mud – lots of mud. This was the fourth of our "hole in the middle tour" hills (along with Oxfordshire, Wiltshire and Warwickshire) and was the muddiest of all the 48.

The 17th century Windmill Inn is built in the local Yellowstone with a thatched roof and is on a lovely green in the picturesque village of Badby. Parking is available on the street nearby.

With the pub on your right, proceed in an orderly fashion down Main Street, then the second right which is Bunkers Hill. A lot of this walk is, again, road and verge-walking.

Bunkers Hill you follow for about 400 metres before it meets the A361 (A), which you cross and take the nameless little road almost opposite, which is signposted for Catesby (2 miles). Follow this for half a mile and then some choices present themselves. You could skirt around to the north for a slightly shorter if steeper ascent, but much the most logical (and public-footpath-based) is to heed the field gate and footpath sign on the left (B) which bid you go that way (remembering to keep the trees to your left and following the direction of the sign); Follow this, tree-lined, path for about half a mile as it slowly climbs from about 160 to 200 metres. After the second tree-lined field boundary to the right it is time to *turn* right (C) and take on the last twenty metres of extra altitude.

This area has various paths and scratches to take you north and passes through and around an area which has been scraped for what looks like BMX or quad-bike or some such, I don't know (D).

The top itself is indistinct and is just beyond the scraped soil, with an arc of trees to its north and west and the views are pleasant enough down towards Daventry, Warwickshire and, at a snip, Oxfordshire and all over the middle of England (and only Bette can get middler than this).

These slopes drain in to three different rivers: the little-known Leam, which flows in to the Severn – Britain's longest river, which finds the sea over west between England and Wales; the Cherwell, which feeds the Thames and goes east to the North Sea and the Nene which flows north to The Wash. Whilst not having another river flowing south to complete the set, this is the very essence of central England.

Whilst at the "top" it may be worth doing a quick circuit and seeing if you can find what is apparently a very square ditch and embankment about 200 metres across. This apparently, marks the remains of an iron age fort – although not everyone can agree on that point.

The one point to be agreed on, however, is that the Windmill beckons. Down the slope and right along that nameless track, now crossing the A361 again and left then right down Bunkers Hill, sweeping around to the left and soon enough you're there.

The Windmill Inn is one of those pubs with outside seating where it would be an absolute crime not to capitalise, especially on a God-given, sun-burnished afternoon such as this. So that is what we did, coffee and chocolate mint biscuits to the side. We did not eat a full meal here and, reading some reviews, the pub did go through a bit of a downturn.

However, recent reviews show that service has improved and the food is good.

The Windmill Inn is back on track then – so must we be now, as we shape up for the rest of our discovery of the bit in the middle.

This was the last of four walks in two days and the mud of Northamptonshire was such that Wife decided that my walking boots had to be thrown out (precious walking boots which had climbed many hills and mountains, including one in Greenland).

In an added twist, Youngster reset the code on the iPhone and forgot what it was, so the memory had to be wiped and most of the photographs of the weekend were lost. Hence my constant reference to "the ill-fated hole in the middle tour."

Never mind. Onwards and northwards to Leicestershire.

Leicestershire

Bardon Hill

Height: 278m (912 ft)

Pub: The Birch Tree, Bardon Road, Coalville, Leicestershire LE67 1TD (01530) 83213

Parking: Near to pub (free)

Walk: 3 miles

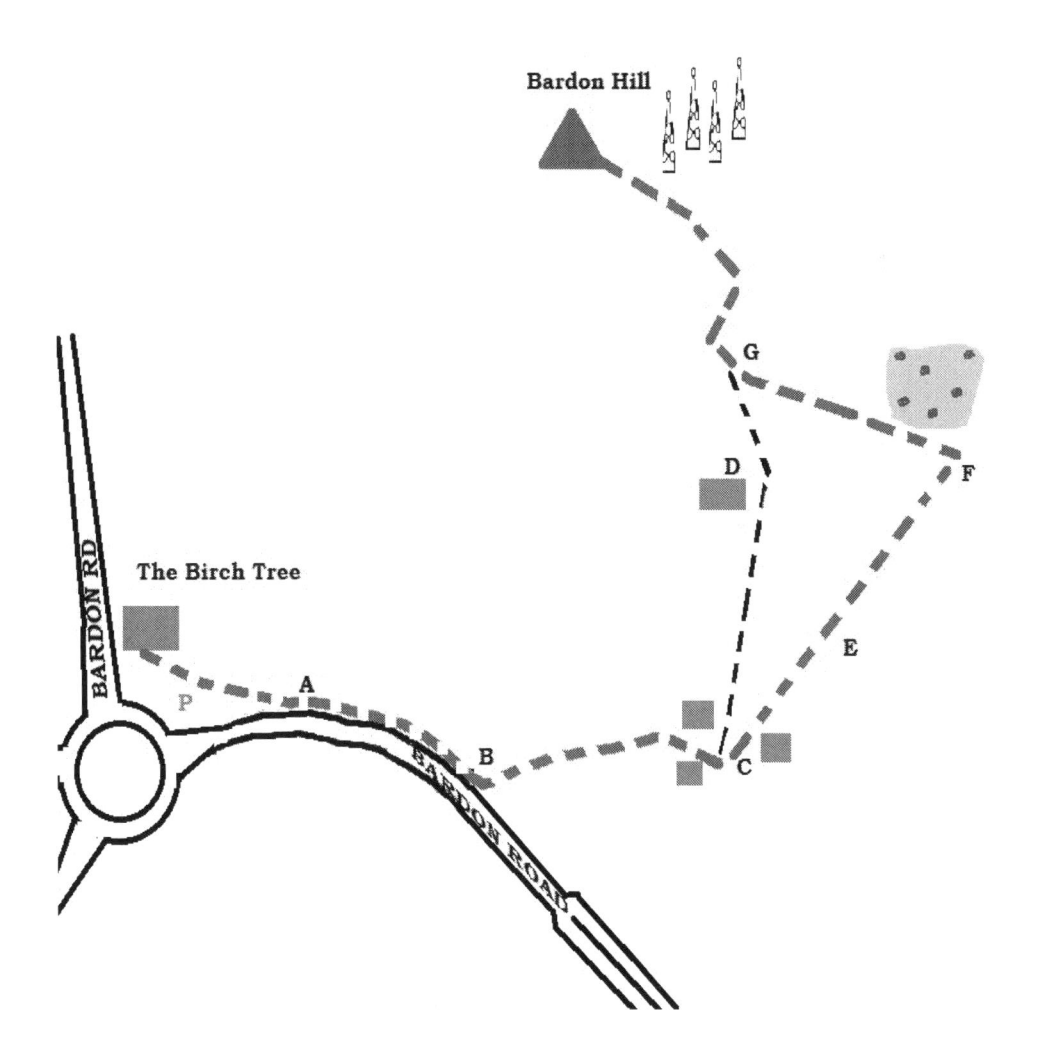

Imagine a hill cut half away; naturally sloping on one side as God intended, but with the other just sliced off. Bardon is one such hill. Naturally "blessed" with mineral deposits, its western half has been scoured to within an inch of its life with the result that views across that aspect are open, but stark and industrial.

The walk begins just to the east of the small Leicestershire town of Coalville about seven miles west of the county town. Parking is a breeze, but you will be asked not to park *at* the pub which, as we found on our return, having been empty was by this time rammed – a very popular establishment. No worries, just outside of the pub is an area of road, parallel to the Bardon Road/A511, which has been mercifully stopped up. With the pub on your left proceed along this stub road for just under 100 metres until you reach a line of boulders designed to stop cars, but not you. With a red garden wall on your left follow the path, a grass verge separating you from the traffic. As the wall runs out, so too does the verge so you are nearer to the speeding vehicles, for a short while anyway.

300 metres in to your walk you will pass the lovely St. Peter's Church (A). Here it is that a very familiar name can be spotted. Attenborough. Those celebrated brothers are from this area and Sir David speaks fondly of his boyhood in Charnwood Forest (which is hereabouts, more below). The name Attenborough, though, is mentioned for more sombre reasons. In a memorial in front of the church, it appears in a roll of honour, remembering victims of the tsunami in Thailand in 2005, of whom three were members of that famous family including Sir Richard's daughter and granddaughter.

We move on, and go past (not up) a track by the graveyard and on passing a footpath 250 metres after the church. This track is a private one to the quarry which, incidentally is never more than 200 metres away, though you would not know it. About 200 metres after *this* though, it is finally time to turn off where a finger-post and stile (B) present themselves and lead you in to the woods.

Staying right, soon enough you cross a narrow wooden bridge and near where this breaks out in to the open you are advised "Danger Deep Sludge Pits" you are also advised of the possible presence of British Longhorn Cattle who may be grazing from April to October.

Take the path rightish (east) and although it is tree-lined you may already be able to see through the tree cover, over to the left, an assemblage of transmitters. "X" marks the spot, transmitter = summit. Now the path nudges gently to the right and you are out of tree cover and heading along a well-marked track east-south eastwards and down a gentle slope towards a group of buildings.

This, when you close in, is a lovely old set of farm buildings at Brook Farm (C), complete with mill-race and all. Over the stile you go and pass through the complex and out the other side. Don't do what we did in blissful ignorance (for t'was in the quiet days between Christmas and New Year, when all was closed) and go turning left after the first building and up the metalled track, for 'tis verboten. This takes you to Bardon Quarry HQ (D) in the shape of the large and looming sandstone-built Bardon Hall, visible at some 600 metres distant. Although this got us to where we wanted, this cannot be relied on as a route.

Instead, having cleared the buildings, hang left and cling to the field edge (trees on your left), striking north-north-eastwards, a pylon on your right a couple of hundred metres along (E). Stick with this path in to a second field, and then where that field ends and you arrive at another pylon (F), go left into a different field, with a small copse to your right.

Keep to the right hand side of the field and eventually you will come out on to a wooden gate (G) and you will see a sign stating "Aggregate Industries – Private Property" and you are near Bardon Hall (but this time having taken the correct route).

There is a reason for the cloak and dagger "thou shalt not pass" approach, this is a working quarry, blasts take place. Be forewarned about when. Actually, this side of the hill is the safe side, it is not being quarried (it is actually a protected area, as much of the signage all around you will tell you), nevertheless there are still restrictions and you should be aware that blasting is 9am – 6pm Monday – Saturday and that usual blasting times on weekdays are "1:45 and 5:15" (should that read "between"?) and you are advised NOT to enter the quarry during blasting. This looks like it is referring to the actual quarry itself (i.e. the other side of the hill), but proceed with caution!

Anyway, once here, your first act is to track rightwards and climb some wooden steps. You then come to a sort of marshalling area for all sorts of vehicles and plant. Having done that, it's up a set of less steep steps.

The route now is up and up and slightly leftwards and towards those transmitters. At one point you will pass a Public Information Notice telling you all about the historic Charnwood Forest. Here, famously, the *Charnia Masoni* fossil was found (I'm saying this, the sign doesn't) by schoolboy Roger Mason in 1957, this fern-like structure proved that life had existed in the pre-Cambrian era when all had been thought to be sterile and lifeless. These are the oldest rocks in the world.

But not all is well in Charnwood, oh no. And why? I shall tell you for why, the dastardly rhododendron, that's what. It's only gone and overrun the bottom of the slopes, meaning that amongst others, the bluebell cannot thrive. And as if that were not enough, on the higher slopes the rapscallion bracken is seeing off the heather and, cheek of all cheeks, the bilberry.

Worry not though, having recognised the threat to the ancient forest, Aggregate Industries have (in conjunction with English Nature – now Natural England) removed the pesky rhododendron and helped preserve and extend the heathland. This is all very well, but they have also eaten half of a mountain away. Ying and Yang.

Further on we saw a touching, and perhaps transient given its delicate looking nature, tribute to one Norman Frank Willett, a cross adorned with green leaves and baubles (and when we were there) snow. Subsequent searches have not shown up who this man was, but what a beautiful place to be remembered by his loved ones.

Now a stile, with a bizarre sign indicating that you should not touch the fence (low-pulse electricity awaiting hapless cattle) and on and up and increasingly the path is rocky until, until the top. The transmitters are on your right. If you turn left after just thirty yards you will see the trig on clearly (but not dramatically) higher ground.

A snowy peak - at last!

The views back east are blocked by trees, but nearer to the transmitters the vista does spread out across Leicestershire. To the west, because of the emasculated topography, they open out cleanly towards Coalville, Nottinghamshire and the Midlands. The very foreground is an industrial wasteland, air where once there was earth, cruel wounds in the once soft soil. But look beyond these matters and all is set fair.

This little mountain rivals Northamptonshire's Arbury Hill for being "in the middle." Geographically there are shouts for both, as the 24th and 25th peaks climbed they straddle the mid-point of the campaign between them, but Bardon is the 24th lowest (or 25th highest) amongst the 48, so has that "middle" claim over Arbury which is a lowly 38th highest. So the Bette Middler joke belongs to it. Sorry Northamptonshire.

Halfway is done, both in the quest and in this walk, and now a slightly easier gravity-fed stroll awaits – this time eschewing that Bardon Hall metalled road.

The Birch Tree is a good lunch pub, offering standard scoff and friendly service, just what you deserve after your conquest of the middlest peak.

Next was a visit to the Welsh borders – with a stop-off in the West Midlands on the way.

West Midlands

Turners Hill – 271m (889ft)

Pub: The Wheatsheaf, 1 Turners Hill, Rowley Regis B65 9DP

01384 253725

Parking: Free, nearby

Walk: ½ mile

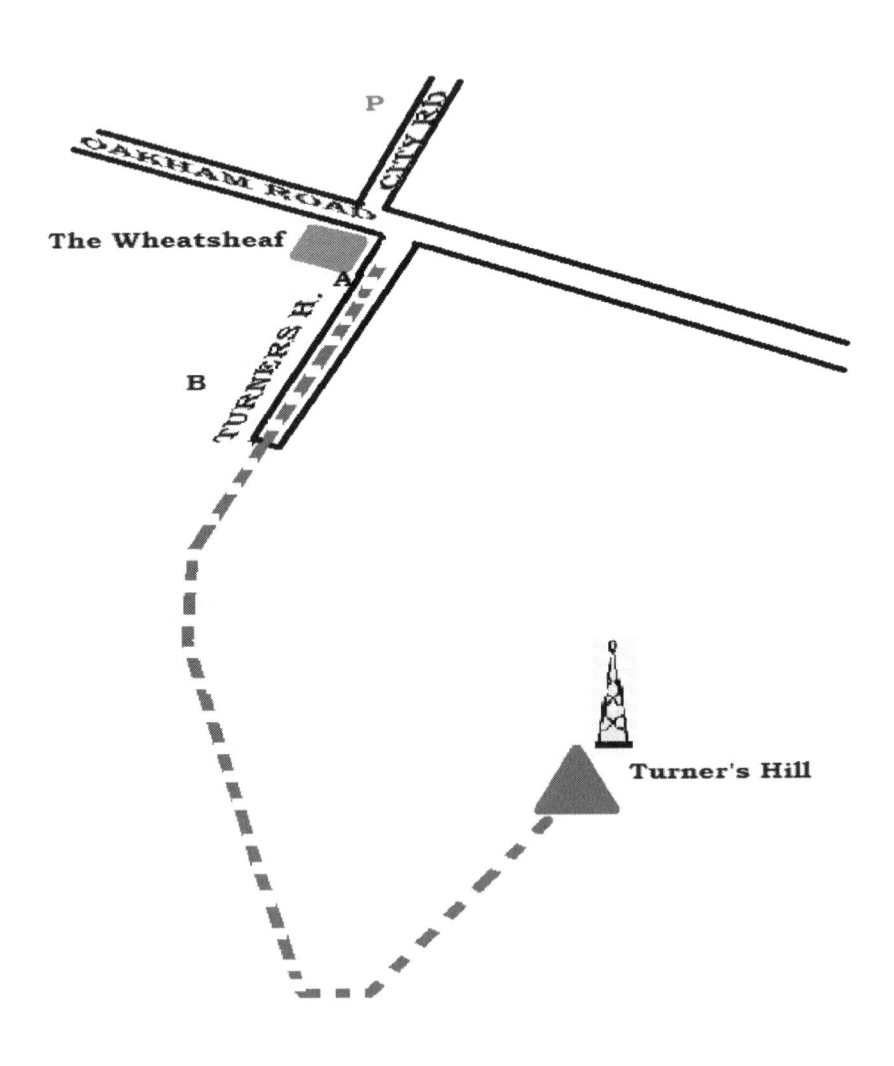

What a funny little walk this is, it's one of those box tickers that the metropolitan counties throws out (or up). Not quite the ludicrously short walk of the City of London, but not much more than it. Imagine a baked potato van and then imagine a transmitter, then imagine that they are five minutes apart (on foot of course) that is today's walk.

Rowley Regis itself derives its name from the Anglo-Saxon "ruh Leah" *meaning* rough, rugged open land. As for the Regis bit, there is not an obvious kingly connection. Once in Staffordshire, it is now in the Metropolitan Borough of Sandwell. Whilst over eight hundred years old, the town is predominantly twentieth century.

Having parked nearby on Portway Hill, or just opposite on City Road, or even right outside the pub itself on Turner's Hill make sure you progress up said hill with The Wheatsheaf on your right. The Wheatsheaf is an unremarkable cream rendered building of no vintage and offers the usual fayre – however, *however* – of somewhat more interest is the potato van. "Tony's Traditional Potatoes" (A) is hitched to a car, but does appear to be there most, if not all days. Worth a nibble on the way back if the ten minutes has led to appetite creation.

This culinary temptation behind you, proceed up Turner's Hill which is from all points dominated by the transmitter masts at the peak, pass a brick and rail fronted garden and then Dudley Golf Club (B) on the right and what looks like part of the course (on the left). Eschew the temptation to climb the field gate and walk across the open land to the left, instead walk on a little way and climb over/around the gate in front of you on the path (designed only to stop visitors of a four-wheeled nature) and carry on just a short while longer. There is then an opening to the left, but so too is there a sign advising you that this is an "Anti-Social Behaviour Hotspot" hmm. Soon after this, the path winds around to the transmitters and you are pretty much there.

This is another case like Great Wood Hill in Suffolk or Hastoe Hill in Hertfordshire – namely, where *exactly* is the highest point? It's not a big plateau, but plateau it is. The answer, however, is academic as the highest land is private and thus (supposedly) inaccessible. A sign from the Wireless Infrastructure Group clearly states "No Admittance, Authorised Personnel Only." You could just get as near as possible and say game over, however for the more adventurous/pedantic/bloody-minded...

There are some reports of a point in the fencing where the barbed wire is raised and a limbo entry is possible. However, on the day we went, the gate had been left open! (almost certainly temporarily) so a straight walk in to the spiky iron fencing around the compound and you're there!

The view is what it is. Given the largely flat landscape the distances seen on a clear day are not bad and various ranges fringe the horizon, but the vista is dominated by the West Midlands conurbation, with Dudley straight ahead and leftish (north and north west) and Brum over to the right (east). Behind you, out of view, the hill is half eaten away by quarry works in a replicating that which we saw in Leicestershire.

That is that, one of the easiest little peaks (whilst still appearing half way down the list due to prevailing land heights) ticked off and time to quickly descend and to the Wheatsheaf for a bit of what takes your fancy, or, if you're in a hurry, why not have a spud? Yes, let's have a spud.

Next – lovely Shropshire!

Shropshire

Brown Clee Hill – 540m (1,770ft)

Pub: The Boyne Arms, Burwarton, Bridgnorth, Shropshire WV16 6QH

(01746) 787214

Parking: At pub

Walk: 4 miles

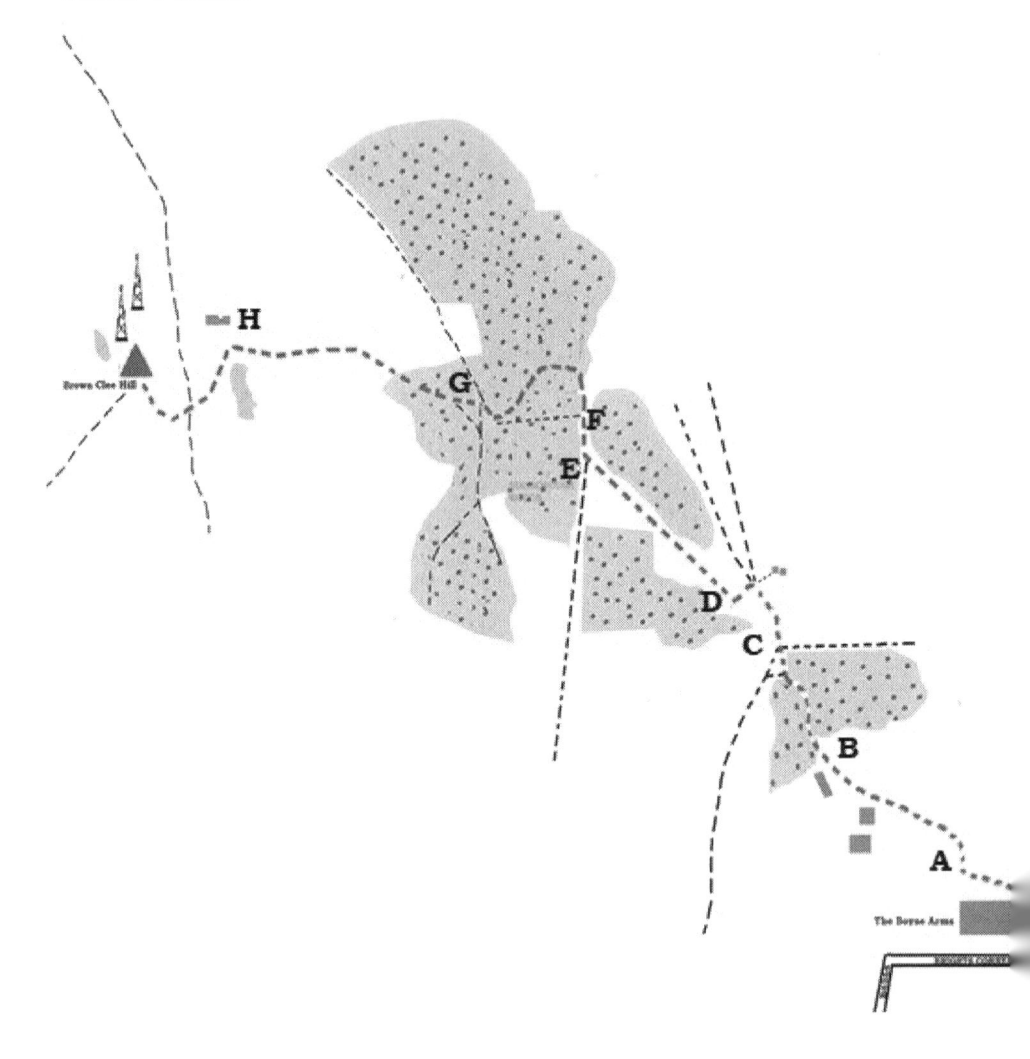

Shropshire, Shropshire indeed. The very shire of Shrop, but what is a Shrop? Well, it appears that it may originate from "Scrob" Richard Scrob. It was this Norman knight who built "Richard's Castle" in the 11th century near to Ludlow in the west of the county.

This is a quiet county of which not much is said, but anything that is said is always complimentary. This is the very county of A.E. Housman's classic "A Shropshire Lad" with its blue remembered hills and all. These same hills are certainly a treat and the walk wavers between gentle pasture and rock climbing and, on the day we walked it, a last climb through the mists to a long abandoned ruin.

You begin in the pretty, but small, village of Burwarton. Not a lot is here, its very essence is its remoteness and tranquility. Of note is Burwarton Hall, home to the Viscount Boyne (a title given in honour of deeds done at that most infamous battle) this name is also given to the public house where our walk starts.

Ask nicely and promise to come back and eat later and you might be able to park up here. If not, there are several off-road places much nearer to the peak, but that would cheapen the achievement wouldn't it?

Having parked up and booked your table, find a gap between the main pub and a separate flint and red-brick quoined building to its right (AKA "The Stable Bar") and you can cut off a pointless corner on your way to the top.

The cosy Boyne Arms

Now you cross an area at the rear which is also used for car parking, keeping the knapped wall to your left. When this wall turns left you do not – carry straight on. Soon, through a gate (A), you are out into open parkland and need to be veering left-ish, ensuring that the few buildings are on your left-hand-side. In fact it would be difficult to go wrong here as you follow a metalled road for the majority of the early part of the journey. Depending on the time of year you will be confronted by farmland animals of some sort. For us it was the ewes and spring lambs and several horses wearing their winter coats.

500 metres on, the openness pauses for a moment as you enter a little wood (B) labelled on maps as "Holly Coppice" which lasts for only 150 metres or so, then you're back in the open. However, a word of warning here. The clue is in the name – coppice. This is an area which is being actively forested, today's woodland may be tomorrow's clearing, about which more below.

Forty metres or so on and you arrive at a junction of paths (C), with Bright's Corner to the right and the ambitiously urban-sounding "The Roundabout" heading north (effectively straight on) along the tree-lined path. Follow this, which then veers slightly left 150 metres on. When you've veered for about 100 metres you will arrive at another junction, with a small group of buildings down the track to your right (D).

Here you must leave "The Roundabout" and head left up a track called "Harewood." The first part of this is in a clearing. When we were there the clearing was more extensive than the maps suggested, with felling clearly an active part of this living landscape. About 300 metres on the clearing narrows and becomes more of a grassy ride between two blocks of woodland before opening out again in this ever changing landscape. Soon you will pass over a culverted stream and half a mile up Harewood you will reach another path junction, with a north-south path arrowing closer and closer to you from the left (E). You are now at Stanborough Woods. Hereabouts you will see a sign erected by the Forestry Commission bidding you "Welcome!" and stating that you are welcome to walk here (F). By taking this path you will go straight through the wood and actually cut off a little bit of the distance. It's up to you, however it was treacherously muddy in places and it is probably worthwhile sticking to the slightly longer route on established paths on slightly higher (drier) ground.

Not long after the above, you will see another footpath going to the left, this loops to the north and around the aforementioned boggy ground and eventually you will reach another crossroads of paths (G). Go to the right – NOT the first, which is a more substantial track, but the second, unmade, track and you are now half a mile from the top.

Proceed for about 300 metres in diminishing woodland and you will now break out into the open in a rockier place and at last you might glimpse the top. On our ascent the mist was rolling in and it was a little longer before the ghostly silhouette of the old quarry buildings came in to view. One last climb up a steep bank and we were there amongst the ruins (H). Only, that isn't the summit.

Gary the dog-walker, with his terrier Midge, advised us in his West Midlands accent that it was "over there" pointing to an unknown place which a breath of wind made briefly visible, transmitters poking out of the hillside at a place he said was ten minutes' walk away. It was tempting to cut straight across the land. However, that would have been foolhardy as this was bog. The metalled track meandered obligingly and took us at last to a place called Abdon Burf.

'Yow can usually see Wales from here" Gary explained, pointing in this direction and that, to all of the things we could not see, ah thanks Gary. We had picked the wrong day for all of that. Never mind, we were at the summit.

If you turn your back on the transmitters which, whilst not uncommon on the highest ground for obvious reasons, do blight the views, you are left with a ceremonial trig which is a cut above the usual obelisk. It comprises a brick and mortar drum about four feet high and three feet across, atopped by a copper plate for orientation. This is accessed by a set of stone steps and lets you know that you are indeed at the highest point in Shropshire.

Just as Gary and Midge dissolved into the mist, the view did clear a little, not as far as Wales, but gave us a golden vista of nearby valleys in the setting sun. Yes, the sun was setting and it was time to make our way back to the Boyne Arms and our table booking (which it was looking increasingly unlikely we were going to make in time).

Wearily, and half an hour late, we did indeed roll up and claim our (reserved, and therefore unavailable for other customers – sorry the Boyne Arms) table and order our food. Delicious, steak and chips washed down with Guinness all in front of a cosy fire.

"Yow can see Wales from here"

What a treat (and well earned) and to look forward to were the peaks of Hereford and Worcester.

Worcestershire

Worcestershire Beacon – 425m (1,395ft)

Pub: The Brewers Arms, Lower Dingle, Great Malvern, WR14 4BQ (01684) 568147

Parking: Nearby (free)

Walk: 2 miles

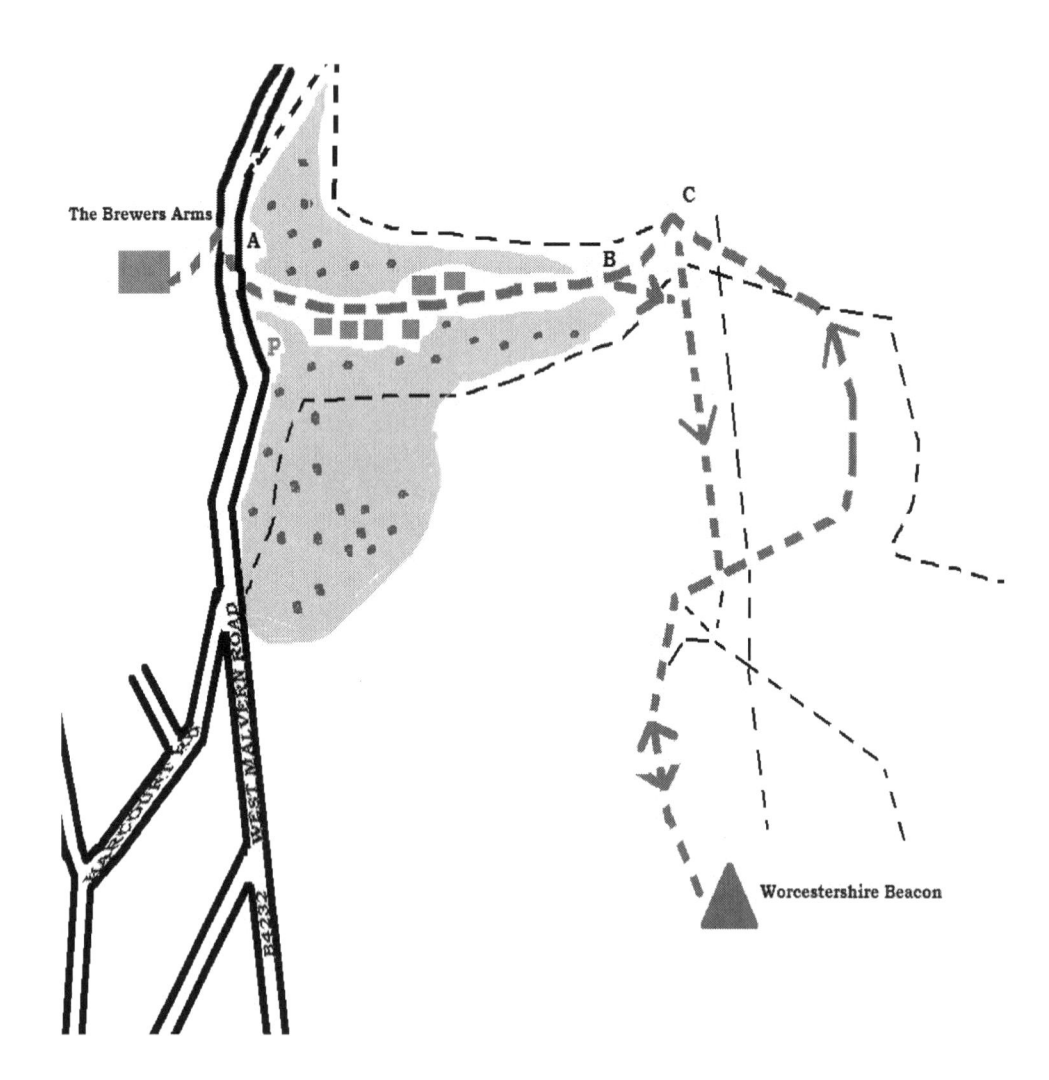

As a maximum yield for minimal investment, this one is right up there with Dunstable Downs – in fact, it even surpasses it.

No sooner have you begun an (albeit strenuous, but nevertheless short-lived) ascent than you arrive at the frontier of heaven with the heart of England laid out all before you.

Whilst the Brewers Arms is sometimes addressed as "Great Malvern" it is in fact in a tiny spit of the village the other side of the hill and is properly speaking in West Malvern.

The pub itself has no parking to speak of, so instead pull up on the West Malvern Road (B4232). If the road is packed, then pull up into a gravelled parking area near to a bus shelter and red telephone box, this is slightly south of the lane where you access the pub (about 100 metres away).

That done, walk back past the telephone box and look out for a footpath (A) opposite the Brewer's Arms sign. The path is well sign-posted noting this as a bridleway and an older sign telling us that it leads to The Dingle, Worcestershire Beacon and Great Malvern.

The path is metalled to begin with and leads to a small group of houses set amongst woodland. The path becomes unmade and then re-metalled as you are taken past some truly lovely dwellings with surely some of the best views in England.

200 metres in, the houses end, the trees peter out and there are rocky outcrops here and there. You have come to the hardest part of this short walk (B). There are choices here to get to the

higher land, you could either carry on ahead and then swing around to the right a bit later (400 metres), or, if you've got the legs for it, head right here and climb straight up the hill (about 200 metres). By the looks of the worn paths, the former is by far the more popular.

Having taken the latter, and with a thumping heart and sweaty brow to prove it, the view begins to open out and you can understand Elgar's inspiration for his many works.

Once at the ridge, which is punctuated by a crag, your destination is about 200 metres further on. The first thing you will see is a monument slightly away from the trig. This metre high barrel is set upon a three-step granite plinth and was erected to commemorate Queen Victoria's Diamond Jubilee. The views south and west, with this subtle structure in the foreground are quite breath-taking and as you marvel at the Malverns rolling into the Black Mountains and away out of sight you have to ask yourself how Elgar could have ever *not* written Nimrod.

On a few metres more, and there it is. The cherished trig point and another county chalked off. For less than half an hour you almost feel guilty about what you've been given, with good views of Great Malvern itself thrown in.

For the return journey, you could vary your fire by taking the main established path down towards a junction of paths (the thicker and more established path to the right swings around outside, whilst another is more direct, but still easier than the one we took on the way up).

Having arrived at the bottom, you will see a barrel shape of cemented together rocks (C), two feet high and four feet across. This has a series of arrows upon it, indicating the different hill-tops and other points of interest all around – The Beacon, Sugar Loaf and so on. After this is the last bit of the descent – remember to take the thinner path which sneaks between the buildings and before you know where you are, you are back through The Dingle and out on to West Malvern Road. Cross straight over it and follow that little path down to the pub.

As a word of warning, Wednesday night is curry night. I say warning, because the local walker's group meets there that evening after their walk and finding a table or even room to stand could be difficult. The garden does have some tables and chairs in it, and this may be worth looking at since the Brewer's Arms is pleased to announce that it has "The Best Pub View in Britain" (2005). Whether the view has got any worse in the last decade, or whether you're only allowed to win it once, who knows? The chips are to die for.

Now to Herefordshire for the only beast of the south – Black Mountain.

Herefordshire

Black Mountain – 703m (2,306ft)

Pub: Blue Boar, Castle Street, Hay-on-Wye, Hereford HR3 5DF

(01497) 82088

Parking: Nearby (paid)

Walk: 11 miles

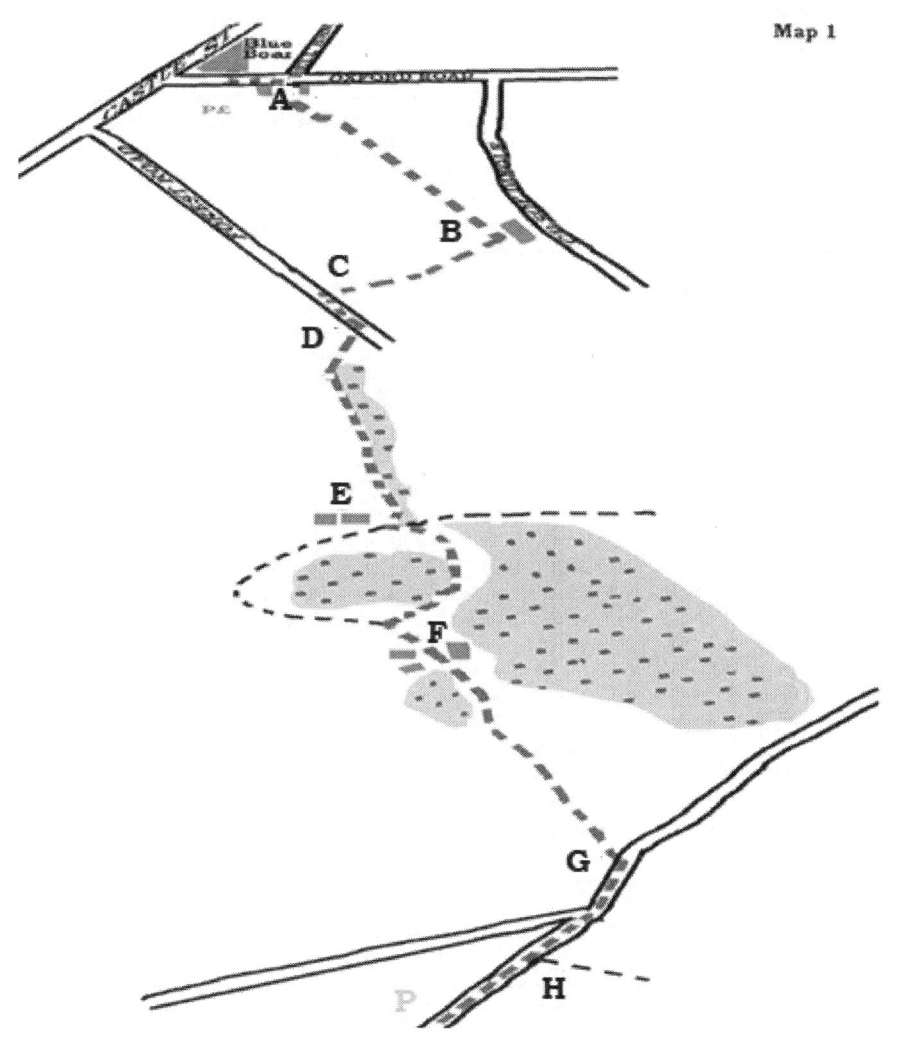

Map 1

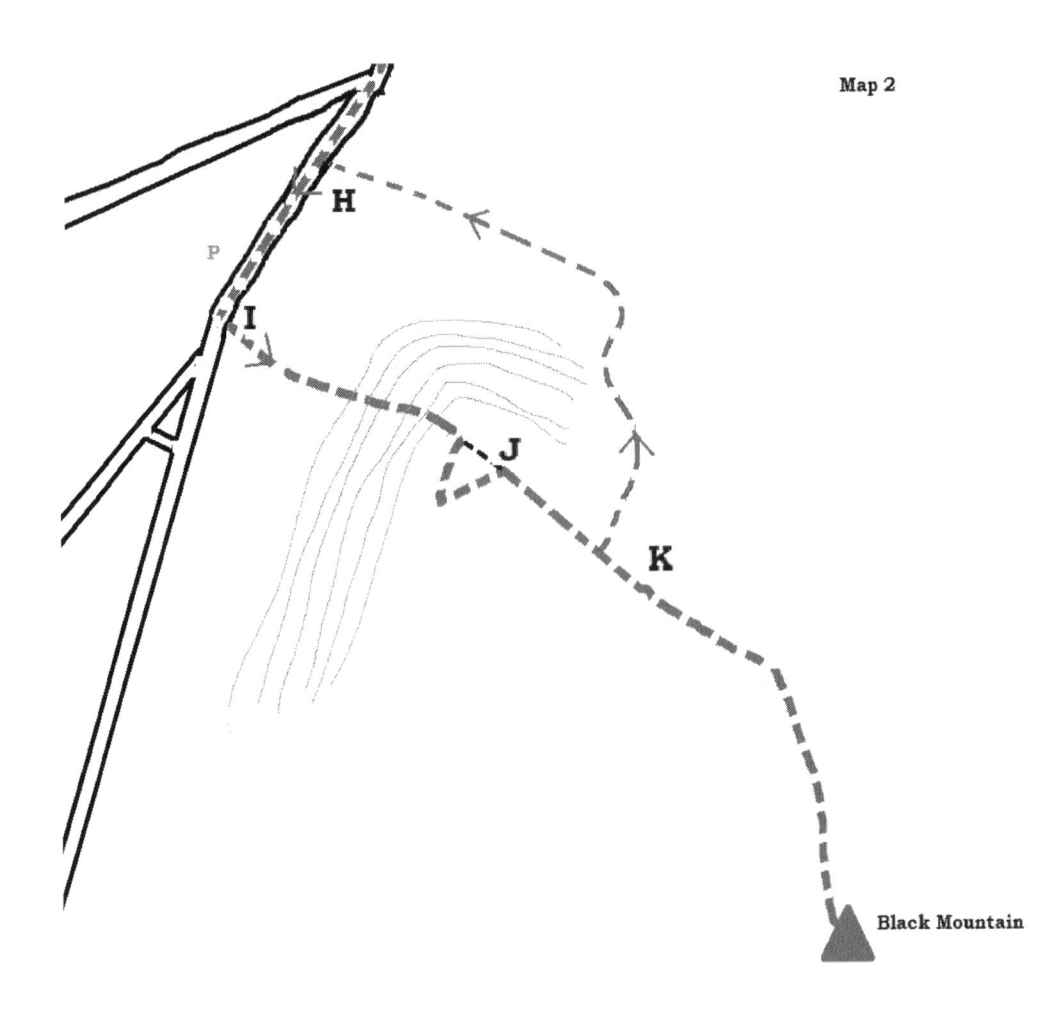

Map 2

This is a monster walk, so stock up on snacks and liquid refreshments and gird your calves and buttocks for some steep walking. That said, it gives so much – lush woodland, soft meadow pasture, climbs which are almost sheer in places, two countries, amongst the most dramatic of views you will find on this entire odyssey and a lovely place to settle once all is done.

It begins in the pretty town of Hay on Wye (of festival fame) which is actually in Powys, Wales. For the only time on this whole jaunt, you are actually outside England as the bilingual signs are testimony and there you will stay for much of this walk, dipping only briefly in to Albion to mop up Herefordshire's finest.

Parking in such a tourist magnet can be difficult, especially in high season (and especially during the literary festival, which we happened upon!) so you will be unlikely to find any free of charge. At festival time there are extra, over-flow options – fields, and even a school which open themselves up to this opportunity for income generation. However, outside of festival time, there is a large parc ceir (car park) on Oxford Road (B4348) just over 100 metres east of the pub.

Turn left out of here and the Blue Boar is 100 metres on, just on the right and on the corner with Castle Street, be-ivied and with signage most redolent of a woodland heraldic past, a wild (of course blue) boar with a standard between its teeth bearing the cross of St. George and other heraldic wot-not, the origins of which escape me.

However, no time, because the walk begins.

Crudely this is an almost due south trek the whole way, and for some parts of the journey our destination is highly visible, albeit that it is over five miles distant. This is a high ridge of land which stretches several miles to the south and rises starkly and obviously heavenwards with little in the way of lesser hills obstructing your view – there will *be* no confusion *which* mountain you are aiming for.

From the pub, go past the aforementioned parc ceir and about 40 metres after this is another matter which will mean you cannot lose your way. Just opposite a bus stop and Bell Bank, and between two buildings (a red brick house to the left, a stone building, use unknown, to the right is a (unmarked at this point) footpath (A) – this is the start of the Offa's Dyke Path which will take you all the way to the top.

This soon breaks out in to fields, and you will follow the field edge for a mile south-eastish with a few kinks and twists, you may hear the odd vehicle movement 200 metres to your left on the oddly-named Cusop Dingle in Herefordshire, England; you may equally hear Welsh traffic 250 metres to your right on Forest Road, but all is mostly silent save for the expected sounds of nature; wind, birdsong, lowing cattle. About one mile in, with a range of screened farm buildings to your left, the Offa's Dyke Path turns sharp right/southwest (B), rightish soon afterwards.

With a lightly-treed area to your left and open field to your right, proceed for about 250 metres until you come to a stile and enter a road (C). This is Forest Road (which would lead you back to Hay central should you turn right). To the left you follow the road for about 120 metres, with no verge - so be seen, be careful, until, just after a field gate, a signposted stile on the right (D) invites you in to a gap underneath the trees.

This breaks out in to the open again and hugs a well-treed field edge to your right for about half a mile until the woods thicken over to your left and you come out into an open area near to some farm buildings (E) over to the right) cross a road and carry on and meander for about another 250 metres, generally south-eastwards until the track joins another road (actually the same road as a few minutes earlier, which winds around the contours in a way that a footpath doesn't have to! feeling smug?)

Rising now, 250 metres further on, the footpath/road passes through a group of farm buildings (F), it feels like you shouldn't be here, but it is a public right of way so you do have the right to "pass and repass", but just not to hang around (here, however, we did meet a friendly Labrador with a slipper in its mouth and did linger and pet for a short minute).

Onwards and eastwards for another 200 – 300 metres the path takes you along a ride between two woodlands – a small affair to the right, a brooding massif to the left.

South-eastwards now, on and inexorably up (it was only by driving up from Hay later on in the day that we realised how much of a climb the whole thing amounted to) for three-quarters of a mile, the destination in full view, you join the road (G) and turn right. Follow it for about 150 metres (ensuring that you stay on the same road and avoid going down the right-hand side of the fork) and you will see a footpath sign on your left with a National Trust symbol, saying Offa's Dyke Path (H). However, if you take this you will find it more difficult (but not impossible) to get to Hay Bluff which, whilst not the highest point is certainly the "high point" of this walk (actually we will pick this path up on the way back). Instead, carry on for just another 400 metres, going past the Stone Circle car parking area (free, and there *is* a stone circle there) and finding the next limb of the Offa's Dyke Path (I) just 50 metres on from the car park and just before a traffic junction with a grassy island (I say grassy, when we were there the local horses were grazing it down to the roots).

Now the climb proper begins! It is over to Map 2.

Cross the road, and the verge and pass over a small fold of land which looks like it could be a stream in the rainy season and now your ascent really begins. This is steep, it is towards the higher end of not-quite-needing-to-use-your-hands, and you can feel those not used often enough muscles tightening by the step, the unwanted ounces falling away from around the belt (no matter, that can be remedied later).

The responsible parties have, by the looks of it, cut steps in to the slope and this does help as you tramp your way up (and there's no hurry, especially if the weather is set fair, if you're tired – stop, turn around, marvel at nature's wonder). Be sure to stick to the given path as soil erosion is an obvious problem here, as a sign planted in the red earth advises you.

500 metres from the bottom, the main path then strikes rightwards (due south). There is a thinner, less well-used direct path at this point which goes straight up the slope. There is probably a reason that it is less well-used, it looks bloody steep. Instead, stay with the main path which rises slowly and cuts diagonally across the mountain for about 400 metres.

Then you come to the mountain walking equivalent of a roundabout and you spin around to the left until you are almost parallel with, and walking in the opposite direction to, the path you have just been on. Now you are facing the other way and have your eyes filled with the glorious views of two nations without having to turn your head.

What you will also see straight away is a bright white object, stark against the blue sky (and sky of any colour for that matter) 200 metres distant. This is the trig point of Hay Bluff (J). On this particular part of the walk you are struck by the peaty bogginess, especially to the left, and are grateful to those who have laid the stone paths. This makes you fully appreciate how difficult it would have been for wayfarers in a previous age, and indeed early pioneers of hill-walking more recently.

Once at the trig, you are left in no doubt which of the two nations you are in. On all four sides a red dragon has been (possibly spray) painted upon the edifice, which sits atop a circular cemented stone base.

But your attention should not linger long on this. Instead look all around you. There in front and to your left are the Black Mountains, there beyond the Brecon Beacons. To the left is Twmpa, to the right and behind you is all of Herefordshire and merry England. This may be a good place to eat your sandwich, but the crisps could soon be claimed by the hungry wind so you may wish to stow things away a while yet – and there is still a little way to go (just over a mile) before England's 5th highest county top can be claimed.

It is, indeed another kilometre before you even *enter* into England at a little way beyond a junction of paths (K) just stay with the same path by the way and as you ride the ridge now you straddle two nations, with some predictable photographic opportunities. In this case it is your left leg which is most relevant. It will, eventually, step upon the highest point in Herefordshire. 703 metres, OS reference <u>SO255350</u>. Finding *exactly* the spot is difficult with no trig, no sign, no nothing, but it would appear to be very near a point where a true stone path is replaced by gravel. However, let your GPS be your guide.

The top!

That is it – what a walk already and only half completed! Enjoy the plateau views which aren't quite as spectacular as those given at the ship's head which is Hay Bluff, and now it's time to turn around and do the easier bit downhill (mind those knees though).

Eldest did turn his ankle not long after the return journey commenced, but manfully (and mostly quietly) soldiered on until the end.

Now to retrace your steps, without a massive mountain ridge as a reference point it is easier to get lost, but the above reference points should be a guide enough – turn right at the bottom, past the stone circle car park, then left between the woodlands, through the farm with the friendly slipper-toting dog (no promises that the mutt will be there) and soon enough Hay will heave in to view. The descent from the parking area at the foot of the mountain takes about two hours.

Once back in Hay, what better reward than to dine at the Blue Boar? To mix animal metaphors, the Boar was rammed, it being festival week, but the food is certainly worth the wait. It is, perhaps, a bit on the pricey side, but well worth it. The pub is an older building, and feels that way too, with low ceilings, a fire and even candles. The menu is traditional and this, combined with a few pints of your favourite ale, will help replenish those lost pounds. Cheers Herefordshire/Wales – we salute you!

As a post-script, we did go to the festival and met the actress Virginia McKenna and comedian Bill Oddie, as well as bumping in to someone who lives in the next road to us.

Next on our journey along the Welsh borders was Gloucestershire.

Gloucestershire

Cleeve Hill

Height: 330m (1,083ft)

Pub: Kings Arms Inn, High Street, Prestbury, Glocs GL52 3AR

(01242) 244403

Parking: At pub or nearby (free)

Walk: 4 miles

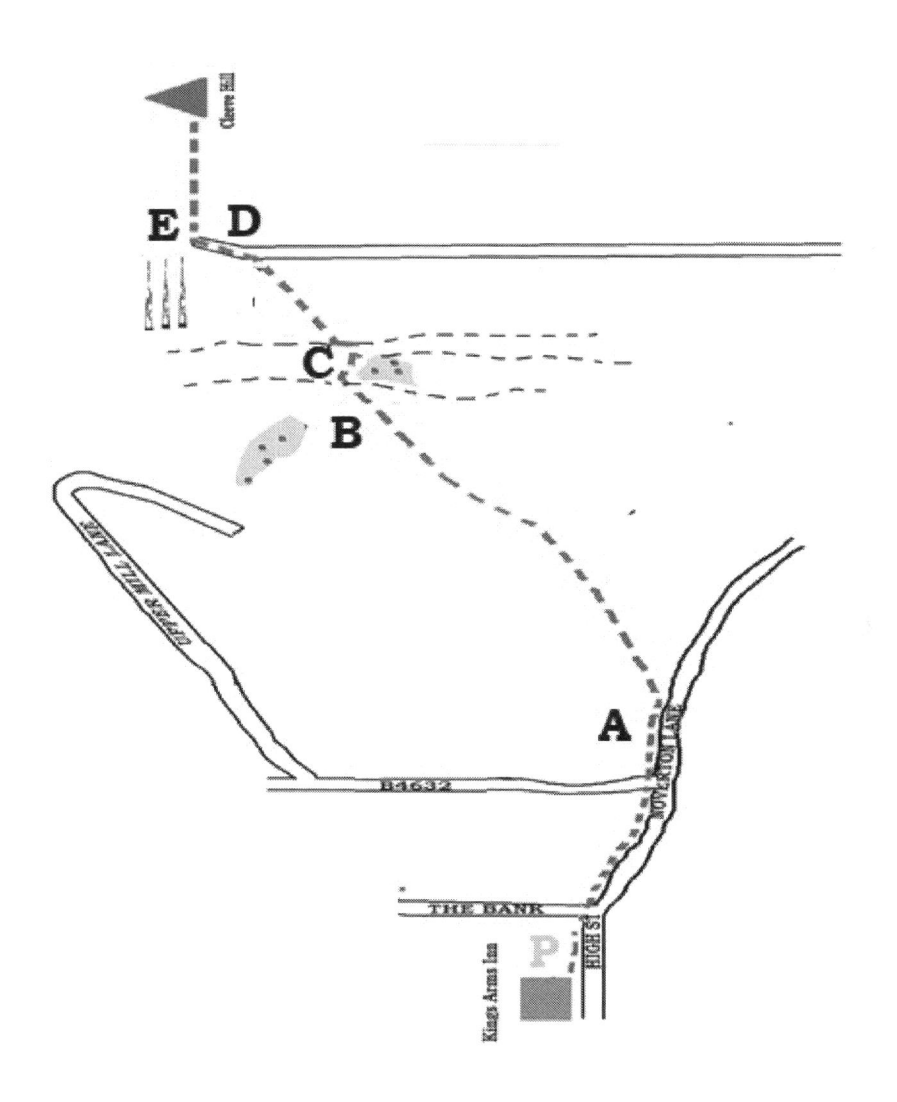

Parking is available at the pub or very nearby on the corner of High Street and The Bank in the pretty Cotswold village of Prestbury. From here, with the pub behind you and on your left, proceed east-southeast along the High Street carrying on across a roundabout, roughly 0.1 miles later you cross the B4632 and the road becomes Noverton Lane.

Carry on east with this and it takes you out of the village, the distance from the pub to when you arch off onto a footpath is a little over half a mile.

By now you are in a newish development of yellow stone houses and will come to a sign which invites you to go left for Desert Orchid Road (don't forget – Prestbury is just outside Cheltenham, of horsey fame) or right for the continuing Noverton Lane. Take the latter and with a narrow glade on your right and the last few houses on your left, soon your time in Prestbury is over. Carry on with the metal track which meanders a little and about 150 metres along, on the left, opposite Noverton Cottage, is a pair of field gates (A).

Take the second of these, this is Southam footpath 20 and follow it north-eastwards for about half a mile, passing Badgers Mount Farm (B) on the left and the path checks eastwards, meandering through a wood and then out in to the open.

About 100 metres along, you arrive at a point where four paths meet (including the Cotswolds Way to the south). This appears as a bit of tangle all scratched in to the grass. The best route from here, rather than carrying on ahead on the Cotswold Way (the more pronounced path on the left) is to head off right which is a steepish climb towards a ridge of broken tree-line. You may already pick out the form of one or more of the masts which penetrate the sky-line. These, at only 600-odd metres distant (and 300-odd metres from the peak) are a good way-marker.

300 metres up the path you come to a kissing gate and a junction with a narrow road, where you turn left. Disappearing in to tree cover, you follow this for 300 metres, until you arrive at the gated compound of not one but three transmitters on the left and, horror of horrors a *car park* on the right (D).

Pick a path between these two affairs and arrive at a field gate (E) and go through it and turn right. Now for the final 300 metres and the trig is next to a low dry-stone wall (made from the local limestone 170 million years old) topped with barbed wire made about five minutes ago.

There it is, the top of Gloucestershire, the peak of the Cotswolds and with a quick visit to the Kings Arms our time in the Bit in the Middle is over, so soon after it began. All apart from the small matter of Bristol.

City of Bristol

East of Dundry Hill

Height: 160m (525 ft)

Pub: John Harvey Arms, Goodwin Dr, Bristol BS14 0DP

07437 619194

Parking: At pub or nearby (free)

Walk: 1 mile

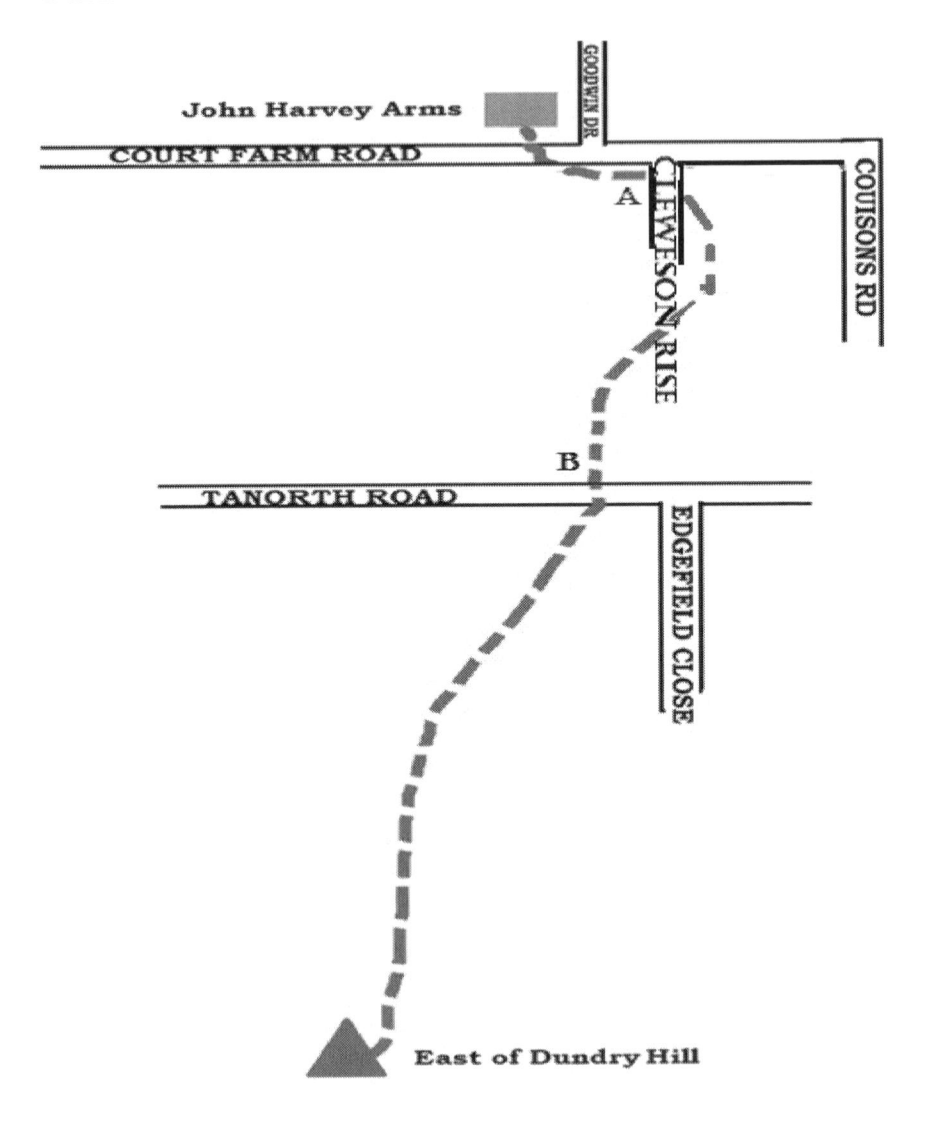

Bristol, a county? Really? For a little while it was the hub of that cosmetic (heh heh) county of Avon, before that it straddled two others – Somerset and Gloucestershire. Whilst it may be more readily associated with Zumerzet (alroit moi luvver? etc..) Gloucestershire County Cricket Club is actually based in the city as well. So, where does it actually belong?

Well, according to Wikipedia it is one of the 48 ceremonial counties, like the city of London, and so (and especially because the hill is bound to be easy in such a teensy-weensy place) it makes the cut.

However, be warned, do not look for a hill, there is not one, do not seek a trig you will not find one – not unless you go to the wrong place, as we did. There is a lovely little trig (next to a scrapyard) with views over the Bristol Channel and in to Wales, near to the lovely Dundry Inn. However, *however,* that is Dundry Head, fully and always within the county of Somerset, always and forever.

What we want is – land "east of Dundry Hill" and that means somewhere in the far south of Bristol, between Whitchurch and Bishopsworth.

The pub itself is very inauspicious looking, a 1960s two-storey affair, surrounded with flat-roofed single-storey extensions and an acreage of car parking. All around are 1960s dwellings, be-dormered on unfeasibly slack roofs. This is a real community pub, though, and it works.

With the pub on your left, proceed along Court Farm Road eastwards for about 50 metres. Soon enough, on the right, you can see the grassy hump that you are headed for. Take the first right at Cleweson Rise (A). At some point after the band of trees on your left, you will have to check over to the right and join a tarmac path. Carry on the way you were going and this will bring you out on to Tanorth Road. Over the road, a very narrow and easily missed path (B) squeezes in between a white blockwork wall and the fence of a very 1960s row of housing.

This path will lead you to open fields to the south and the spot is now only 500 metres away. It's a brief hop to a private track and then some judicious field boundary walking is required, first right to a line of trees, then left along these for about 300 metres. Now to your right, the spot is about 150 metres in front of you, near a point where the trees and hedges meet a path. Again, you may have to circumnavigate a field to get to the exact spot, but there it is, the highest point in Bristol, in a field just north of East Dundry Road at ST593668.

Much ado about not much, that is the end of the middle, the middle which brought us Black Mountain also to a field on the edge of Bristol.

But Bristol is the gateway to the south-west and that is where we are headed – to the dark moorland of Somerset – Exmoor and Dunkery Beacon.

Chapter 4 – The South-West Moorlands

This is a small group of counties, all in common are desolate moor (with Dorset chucked in by geographical expediency). Each of the three moorland counties is dauntingly beautiful, each has its own moor – Dartmoor, Exmoor, Bodmin Moor, all of which are murderous if the conditions are not in your favour.

Not all are made of the same stuff, despite superficial similarities. Somerset's Dunkery is Sandstone, 400 million years old from the Devonian period; High Wilhays in Devon and Brown Willy n Cornwall are both relative youngsters, in 280 million-year-old Granite. To complete the set, Dorset's Lewesdon Hill is Upper Greensand.

These counties are surprisingly mountainous at their peaks, High Wilhays in Devon lays claim to being the highest point in southern England (which it sort of is if you don't count Herefordshire) and with neigbouring Yes Tor and Black Mountain these are the highest points south of Kinder Scout, some 200 miles away. Somerset and Cornwall, at the 15th and 17th highest county-toppers respectively are no titches either.

Devon	**621m**
Somerset	**519m**
Cornwall	**420m**
Dorset	**279m**

Dunkery Beacon

Height: 519m (1703ft)

Pub: The Castle - High St, Porlock, Minehead, Somerset

(01643) 862504

Parking: Nearby (free)

Walk: 8 miles

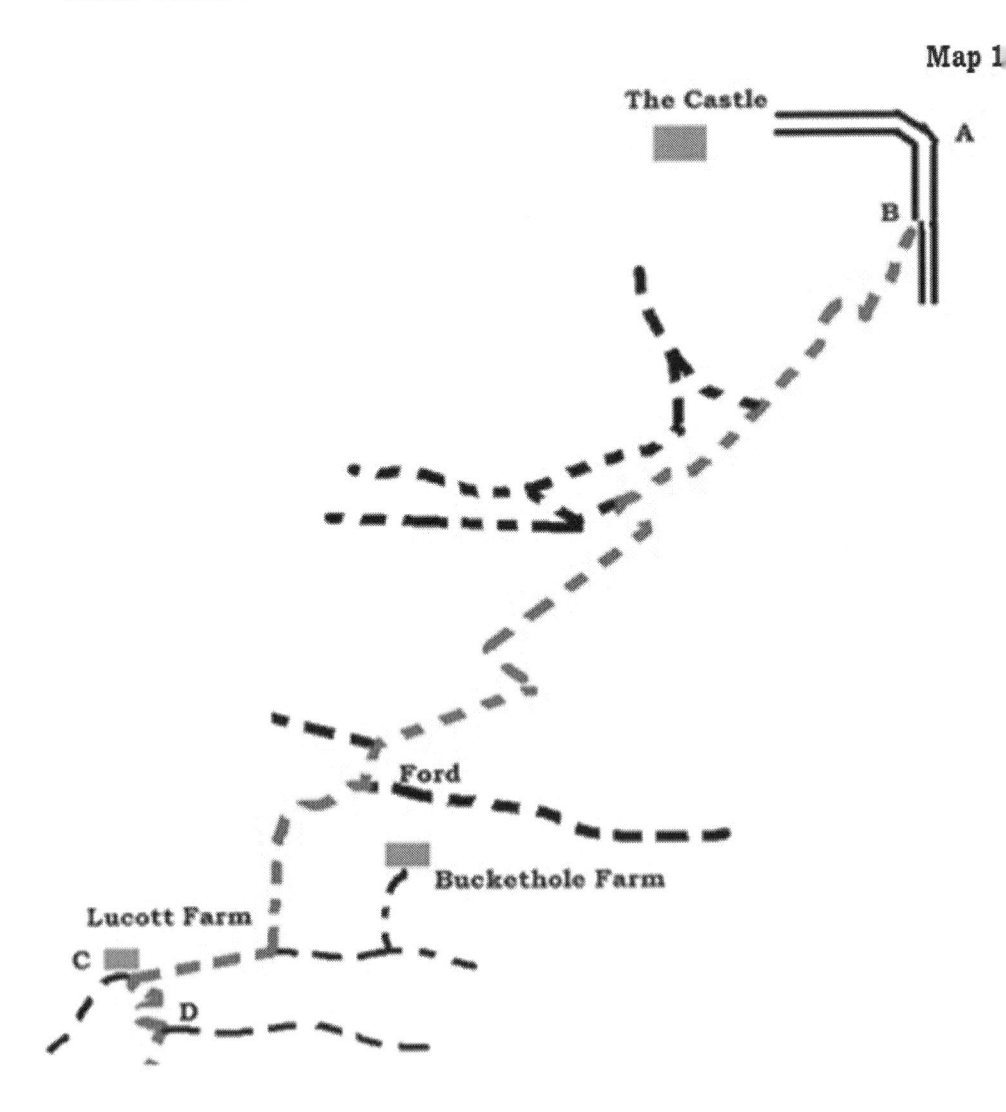

Map 2

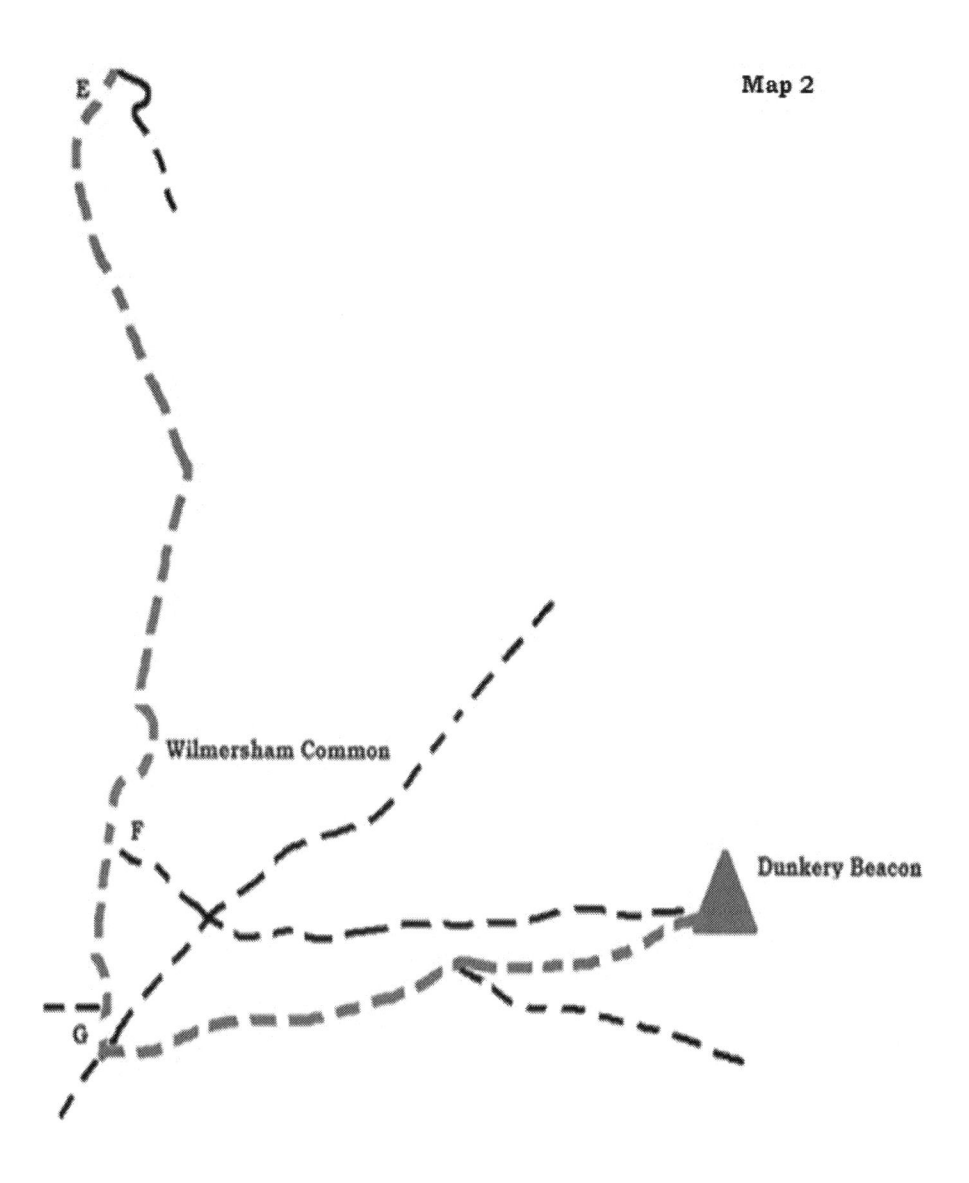

This is the first of three in the distinct south-west moorland group. Of the three, it should be the friendliest of the three moors – Exmoor (the others being Dart and Bodmin) and the easiest (it is near the edge of, rather than the middle of, Exmoor and is not all that far from the nearest decently-sized town – Porlock – at three miles), but.

But, but ,but. If you catch it on the wrong day, as we did as it pelted down with rain, you are reminded just what moorlands are all about, be they in the cold north or the slightly warmer south-west.

Start at the Castle (the Ship Inn, famous for its associations with R.D. Blackmore's *Lorna Doone* is slightly further away to the west – never mind) and begin your walk in the relative comfort of this town's streets, with the further shelter of woodland and then the bitter exposure of bleak moorland, to follow.

With the Castle on your right, proceed along High St. Turn right at St. Dubricius Church on Parson Street (A). It might (on a nicer day) be worth stopping to have a look at this magnificent 13th century Grade I listed building, with its hexagonal spire and its 15th century tomb of John Harrington who fought alongside Henry V. Or on a day such as this, you may wish to press on, with the tree-filled rise of land in front of you.

Heading on south down Parson Street (the church on your left), the Overstream Hotel on your right sort of looks like a pub, but describes itself as a "bed and breakfast" so don't worry about the extra metres walked thus far, the mission is intact.

100 metres down, on the right, just past a white cottage, and opposite St. Dubricius School is a very small car park and just after this is a path in to Hawkcombe Woods (B)

The path heads generally south-west for about one kilometre, meandering a little, with paths joining from the west (right). Carry on with your path until you ford a stream which you keep on your right for a couple of hundred metres, then turning left (south) down the next path you meet, which quickly then kicks right and bends around to the left, before kicking out right (west) again a hundred or so metres later.

Now you are at Lucott Farm (C). Turn left. Heading downhill towards a stream where you cross a footbridge – and now the climb begins. Near the bottom you will have eschewed the hard left (D), which would have taken you east.

On to map 2 and *at* the bottom of the fall of land, the path forks, take the *right* fork (E) and climb up Tar Barr Hill.

The walk, if an exertion, is at least more straightforward now. This path is followed for a couple of kilometres with no distraction or possible wrong choice of path. Over to the left you may see promises of other, perhaps shorter-looking routes to the top, particularly one about 1 kilometre early (F) from the next instruction but these are topographically challenging and do involve some down as well as up.

You are now at Wilmersham Common as you cross the Thurley Combe and gain 100 metres more in height, climbing to 456 metres.

Now at a junction of paths, it is time for the final assault (G). You need to go hard left (east) and walk the last two kilometres, almost on the ridge (you will only rise another 60 metres the whole way there). The rain and mist were such that, on espying the summit cairn I believed it to be a distant massif another kilometre's walk away with perhaps another valley between us until Eldest advised me that it was "just there", which it was, thank God, just feet in front of us.

On a banked up rise of land stands the (sensibly) cemented together stubby cairn with its plaque advising you of this place of "Historic Interest or Natural Beauty." Set a few metres away, superfluously, is a trig.

Dunkery's boast, apart from being a county top, is that it is "the highest point in southern England outside Dartmoor."
The view, usually, is amongst the most dramatic, crumpled carpets of purple heather sitting atop 400 million year old sandstone, views in all directions including north across the Bristol Channel and in to the Vale of Glamorgan. Not today of course, for the second time "views in to Wales" were denied us by the weather (remember Gary the Brummie in Shropshire?).
Apparently also red deer are to be seen up here and Exmoor ponies, not today though, they aren't stupid. Also not stupid, but very brave, was the man we met just yards from the monument. I say man, the first we saw was a tiny dome tent with legs sticking out of it. Worried for his safety, I asked if he was alright. No answer to start with, but then a bearded man emerged wondering why I had disturbed him. He was a leader for some Duke of Edinburgh's expedition and was awaiting his troop. These we saw a little later, utterly soaked after a longer walk than ours and trudging back to the dry of Porlock.

And so the return begins. West to that junction of paths at (G), then second right (north) and the same long path to Wilmersham Common, back on to map 1 and eschewing the hard *right* turn at (D) and descending down to the footbridge, turning right and uphill to Lucott Farm (C). Then right, left and right with the stream on our left, which you then ford.

Paths join from the west (left) and you stick with your meandering path north-eastwards for a kilometre until you break out on to Parson Road with St. Dubricius school and church opposite. Round to the left on to the High Street and you are there, ready to sample the delights of the Castle.

Or, ready to kick off your outer clothing and just drive away to Cornwall with the hopes of a sunnier day and the next conquest.

It's time for a bit of Brown Willy!

Cornwall

Brown Willy – 420m (1,378 ft)

Pub: Masons Arms, Camelford PL32 9PB

(01840) 21330

Parking: Free, nearby – or paid at Rough Tor Car Park

Walk: 9 miles (4 miles from Rough Tor Car Park)

Map 1

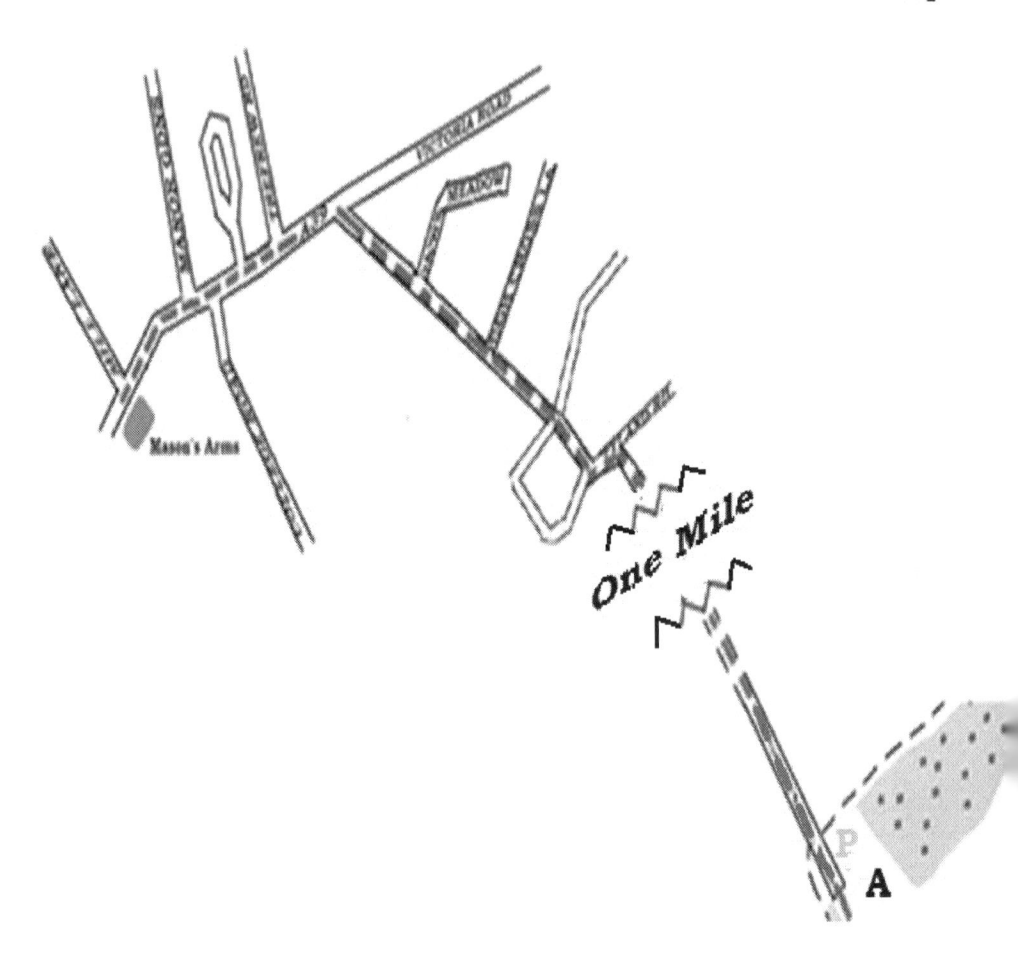

Map 2

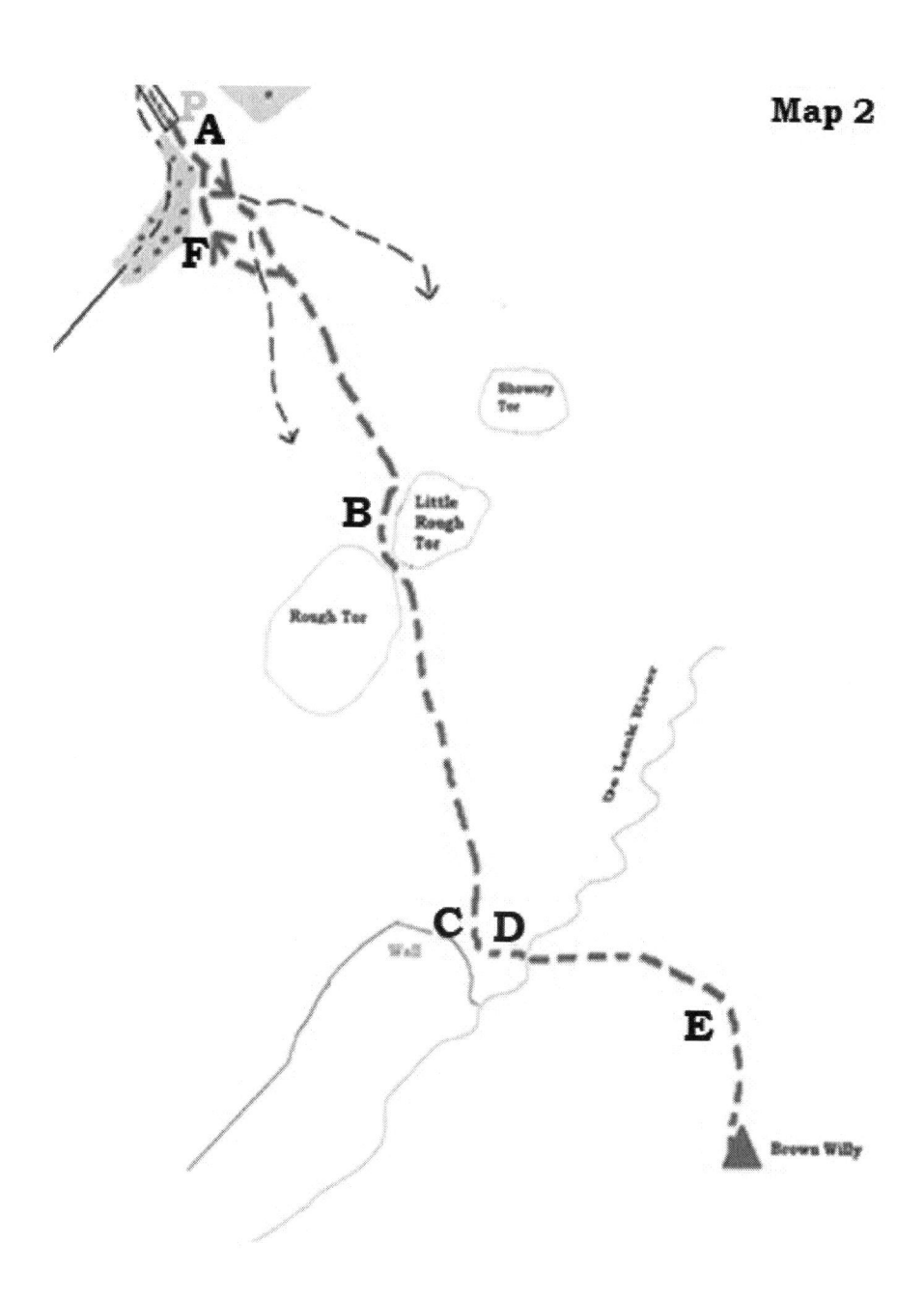

Now Stop giggling!

This was a warmer, sunnier, clearer day than Somerset and Exmoor had offered us – thank God.

Access from pub-to-peak for this rude-named summit has two possible options – one from Camelford, the other from the magical Jamaica Inn at Bolventor. I was up for the latter, but the wife (perhaps sensibly) made me take the slightly shorter route from the north (because we used the car park, rather than walking from the pub!), which meant that this most literary of starting points was denied us.

Any way you look at it, Brown Willy (alternatively known in Cornish as Bronn Wennili - "hill of swallows") is the highest point on the desolate Bodmin Moor and is a beast of a mountain and if you catch it on the wrong day the weather is cruel and unforgiving, the wind merciless and the mist treacherous. Alternatively if you catch it on a good day it will give you one of the most rewarding walks of all, stunning scenery and views and, although there are some fairly pronounced ups and downs, a clearly defined hill to climb – "proper job."

The day we went was God-given, with only a brief moment of very light rain the rest of the time was clear and sunny, just the right side of fresh, and it was a joy to be alive.

If you wish to dogmatically adhere to the <u>from the pub</u> edict (you don't have to you know) then you should start from Camelford. With the Masons Arms on your right, proceed up the A39 (Market Place, becoming Victoria Road) for about 1/3 mile, then take the second right which is Rough Tor Road. This you follow for two miles south-eastwards across stark country until you reach the Rough Tor Car Park near Tregoodwell.

Or.....

Go straight to map 2 and park up at the Forestry Commission's Rough Tor car park (A) near Tregoodwell! This has a laminated sign from Cornwall Council, with a slab of granite as its backing, asking you to respect country ways and try and "disperse across the moor" in order to avoid erosion. With a specific route in mind this is not always possible, but should be heeded as much as you can.

The first part of your walk is actually *downhill* towards a glistening, braided stream, with a pinewood to your right and various tors hemming the horizon in front of you. There is a memorial menhir over to the right which we shall have a look at on the way back.

Depending on the time of year, the length of grass and the amount of foot traffic, you may or may not be able to discern your path, snaking its way forth between two distant summits. These are Little Rough Tor to the left and, the larger Rough Tor proper on the right. Head for the pass between them (B).
Once in that lower land between the peaks, strike south-eastwards (leftish) towards a little river. To help you, look out for a wall to your right (C). Your progress, and that of the wall across this barren landscape, should before long coincide and soon, with the wall still just on your right, you will reach the river bridge crossing (D). This river oddly named "De Lank" (Dowr Dinlonk in Cornish, meaning ravine fort river – apparently.

Now it's all straightforward, and as the land rises with you again, drink in the good, sweet Cornish air, air as pure as the Atlantic from which it is driven in, air which has had three thousand miles of ocean, brine and pristine nothing to make it the purest you could ever hope for anywhere in these islands, let alone England.

At a stile (E), note the arrow pointing forwards, now you will feel a greater sense of remoteness with each step and soon the ascent runs out and there is nothing left to do, nowhere left to go, for you are at Cornwall's highest point. Here is a trig and next to it a crumbling granite cairn beneath which (it is rumoured) there is buried an ancient Cornish king.

Whilst coastal views are possible (the sea is about eight miles away at its closest), these are for the purest of days (crisp, cold, winter days). We had a good view, no doubt across the heathery granite landscape, but it was tempered by a thin milky haze.

The walk back is no less rewarding, especially as the car edges ever in to view. As a last port of call, do go and look at that menhir (F). It remembers poor Charlotte Dymond, murdered by her spurned lover Matthew Weeks in 1844 on this very moor. A book recounting the tale was for sale at Jamaica Inn which we *drove* to later.

This one is definitely worth coming back to another day and taking from the south, from Jamaica Inn.

Next, to complete the trio of the south-west moors, is High Willhays in Devon.

Devon

High Willhays – 621m (2,039ft)

Pub: White Hart, Fore Street Okehampton, Devon EX20 1HD

(01837) 658533

Parking: Nearby (Paid) Some free ¼ mile away (High Street)

Walk: 6 miles

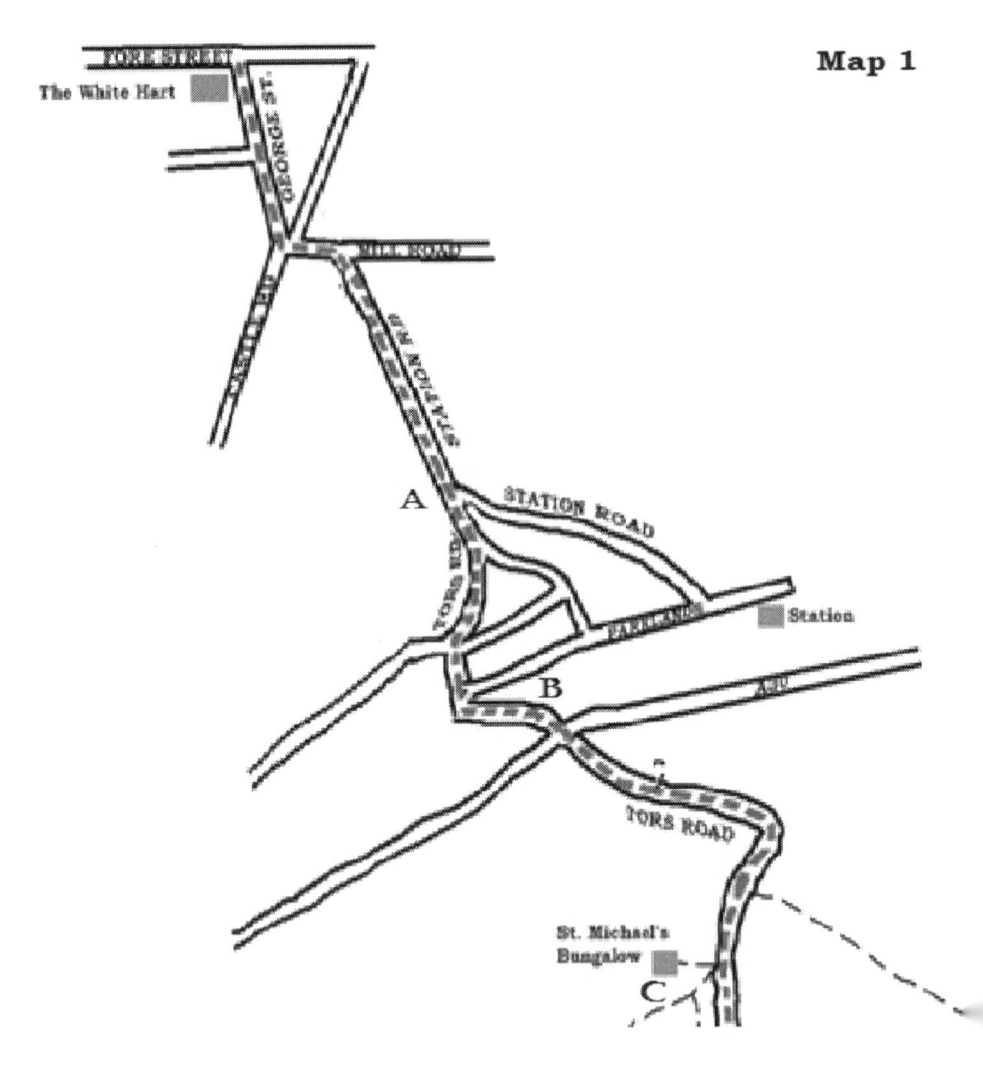

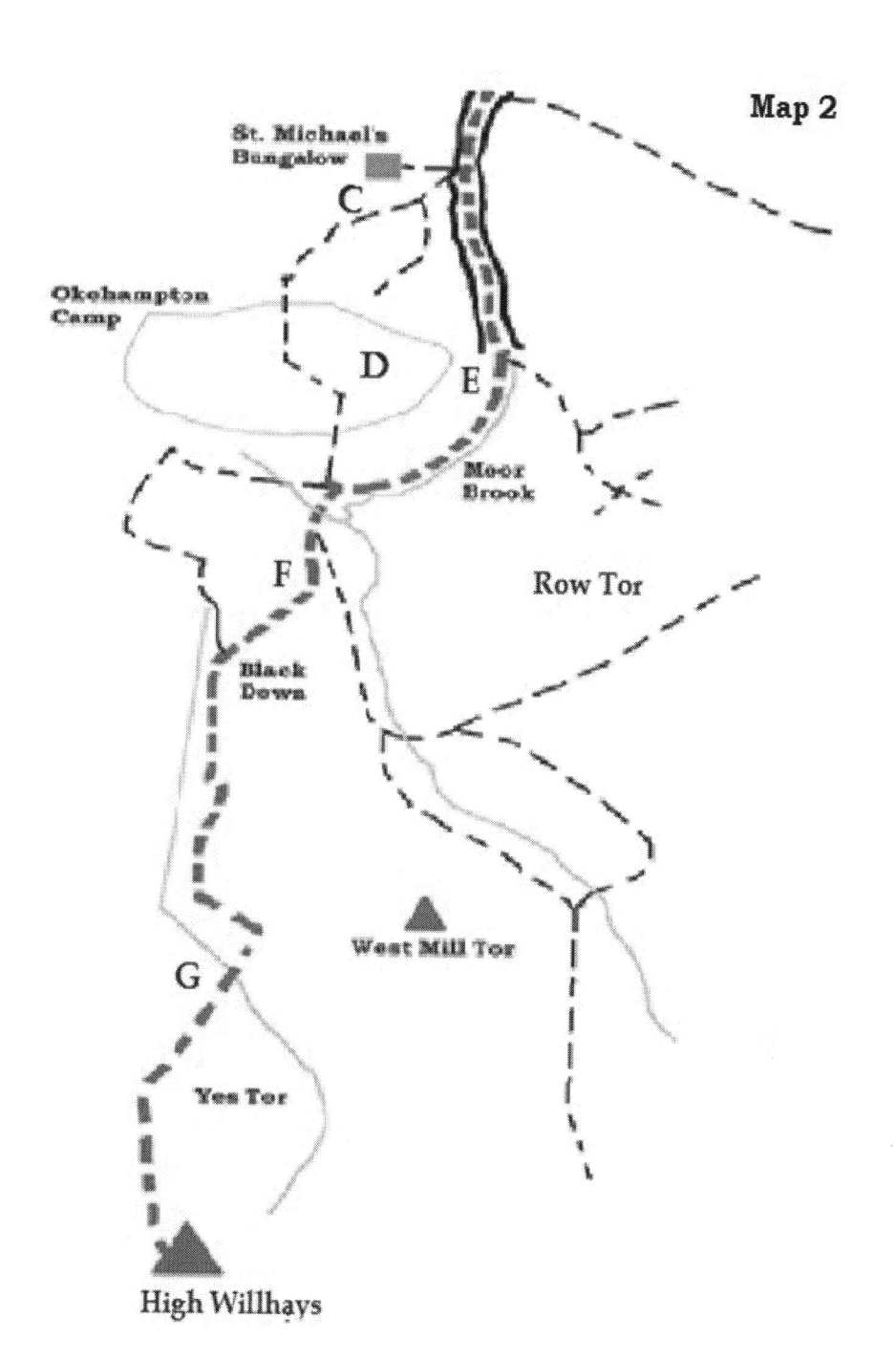

St. Michael's
Bungalow

C

Okehampton
Camp

D

E

Moor
Brook

F

Row Tor

Black
Down

West Mill Tor

G

Yes Tor

High Willhays

Map 2

This is the highest of the southern moorland peaks, it is the highest in southern England (sort of) and is in the top ten county summits of England (eighth, actually).

As with Brown Willy, if you catch this beast in a bad mood then you will be in for a torrid time. Whilst slightly less bleak than Cornwall's peak it is, nonetheless, just as exposed to the elements – mist, rain, wind and all else that mother nature has to throw at you; as with Brown Willy, though, if you catch it on a good day the visual rewards are almost limitless.

As with Cornwall, you're left with the temptation of starting *a little way along* the route, rather than at the pub itself as you could knock three miles off the round trip. However, should you resist temptation then you can begin in the pleasant little town of Okehampton and the White Hart Inn.

Actually parking is at a premium and to find a place without double yellows you may have to park a little way from it. Some spaces are sometimes available up the High Street about quarter of a mile to the west, but why not make life easy (and assist the local economy, a bit) and head up Market Street (just opposite the pub) and use the paid parking facility? Job done, on with the walk.

The White Hart faces on to Fore Street, but is on the corner of George Street. Take the latter southwards and it then kinks slightly left. 50 metres beyond this, turn right up Station Road which meanders slowly uphill for about half a kilometre. Station Road then takes a sharp left, which you do not, instead carrying on southwards (A) with the, albeit differently named, Tors Road (whose name suggests something a bit "moor-ish"). Tors Road wends its way ever south and south-eastwards, out of the town over first the railway line about 500 metres on (B), and over the A30 about 150 metres after that. 500 metres after the A30, the road veers right (southwest) then taking on the name Camp Road. Careful though, according to the maps, near to St. Michael's Bungalow, there appear to be two bits of road with that name, you want the left or easternmost of the two (C).

Referring to map 2, you will now the Okehampton army camp (from which the road gets its name) on your right (D). You are near to the entrance to the Dartmoor National Park and if you still have your car with you, this may be a good place to leave it (considerately) although there is scope to drive on yet further as some did, but what would be the point?

Now begins the long, slow climb of the several tors (Row, West Mill and Yes) before the final conquest. As landmarks, proceed with the little stream (Moor Brook) on your left and a wall on your right. Following the route southwards, note the path which is visually between the smaller Row Tor (468 metres) and the higher West Mill Tor (541 metres). You will soon meet a crossroads of paths (E) and may see that there are two routes to choose from, logically take the right hand-side (western) one which reads as a "straight on", this is a little shorter and cuts through fewer contours to begin with, but at the end begins to climb around the edge of West Mill Tor. About one kilometre along, you will reach another junction of paths (F) and need to turn right rather than proceeding straight on. At this point you will see two peaks of note – to the left (east) is the less illustrious of the "Mill Tor" brothers, East Mill Tour, at a paltry 513 metres, more to the right, and the way you are heading, is Yes Tor. So that's positive.

You climb up and around this and ford Red-a-Ven Brook (G) and almost reach Yes Tor's peak (in fact, your path takes you to 590 metres in height on this hill, and you may be tempted to turn around and climb to the 619 metres – agonisingly close to being the highest point in Devon - required to reach its summit.

Eschewing such temptation for just a moment more, take the path the last few hundred metres until you reach the plateau of High Willhays. In fact, having got there, you will need to push on a little further as the point itself is at the southern edge of the plateau marked by a cairn.

This is the highest point in southern England (so is the claim, but you'd have to categorise Herefordshire as being other than in the south and that is open to interpretation). Views are remarkable, looking south and indeed east and west across the desolate swampy granite of Dartmoor, but you might want to save your oohs and aahs for Yes Tor on the way back, a more pronounced peak, with a trig point, and views north towards Exmoor, as well as presenting the full panorama described above – the advantage of a true peak rather than a plateau. This can be accessed by a directly north-facing footpath from High Willhays, about one kilometre long, and dipping barely below 600 metres at any point.

That done, find your way down the steep-slope to the footpath east of Yes Tor and back to the way you came in earlier. God willing the weather will hold for you as it did for us, and whilst good weather cannot be guaranteed, it would be a good idea to ensure you go in summer. We had done the three south-western moors and it was us 2 weather 1.

The south-west was done, apart from the small matter of Dorset.

Dorset

Lewesdon Hill

Height: 279m (915ft)

Pub: The New Inn, Stoke Abbott, Beaminster, Dorset DT8 3JW

(01308) 868333

Parking: Near to pub (free)

Walk: 2 ½ miles

Lovely Dorset, Hardy's (best writer ever) own country, lush meadows and local stone houses, winding lanes and sleepy woodlands. It shouldn't really be in the "South West Moors" section, but it isn't chalky, there were too many in the "Bit in the Middle" section and not enough in this one. Plus, it is in the south west, so it's going in.

This is a charming walk, split roughly half-and-half meadow and woodland, and the climb is mostly gentle, with pleasing views once at the top.

No need to worry about parking at the pub (although there did seem to be ample on our visit) as there is plenty just outside it. The New Inn has an old-worldly feel to it, local stone making it meld with its surroundings and the few houses in the vicinity. The pub sign shows a shaven-headed abbot tending cattle and proudly explains that "the former name of this village was Abbott Stock and is said to relate to the dairy farm of the Manor of Abbots which no longer exists."

With the pub on your left proceed about 100 metres with the village hall to your right before turning left (southwards) and walking amongst thatched cottages on your left and right then passing a junction on the right signposted for Bridport and Beaminster (A) this is Norway Lane. Soon you will see signposted on the right (but pointing left) the "12th century church" this is St. Mary's and possibly something to look at on the way back (B). At the southern end of the village near Higher Farm, the road bends right, but our trail carries straight on briefly (C) with some stone houses to the left before taking a right-hand footpath.

Soon the path becomes indistinct and you are left instead in a grassy meadow heading the same way first slightly up, then slightly down, arriving at a gate, the whole field walk having been no more than 150 metres. At this point you may see signs telling you that you are on the "Jubilee Trail" celebrating the Diamond Jubilee of the Ramblers' Association (1935-1995).

Carry on through said gate, downhill to a second, then a third, now downhill further (*why* downhill?) pass to the right of a large pine-type tree and now to *another* (kissing) gate. After this a boardwalk (D) passes over a (thankfully when we were there) tame stream and now, at last, uphill again.

Once at the crest of the hill, bear right and keep a group of farm buildings (Brimley Farm) on your right (E) some maps also show this as Stoke Abbott Fruit Farm, although at the time of our visit it proudly bore the name of Brimley. Beyond the buildings, carry on the way you were going, joining a road which you follow for 100 metres and enjoy the lofty views which open out in front of you, until the road reaches a crossroads at the B3162 (F).

Cross the B3162 and begin to walk along the road opposite where you have just come from (a finger post over to your left advising you that this is the way to Blackney, Shave Cross and Whitchurch), ignore the brown sign pointing you towards the New Inn which you have walked from and after about 40 metres, on the right, is a metal field gate (G) which you should take.

Now climb slightly leftwards aiming for the trees and the crest of the hill. Soon is a gate, and soon beyond that a metalled path which goes by the name of Coombe Lane (H). Turn right along it, then soon left, on to a bridleway, disappearing in to woods. 500 metres on (I), are several paths of varying permanence, just keep on straight though as you head upwards and woods-wards including sets of wooden steps. The path jolts around a little leftish.

Soon is an information board, and almost as soon is the final ascent to the plateau itself of Lewesdon Hill. It is in a cleared green area, which you could almost believe was a part of someone's garden (albeit a large, grandparents' type of garden, rather than your being at the peak. You'll need a GPS to tell you exactly where it is as it is unmarked (no trig, no sign, no nothing). It is described by the Hill Baggers as "grassy mound at east end of ridge" and "marginally higher than mound under tree 60m NNW."

The views are special, if a little closed in by trees, and the sea is six miles distant to the south.

As we climbed back down again we knew that the south-west was done, that the whole of southern England was done, the fat bit with most of the counties. 34 peaks out of 48 slain, with only the 14 in the skinny bit to go

The trouble is, those 14 included all of the Peak District and all of the beasts of the north. Just a couple were tiddlers, but there remained ten of the top twelve to conquer. The hard work had only just begun.

Next was the Peak District, beginning with a combined Cheshire and Staffordshire walk.

The Peak District

The name says it all really. At the southern end of the Pennines, the Peak District became England's first national park in 1951. The park covers an area of about 1,400m2, which sounds like a lot, but none of the county peaks is more than 20 miles from the next, mopping up six high points in the most concentrated area of the same anywhere on our journeys.

The geology is sedimentary, from the Carboniferous period (60 million years ago), limestone on gritstone. A folding of the land shortly after this time crumpled it in to the range of peaks you see today, but the mountains are old, rounded by time. This is high country indeed, in fact to flog a dead horse it is the biggest concentration of high land in the odyssey, with the result that individual peaks tend to fail to show themselves in the way that soaring peaks might in other regions.

A key differentiator, though, is the split between the Dark Peaks and the White Peaks. The latter, in the central and southern section, has Carboniferous Limestone near the surface, whilst the more forbidding sounding Dark Peaks area (which does take in most of the county toppers) is higher and dominated by moorland caused by saturated soil due to the impervious millstone grit.

In common with the chalklands of the south, there is not an enormous range between the peaks here, although those topped by the grit reach greater altitude, with only about 100 metres difference between Cheeks Hill in Staffordshire and mighty Kinder Scout in Derbys.

Derbyshire	**636m**
West Yorkshire	**582m**
Cheshire	**559m**
South Yorkshire	**550m**
Greater Manchester	**542m**
Staffordshire	**520m**

Cheshire and Staffordshire

Cheshire: Shining Tor Height 559m (1,834ft)

Staffordshire: Cheeks Hill 520m (1,1710ft)

Pub: Cat & Fiddle, Buxton Road, Macclesfield SK11 0AR

(01298) 78366

Parking: Nearby Free (on road and at pub)

Walk: 7 miles

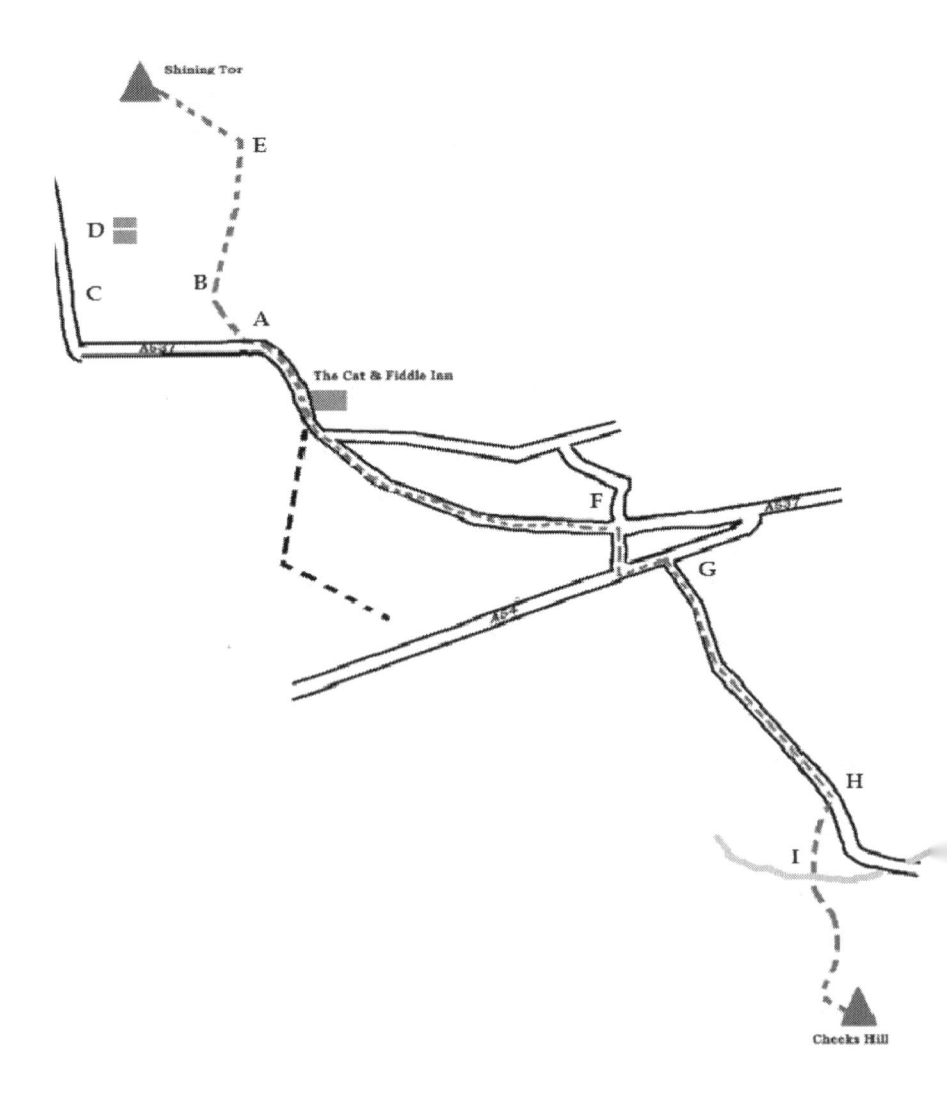

When listing the mountainous counties of England, you would probably go for the old favourites: North Yorkshire, Durham, Northumberland and Cumbria, always Cumbria. It's probably a safe bet, unless you're a local, that Cheshire isn't on your list, but you'd be wrong, as I was. Cheshire is of course a "nice" county by reputation, pretty countryside up there on the Welsh borders, nibbled away at by the conurbations of Liverpool and Manchester yes, but otherwise unspoilt (exception Warrington-Runcorn new town perhaps? Just saying). And then, of course, there's lovely Chester. Perhaps less well known is its rugged north-eastern edge. The Peak District, whilst traditionally associated with Derbyshire and the Yorkshires also shows its face up here – and to dramatic effect.

The walk itself, whilst it will cause you to break into a sweat, is a relatively straightforward one to follow and, whilst giving spectacular views, is not treacherous. When coupled with Staffordshire, though, it does amount to an honest afternoon's stroll.

The Cat & Fiddle Inn itself is a marvel. At a height of 515 metres It boasts that it is the second highest pub in the country (curse you the Tan Hill Inn, Swaledale at 528 metres!) and is the highest pub we will see on our walks. Parking couldn't be easier, there is a pub car park which seemed well used with cars and countless bikers, and there is also a small parking area opposite (although part of this is supposed to be a bus stop!).

Standing parallel to the road, and with your right cheek (face, not the other sort, more about that later) resting against this lovely

200-year-old building you can already see your destination up high and straight ahead and so the walk begins.

For the first few minutes (250 metres) you will need to follow the fast-flowing A537. There are unmade paths on left and right, but it is preferable to take the right-hand-side one as the former does fall away in places.

Soon, as the road veers to the left you will meet a footpath to turn right off of it (A) with a sign declaring that this is "Access Land" leading you up the gravel track as the ascent proper begins – this is the first swish of the "Zorro" path you will be taking.

The shortest of the swishes, and heading north-west this lasts for about 250 metres before you then take the right-hand-side option (B) of two footpaths and strike north-north-east for about half a mile. To your left, down the slope, you may espy the Peak View Tea Rooms (C).

Try not to think about tea and cake yet. A little later the Stake Farm buildings (D). Along here you may find Shetland Ponies, grazing the short grass and heath with the odd Skylark floating and sinking before scurrying to its nest.

Only a mile in to the walk, and already you are on the final "swish". At a finger sign (E), which clearly tells you where Shining Tor and the Cat and Fiddle are. By this point you would have crossed from Cheshire to Derbyshire and back in to Cheshire again, although there is no clear signage to this effect. Turn left now and for half a mile walk north-westwards and upwards with a drystone wall to your left. Here and there are small moments of climbing where the thighs will feel the strain, but these are fleeting on the well laid surface.

Then suddenly you are at the top, through a gate you will find the trig in glorious white with the view as your reward. And what a view!

Shining Tor - the roof of Cheshire - an unexpected highight

If the walk did not take your breath away this will.

A few feet on from the trig, across the grass, sit near the rocky promontory and gaze at all before and beneath you. It's almost embarrassing that, after so little effort, we have been given so much, including a top-tenner.

For all that this is "the north", it does not quite wear the desolation of Dartmoor and High Willhays (which is just sixty metres higher than it). This might be due to the friendlier sandstone on which the soil lies, it might just be the power of suggestion as surely more has been written about Dartmoor than here, but all is a light and friendly green.

To the southwest is Shutlingsloe ("the Matterhorn of Cheshire") and the dark brooding sylvan massif of Macclesfield Forest. Also in view, Macclesfield itself, Jodrell Bank and the so many glorious peaks of Cheshire and Derbyshire – not to mention Staffordshire – and it's there that we are headed next with its oddly named "Cheeks Hill" topping out the potteries county.

It's a toss-up as to which pub is closest to Cheeks. If you are looking for a stand-alone experience then you could do worse than to go to the Knights Table at Quarnford near Buxton, post code SK17 0SN. However, as you're already parked up, why not go back the way you've come and resist the temptation to get back in the car? Then you just need to use the network of roads and paths to find your way to the next peak.

Opposite the Cat and Fiddle, and amongst the parked cars/bus stop, is a tiny gated track. This is one option, but is longer, if quieter. We will meet up with the end of this route later, but for now follow the main A537 downhill for just under a mile. It is noisy and there is traffic rattling past you, but you can walk down on the right and be a comfortable distance from the vehicles (sometimes having to duck a bit closer to avoid stream and bog). Crossing once more into Derbyshire you will pass a large road sign for Buxton and Congleton and soon after that a cross-roads stating "Derbyshire Bridge (Only)" to the left – take the turning to the right (F).

This small road links the A537 with the A54 to the south and runs for about 85 metres. Turn left along the latter for about 75 metres, then turn up the first metalled track on the right (G). There is a 7.5 tonne limit here, so if you ate well at the Cat and Fiddle (snigger..). Over the grid, like cattle, you go next to, and amongst, the purple heather, the road barely rising. About half a mile along you will be confronted by a number of choices of paths to the right and to your destination.

The best you will see is a small gravelled area (H), supposedly a passing place, but with perhaps a car or two parked up – psst, if you're tired you could always drive here from the Cat & Fiddle, just saying. Find your way past this onto the grassy path and the rest is easy. Head almost directly due south the whole way there for 1/3 of a mile (450 metres), the only deviation being about 150 metres in when you must veer slightly left and clear the river Dane (I), a greater or lesser challenge depending on the time of year.

You're almost there now, and in fact whilst there is a lightly – trodden path, you can pick your own route as the destination emerges, it is a dry-stone wall enclosure, with a gate in the middle.

Just at the very end of your walk you pass, un-signposted, in to Staffordshire, for the first and only time on this walk, a sword of the potteries county thrust in to Derbyshire, with Cheshire just half a mile away.

That's it. No trig. Just next to the enclosure is the highest point in Staffordshire. This is Cheeks Hill and, seeing that no-one else was around, I did the obligatory, to the a(be)musement of my family.

Hey Diddle Diddle!

The peak is not one of the most significant you will see. However it does give, from a lower perspective, a panorama of the dramatic peaks around it – Shining Tor, Shutlingsloe, Axe Edge et. al.

Now back to the Cat & Fiddle to eat, if you haven't already, or even if you have – you've definitely earned it, you just need to walk a couple of miles up that hill again though.

Two Peaks from the district down, four to go.

Next, South Yorkshire.

South Yorkshire

High Stones – 550m (1804ft)

**Pub: The Waggon & Horses, Langsett, Stocksbridge S36 4GY
(01226) 763147**

Parking: A distance from pub (free)

Walk: 10 miles

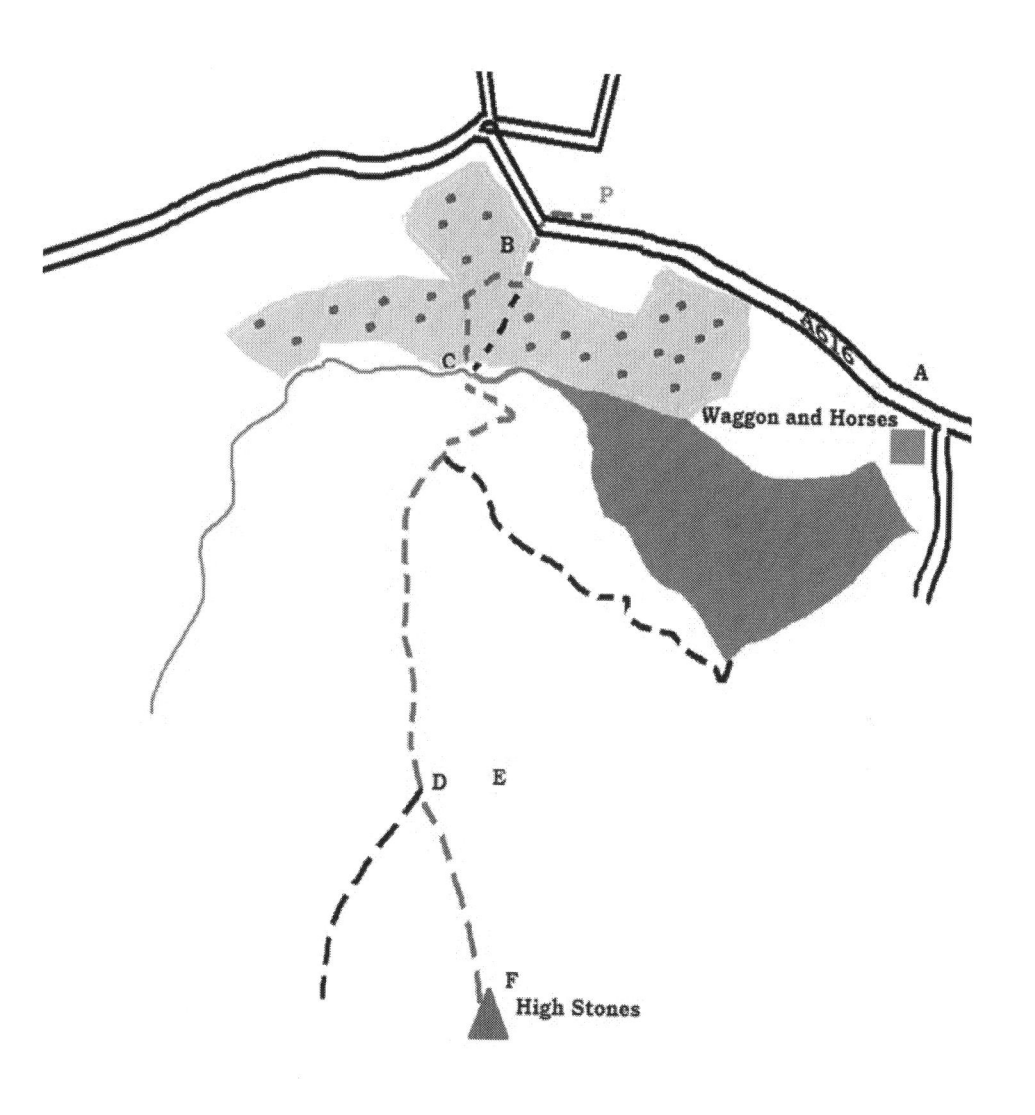

This is the Dark Peak area, along with Derbyshire this is the wilder and generally higher part of the Peak District (although, conversely, High Stones is about ten metres lower than Shining Tor). It gets its name from the difference in rock. The limestone bedrock is covered by "Millstone Grit" which leads to saturation in winter and boggy black peat all over the place. It is fairly featureless and this walk in particular, though very long, is devoid of many points of interest, hence the paucity of annotations!

Unless you get the permission of the owner of the Waggon & Horses (or of the gaily-coloured Bank View Café opposite (A) – bit of a cheek though if you're not going to go in) you are left looking for somewhere to plonk your motor.

Midhope Cliff Lane takes you to the start of the lakeside walk, but there is nowhere to park, not even remotely nearby. Parking on the road itself is not an option as it would lead to utter traffic chaos and hunting further east for somewhere takes you right away from where you wish to be.

Therefore, alack and alas, you need to proceed west (i.e. leaving the pub on your left). Little Gilbert Hill produces the same issues as Midhope and don't even think about trying to pull up on the fast but narrow A616. Instead, proceed west then northwest for just over three quarters of a mile where you will see a parking and picnic finger board on your left pointing you towards a car park which has a light blue sign at its entrance announcing Langsett's Flouch car park, which is on the right. Parking here means the round journey has about a mile-and-a-half cut off, arriving at the figure of about ten miles. Short of walking back to the pub and starting the walk from fresh, this seems the best deal.

Once in the car park (free of charge) do not proceed back to the entrance, but instead carry on the way you have just driven in. After the parking area a path carries on for about 50 metres across the grass and on to the A616. Needless to say "be careful" the traffic (thin though it is) does come by at a pace. Be patient, take no risks, your opportunity will present itself. Cross over and carry on straight over down Brook House Lane (B) which has a blue gate barring unwanted vehicular traffic. To the left of this is a pedestrian gate and for the next couple of hundred metres proceed through the woods.

Now there is a mesh of paths going here and there; whilst one of these could provide a shortcut you would be advised to just carry straight on over and continue with Brook House Lane which jogs over to the right and then checks back left again.

This carries on for another 150-odd metres, then turning left. Then continue about 300 metres more, almost due south before the stony path breaks out into the open and rolls down towards and over a pretty stone bridge (C) over the gurgling waters of the amazingly-named "The Porter of Little Don River." An orientation board welcomes you to Langsett and informs you about "Conserving the Dark Peak Moorlands." Then it is left through a heavy gate.

The next part of the walk is a pure climb and brings you around in a loop. First carry on along the partly-stoned path, cut through the heather, for about 120 metres towards the trees, then swing around 90 degrees to the right for about 40 metres, then right again for 80 or so metres until you come to a point level with (though about 30 metres higher than) the bridge over (let's say it again) The Porter of Little Don River.

Over the next four and half miles you will gain less than 300 metres in altitude and thus most of the way will be a long moorland plod averaging a one in 25 gradient and feeling generally flat-ish, although with peaks and troughs.

On a clear day you will need little instruction on how to proceed from here. The path, in common with many moorland tracks, has been shaped by some thousands of feet, finding the easiest most logical way to get from A to B and there is no earthly reason to disagree with your forebears and wander off of it – not when there is bog and peat abroad. Here and there stone has been laid to ease the way, but generally the path is a wound cut deep into the heavy soil.

As you gain height you will clearly see Langsett Reservoir over to your left, but the main geographical reference point is to your right, the deep-gouged valley of TPOLDR (I love it, but I couldn't say it again).
About 1 kilometre in, there is a path to the left (to be ignored), the path nears (but rounds) the summit of Hingliff Common at 350 metres, passing near the strangely-named Ratten Gutter which feeds Langsett Reservoir. Keep going south-west and cross the Haslingshaw via a ford.

Now, on the right, the path is close to the steep-sided valley of the Mickleden Edge (a tributary of TPOLDR, yes, even that has its tributaries). Another path joins you from the left, another path to be ignored. At about 191:985, the maps show the path you are on to be called "Mickleden Edge."

Hang on to your children, because the next point at 195:977 is called "Lost lad" and the path becomes known as Cut Gate. Here there are odd little cairns which don't seem to represent any summit or anything of consequence (devoted to the lost lad perhaps?); the contours are sparse and the land boggy as it flattens out. The Great Grough is forded and the path goes on.
At about 186:960 it's time to leave the main path (there is a better path further on, but this would require a big drop then a rise of about 130 metres – a climb which is avoidable). So strike left along Howden Edge and soon you will be close to Margery Hill

(E), the almost (but not quite) highest peak in South Yorkshire. You could detour up to the left with very little effort and note that this is a bronze age Scheduled Ancient Monument.

The peat in this area has been dated to around 3,500 years of age (thus denoting an artificial – and therefore man-made – structure) and is thought to be a burial mound. So precious is the site that it has been fenced off, although you can get to within feet of the great stone sitting astride another great stone.

Back to the main route, you are now on Wilfrey Edge (D). This is the last knockings of the journey (about one kilometre left now) and keeping to the same height of about 540 metres, the climb, such as it was, is over. High Stones sits on a saddle of high land with tremendous views south towards Howden Reservoir and dam, the Upper Derwent valley and per chance Kinder Scout, Derbyshire's highest and number six on the list (though that is to follow). A cairn (F) marks "the spot" but in fact, this is not the highest point. A subsequent survey showed land just to the west of this to be a couple of metres higher. If you're using a GPS, the location of South Yorkshire's highest is SK188943.

Incredibly, because of the crazy way in which boundaries work this is the highest point in "the City of Sheffield" but it must surely rank amongst the most remote of all the county tops.

Howden Reservoir - as seen from the summit of High Stones

It's time to turn back now where the view is limited because of the plateau, but does open up in the later stages and provide views of, amongst other things, a sea of wind turbines – exploiting a potentially limitless commodity.

A drink at the Waggon and Horses is well-deserved at this point and once parked up at the pub, that's exactly what you should do.

This was the longest walk so far and boy did we sleep long and well that night! It was thankfully a while until our next big walk and when we did return to the Peaks it was to scale the heights of West Yorkshire.

West Yorkshire
Black Hill 582m (1,908ft)
Pub: The Fleece Inn, Woodhead Rd, Holme HD9 2QG
(01484) 683449

Parking: Nearby Free
Walk: 4 ½ miles

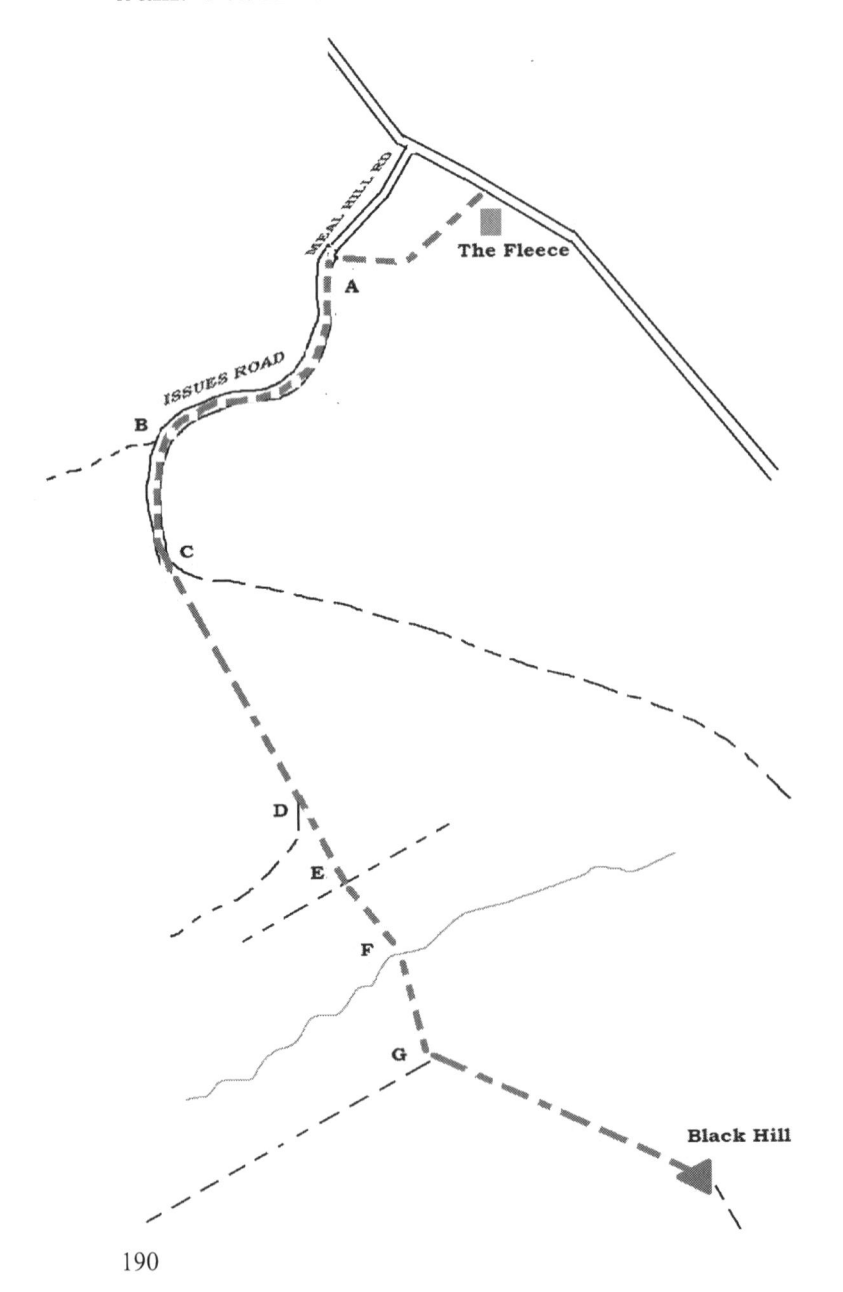

Black Hill was historically Cheshire's highest point, before things got all messed around with, and is now in the Metropolitan Borough of Kirklees, just inside West Yorkshire, but on the border with Derbyshire.

Higher than the already climbed Cheshire, Staffordshire and South Yorkshire (and the yet to come tomorrow, Greater Manchester) only Kinder Scout tops Black Hill within the Peak District. West Yorkshire's finest comes in at ninth highest overall and the walk is not too demanding.

The Fleece Inn is a polite little building in the village of Holme. A bit of a late start to get a table, still why climb on an empty stomach? Quick refreshment there, and armed with chocolate bars, we were off.

A tarmac path to the right of the pub, between the building and a stone wall takes you through the car park and gives way to a grassy track that eventually leads out on to the oddly-named Meal Hill Road (A). Then a quick left on to that narrow road and all feels very traditional, Methodist, hill country. Past the austere Holme Liberal Club and a slow climb begins alongside groups of stone houses, the road now becoming the not quite as weirdly-named "Issues Road." Past the Holme Junior and Infant School on the left the buildings soon run out. About a quarter of a mile on, the road curls around to the left. Go with that curl and ignore the turning to the right which goes to Bilberry Reservoir (B).

A third of a mile on is another choice, the road ends and the path tempts you around to the left, with a peak and a mast in full view, don't take this, it leads to the wrong peak. Instead take the gate and stile to the right (C) and begin the long, straight, obvious path towards our goal. This is a line you will take for a further three quarters of a mile.

This takes you through relatively friendly flat, agricultural land with the odd building and structure. However, soon the land becomes more barren and there is a junction of paths (400 metres from the arable land). One of these sweeps around to the right in a circular pattern (D) – ignore this. 70 metres on is a cross-road of paths (E) - still push straight on. Now is a descent and 150 metres on from the cross-roads is a brook to cross (F) which seems to carry the name "Issue Clough." There is the option of a path veering to the right, but again head straight on (unless the brook is a torrent, of course). By now the end is about one mile away. Carry on in the same direction as the land rises sharply and 300 metres later, much gladness as you hit a well-known footpath – the Pennine Way! (G) Now go left along this legendary trail and, for almost three quarters of a mile, follow. This is pretty much a plateau and the hard work is done. For almost half a mile, the land rises only twelve metres. There is a path, but it is boggy to the sides. The land is peat, sitting on flat areas of Midgely Grit Sandstone with putrid standing water everywhere.

Torrential rain - for just one minute!

The whole area is dark and unfriendly looking, more so as the skies turned slate grey and, with little warning, dumped their load upon us, saturating us. As quickly as the rain started, just as we reached the top, it stopped as soon as we walked away. Were the Gods trying to tell us something?

There is another county top – Greater Manchester's Black Chew Head – just over two miles away as the crow flies (three and a half on foot, if you're not a crow). I'd had reservations about this, it is a quite breath-taking route, but part of it incorporates a walk along the edge of the lethal Laddow Rocks, a sheer drop of hundreds of feet, slippery when wet. I was worried for the boys as much as anything and the fact it was now raining put the tin lid on that one. No matter, we had planned to do it separately anyway, the Premier Inn in Halifax awaited and we would return tomorrow from the other side, eschewing the "attraction" of those rocks.

Wet to the skin (for only the third time out of 39) it was time for us to tramp back, along the Pennine Way until that right hand turn and down the steep slope, over the oddly-named Issue Clough and along that long straight path towards Issues Road, Meal Hill Road, then back through the car park and to the motor.

The pub was done, the peak was done, and our hotel was invitingly just ten miles away, with its hot shower and its dryness and food and all. An evening of comfort awaited us, but tomorrow was another, and our last but one, Peak walk.
Greater Manchester and Black Chew Head awaited us.

Greater Manchester

Black Chew Head 542m (1,778 ft)

Pub: The Clarence, 180 Chew Valley Rd, Greenfield, Oldham OL3 7DD

(01457) 872319

Parking: Nearby Free (limited) or at Dovestone Reservoir Car Park (half a mile away) £1.30

Walk: From Dovestone Reservoir 7 miles – 9 miles from The Clarence

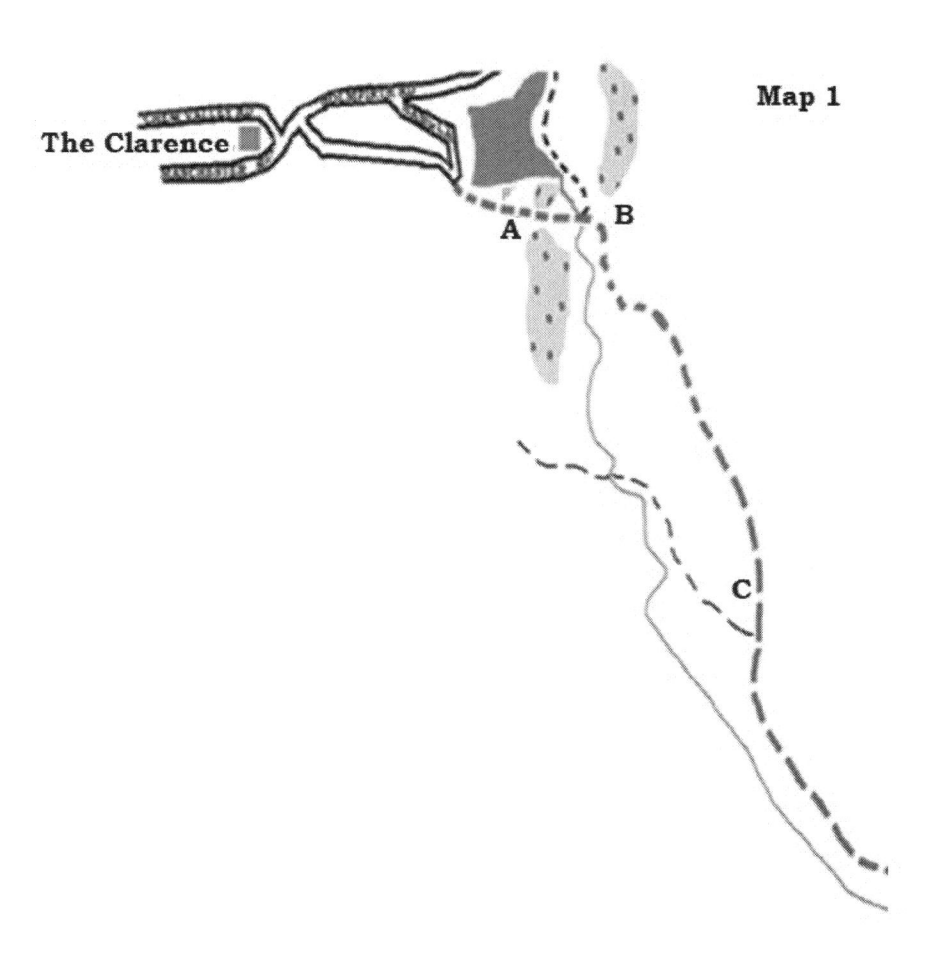

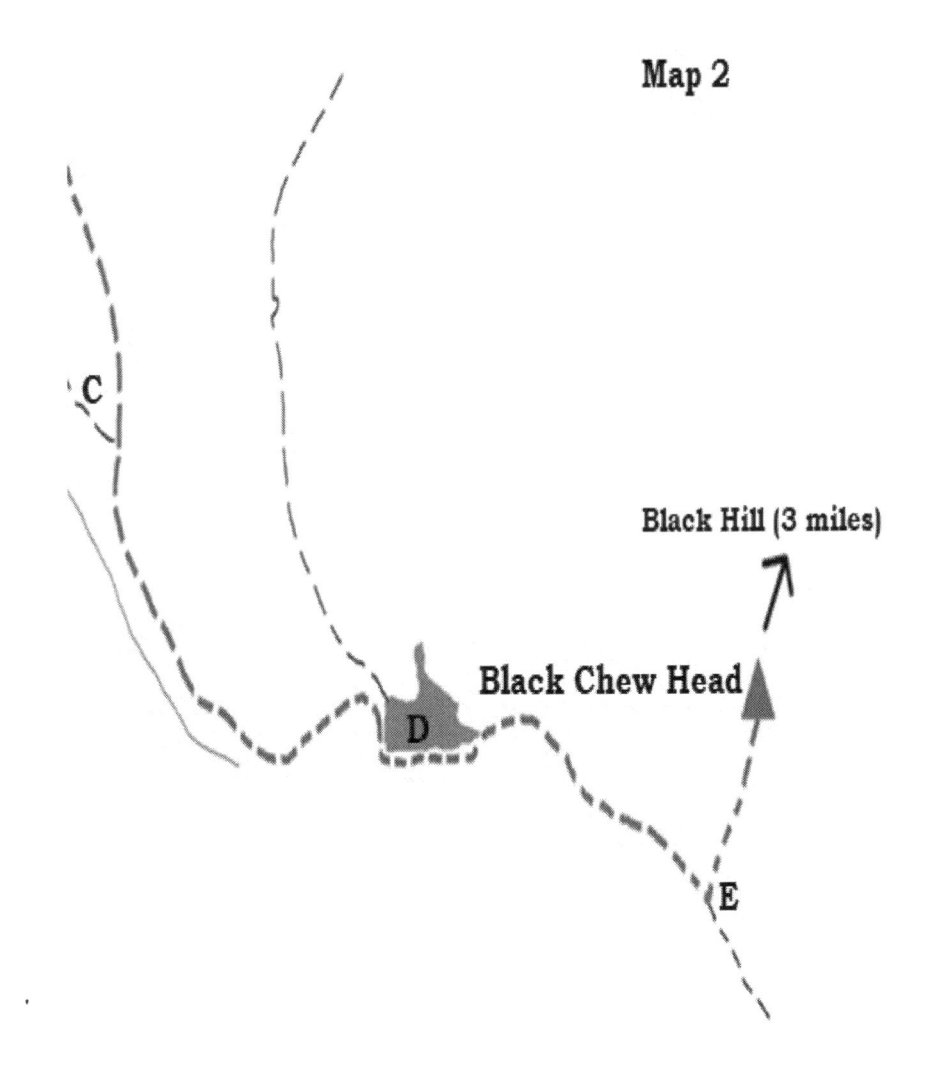

Map 2

Black Hill (3 miles)

Black Chew Head

C

D

E

Believe it or not, this isolated moorland is still in the metropolitan county of Greater Manchester. But there is nothing metropolitan about it. The second part of the assault on the summit counts as possibly the loneliest and most desolate place encountered on any of the walks.

This hike can be coupled with Black Hill in West Yorkshire, but would entail that perilous walk around the Laddow Rocks. So we did it as a stand-alone.

The pub, The Clarence, a politely composed gault brick building at the eastern edge of the little town of Greenfield, was offering a Friday night quiz and "open the box" (what's that then?) with live music on Saturdays. It has a car park with about twenty spaces, but the message is clear – "Polite Notice – WALKERS & RAMBLERS – Please do not leave your vehicles whilst you are not in the pub."

Ah, we won't park there then!

Parking elsewhere about is scarce (and for that reason we did not manage to properly visit this particular pub), so you may as well carry on eastwards along Chew Valley Road and take the first exit on the mini-roundabout to Holmfirth Road for a third of a mile before turning right down Bank Lane. This soon bends around to the right and takes you to the Dovestone Reservoir. Here, amongst many others if you hit it at the right (or wrong) time, you can park up for just £1.30 for the day. There are some limited facilities here, including an ice cream van, but beware the toilets, these are swimming with unpleasantness and with odours which carry far on the wind.

On arriving, you are confronted by a steep grassy bank and with no indication of the reservoir. Climb it if you wish, or save your legs for you will soon see this man-made lake on your left in any event, as you walk past the fragrant toilets.

Now you come to a barrier to any further vehicular progress, a gate to the Dovestone Sailing Club (A) stating on a bright yellow sign "Private Road, Members Only". No matter, you could only have realistically gone another 100 metres or so, so don't fret. This is the Chew Road and with glimpses of boats through the trees to your left carry on and enjoy, for soon the climb will begin.

In about 300 metres, Chew Road bends around to the right (B) and up the steep hill, the gentle stream far and further below to your right, views opening up to the right and behind

Whilst unforgiving and unrelenting, the walk does not compare in steepness to some of the hikes and it is at least (at this point anyway) on a hard surface. Also, to put you in your place. we saw a cyclist climbing it with grit and vigour – the fool, the fit and lucky fool!

To the right is the Chew Brook which meanders to and away from our path. Also coming in from the right is Oldham Way, which eventually joins Chew Road (C); onto map 2, and still we edge ever higher until a final bend and a small building and the next body of water – the Black Chew Reservoir – heave in to view. Once at the reservoir (and, again, you can climb straight up the slope or save your legs) turn right and keep it to your left (D).

At the south-western corner of the reservoir, do not be dispirited by the hardstanding area and the possible presence of a vehicle or two and think you could have cut out that long walk (and why should you want to anyway?). They really shouldn't be here and if they are it's all to do with works at the reservoir. Turn left and track the southern edge of the water and you may want to flop down and have your sarnies here, for you are now well over half way in distance and have completed much of your vertical ascent, but the second part is about to begin.

If you strike a line almost exactly due east from the eastern most tip of the reservoir (for it is so shaped) your goal is just three quarters of a mile away. However, a straight line isn't quite possible as this peak, along with most of its close relatives and the giants, is pitted with peat bogs – not as bad as some, but certainly bad enough to be avoided if feasible. However, east is possible to begin with on this part of the trek as you follow the variously made and unmade, and occasionally lost, paths just south of the stream which feeds Chew Lake.

With about half a mile left, and as the path edges towards the stream and in fact seems to invite you to cross it, you have two main choices, either head south-east (i.e. the way you were going) and try and rediscover the designated footpath, or leap the stream and charge across the morass towards Eldorado. In drier weather, the latter is possible, however the former (if longer) will take you to the proper spur path along a wire fence until you arrive at the summit. Summit is a misleading phrase at this point as the "climb" is generally very gentle.

Very soon you will feel quite alone and words such as "bleak" and "desolation" creep in. Then you remember that this is Saddleworth Moor and all which that evokes, the names of those evil two and all their victims etched forever in our collective memory, poor Keith Bennett still unfound. You would not want to be here in the dark, you would not want to be here in the cold, you would not want to be here alone – still less would you want to be here with somebody you did not know.

When youngest kept running off ahead I did feel it my duty to tell him a summary of what had happened back then. He did keep close at heel after that point. My real concern was, of course, those lethal Laddow Rocks which were just a few hundred feet away, but it did the trick.

This is amongst the loneliest walks of any; after Chew Lake (where we saw three people) we saw only one more, a lone walker near to the top and walking away from the Pennine Way. Also, oddly, a small dome tent in the distance, perhaps on another mad-cap Duke of Edinburgh expedition.

For a short while you lose view of Chew Lake and there is very little visual reference leading to potential disorientation. If this should happen, remember the lake is due west and that is the way out of this.

Soon enough and dry shod if you're lucky, you crest the final fold in the land and a stick in a small cairn offers itself up (not many stones here to add to the cairn, hence its diminutiveness) no trig, but at least something to aim for.

The plateau location means that the views in some directions (particularly south) are less than spectacular, but in some directions you get a sense of the shape of the land, a drop over to the east indicating Laddow and to the north-east just about three miles away is the Black Hill of yesterday.

Now south again and within just a few minutes, Chew Lake is in sight and easy visual orientation is your friend. The views on the way down, and especially just after Chew Lake are superior to those on the way up as the land opens out all before you. Between the lakes there is some light foot and cycle traffic with a single airplane overhead making its way from Manchester airport and then, oddly, a smell of paraffin, which stayed with us for a mile, soon melting in to a whiff of sausage, smoke, Indians in bright clothing enjoying their Sunday lunch and giving the place a sacred, exotic air and finally at the bottom an easily deserved ice cream.

Black Chew Head, one of the big ten and a long hard walk. Neither the longest, nor the hardest, but by God the loneliest. That was the Peak District almost done – all apart from the daddy of them all – Kinder Scout.

Derbyshire

Kinder Scout   636 m (2,088ft)

Pub: The Old Nags Head, Edale, Hope Vale S33 7ZD
(01433) 670291

Parking: Nearby Free

Walk: 7 miles

Map 1

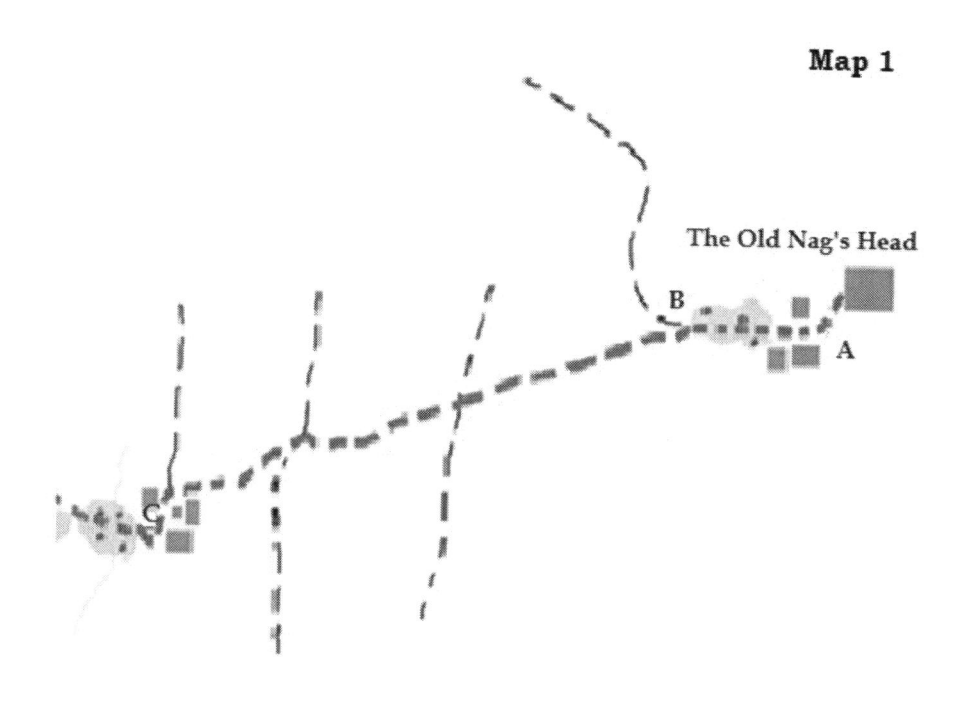

The Old Nag's Head

Map 2

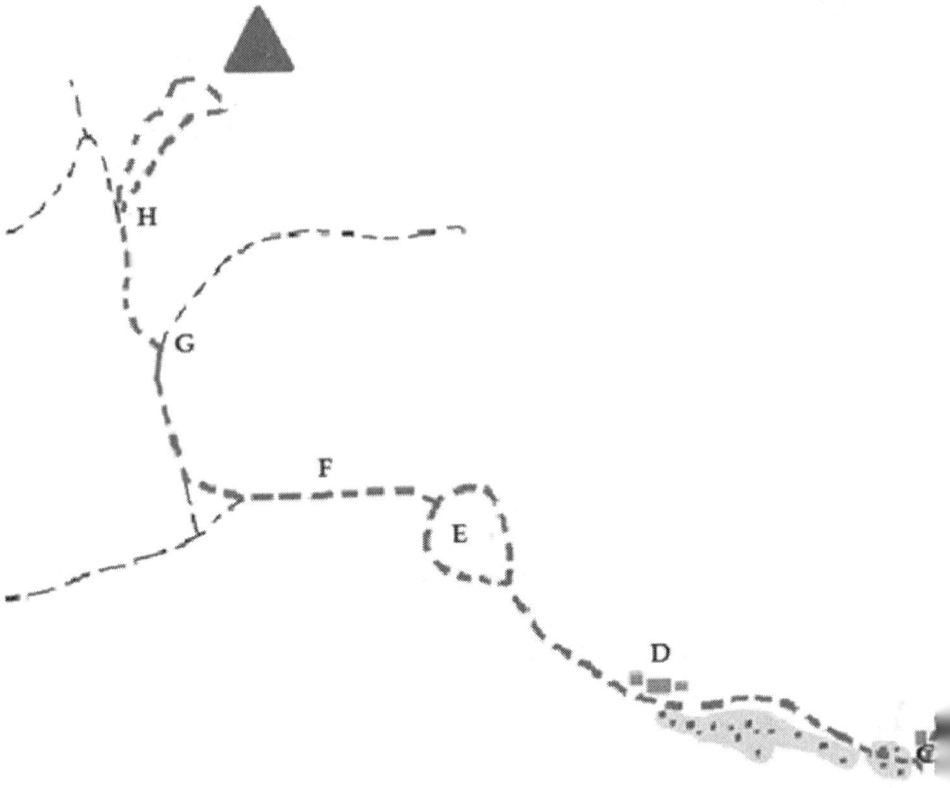

This is the highest peak in the Peak District, Derbyshire's top and the sixth highest county top of all (pipped to fifth place by that surprise package Herefordshire). It is a long enough walk and the definable walk proper begins right next to the pub.

Navigationally it is reasonably straightforward, although there is a twist in the plot right at the end – a very swirling, misty twist too on the day that we climbed it.

We were lucky enough and (for a change) early enough to nab the last parking bay outside of the Old Nags Head Inn, towards the northern end of the straggly, but picturesque, village of Edale. Failing this, you are probably looking at parking at or near Edale railway station, half a mile's walk to the south.

Having alighted at, or walked to, the Nags, depending on your luck, it couldn't be simpler. The beginning of the Pennine way is just a few feet away. Opposite the car park, if you can avert your attention from the allure of Coopers Café; there, between two stone houses, is a multi-fingered finger post (A), clearly showing you the direction you must take. Fifty metres on and the buildings have finished, you are now at a field edge, amongst and next to lines of trees which will be with you for about 250 metres. As the trees run out (B) you are faced with a choice of paths. Both will lead you ultimately to your goal; to the right is via Grindslow Knoll, to the left is the Pennine Way which takes you via Booth and all the fun of Jacob's Ladder. Take the latter path.

Things are straightforward for the next mile, the Pennine Way carries on generally westward, with the odd thin path shooting off here and there. Stick to the main path.

The next point of note is Upper Booth Farm (C), through which the Pennine Way picks a path between buildings. As you emerge from the farm on a stony path, note the old red telephone box on the left and a finger post on your right, bidding you that way (right, that is) on to what is actually a road. On you go, into a small wooded area, bridging a small stream, then out the other side. Now the road goes on just a little way more (less than quarter of a mile), before a gate brings an end to car-borne (and cloven-hoof-borne) travel.

Now you are climbing, woodland fading away on your left-hand-side, your path rising north-westwards, now on Map 2. Half a mile after Upper Booth Farm is another group of farm buildings (D), half a mile more and the path loops around in a complete circle (E), with a continuation on the far side of it, why not take one side on the way up, the other on the way down? The right hand bit is quicker.

On a third of a mile and you are at Jacob's ladder (F), which might as well be called the Devil's Bastard, an endless and knee-crunching (but still beautiful) set of steps cut in to the rock. Soon after this is a cut across west and then the path kicks up north. 300 metres on is a divergence of paths (G) and what seems like a wider one going off right (east), do not take this, carry on instead with the Pennine Way.

Within 800 metres of this, you have arrived at the trig (H) – time to celebrate! Well, no actually. This is Kinder Low.
And there the confusion starts. This celebrated, ceremonial place is *not* the high point of Derbyshire – no siree. That is about half a mile away to the north-east. By legend this point is a bit on the difficult side to find, across the featureless bog. It's even worse in mist. It was misty. Very misty. The worst we had had on all of our forty peaks. It had begun about half way up and came and looked at us and swirled away again, naughtily waiting for the moment of maximum impact. As we stumbled across the peat in the general direction (my phone having lost all power due to over-zealous photography and, thus denying us the "red blob" on the OS map to tell us where we were) we went around in an arc, at one point going with some people who were "going to Kinder

Scout". What that meant, I don't know, but it didn't mean the peak.

Otherwise known as......... The Devil's Bastard!

So we broke away from them and couldn't see a bloody thing. We were so close. It was freezing, bone-chillingly freezing, it was still April. Easter is supposed to have good weather, isn't it? Seeing a tall stone-shape looming in front of us, Eldest made a run for it and got there first – only it wasn't "there", it was the trig at Kinder bloody Low! We had gone around in a circle, just missing the spot. I should have brought my fleece lining to my cagoule, I was shivering with cold and I wasn't alone.

I called it.

It was the children you see (won't somebody please think of the children?) We had as near as damn it got there, we were on the summit plateau, just yards from the right place. As far as I was concerned, we had done Kinder Scout in not very friendly conditions and anybody who says that we didn't, well.....just don't.

Orientation back down was a whole lot easier, the Pennine Way is clearly marked. The Devil's Bastard was not kind on the knees of one who is just clinging on to his forties. By the time we had descended the ladder, we were in the clear again and the weather was reasonable, sunny even, for a while. but the wet and rain did come again and we were chilled to the marrow.

The next bit to Upper Booth did seem to take an age, as did Upper Booth to Edale on that long, flat walk. We noted a heavily-populated campsite and had huge respect for those who were actually *on their holidays* on such a day as this, camping facilities including a shower block where it must be impossible to ever get completely dry. As for us, we were staying at my Aunt's house in Eckington just an hour away, with all the lovely warmth and comfort which that entailed.

It was with a glad heart that we cut through that final path and found again the Old Nag's Head. It had to be hot chocolate by the fire and before long things were not so bad.

That, then, was the Peak District and we had come within a few metres of absolute triumph, but it was triumph enough. Now all that remained were the beasts (and a couple of tiddlers) of the Savage North.

The final chapter was about to begin – and it began in Merseyside.

The Savage North

We had taken a stroll down the garden path, explored some rooms on the ground floor, then climbed some steps and taken a look upstairs.

Now it was time to climb up on the roof – of England.

Excepting the smaller hills of Merseyside and Tyne & Wear, which are included here for geographical convenience, everything now was big business – the big four, plus Greenhill Lancashire at number seven; 627 – 912 metres....big stuff indeed!

These big boys are absolute brutes, their relative heights (The Cheviot, for example 556 metres higher than the surrounding land) make these a day-long undertaking (although there is a two-in-one) and you really feel like you've been there when the walk is done. Just what hill....*mountain* walking is all about!

Cumbria	**978m**
Northumberland	**815m**
Durham	**788m**
North Yorkshire	**736m**
Lancashire	**628m**
Tyne & Wear	**259 m**
Merseyside	**179m**

Merseyside

Billinge Hill – 179m (586ft)

Pub: Eagle & Child, 38 Main Street, Billinge, Wigan WN5 7HD

(01744) 892453

Parking: At pub, pay at car park or free a little walk away.

Walk: 2 miles

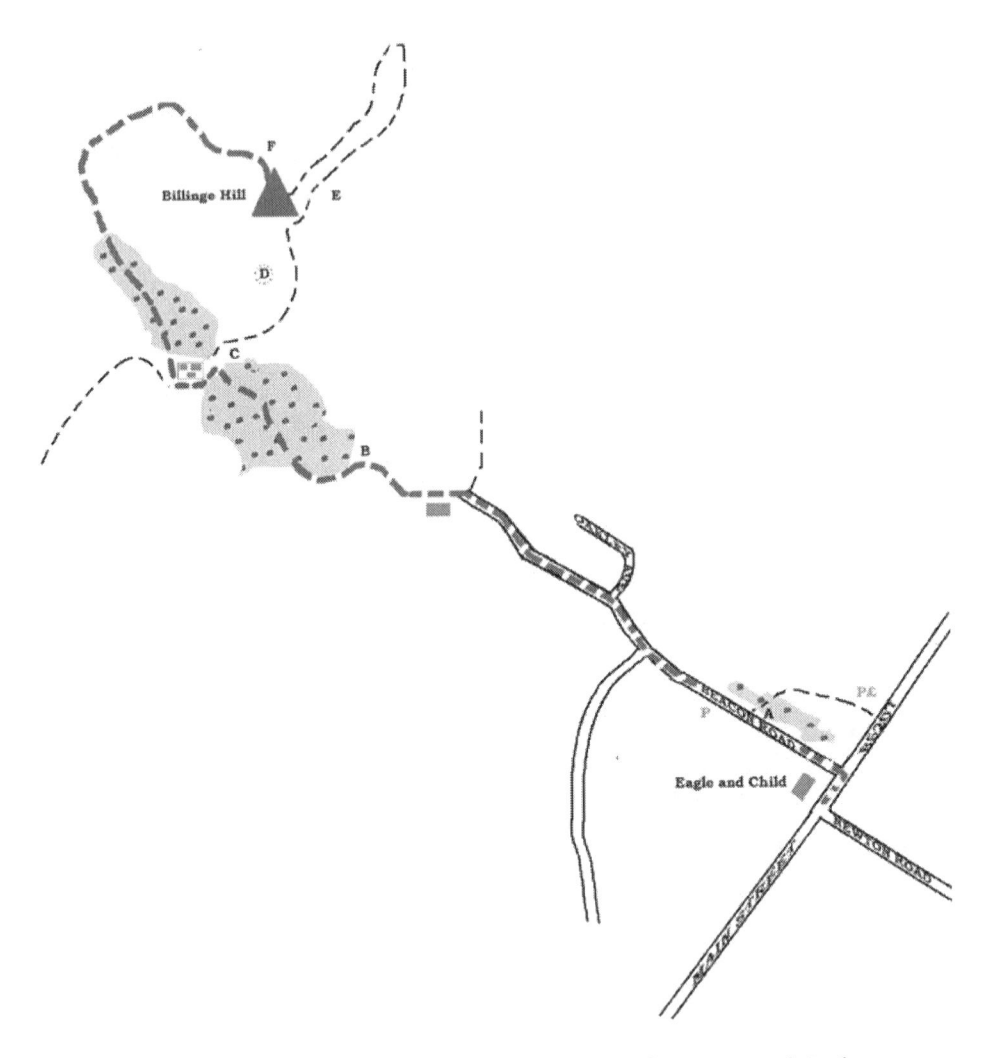

Billinge Hill is a distinct feature in the landscape and is known by locals as "the lump."

After Saddleworth Moor, Kinder Scout and all, and before Whernside and the other northern beasts, this little walk was a bit of light relief. Just a mile to the summit (much of which is road and flat field walking) and hardly any climb at all, barely breaking in to a sweat before the trails and trials ahead.

At 41st in the rankings it is far beneath any of its neighbours (all in the top twelve), still it has to belong somewhere and here it is, the little brother of the north.

This walk itself would actually be a lot more straightforward and a lot briefer if somebody hadn't decided to fence off most of the summit plateau.

Having said that, given that this is a supposedly metropolitan county, the peak itself and the views are of a fairly decent quality. Billinge itself is littered with pubs, several vying for "nearest to the peak" status. Nearby is Squires Bar and just opposite is the Stork Inn. It is, however, the Eagle and Child near the corner of Main Street and Beacon Road that wins by a short head. There is parking to the rear, but you are faced with the usual situation of asking first and the sign clearly states "Car Park for Patrons Only" you can but ask. If the promise of future custom is not sufficient you are left looking for elsewhere, and unlike pubs, parking spaces are at a premium. You could shoot past the Eagle, across the entrance to Beacon Road and about 100 metres along is the entrance to the paying Bankes Park car park, fronted with sandstone slabs reminding you of the now-gone nearby quarry. Failing this, you could just drive around until the double-yellows run out. If you're doing this, why not drive the first 150 metres or so up Beacon Road until spaces appear both left and right?

Either way, you will be going past this point anyway. This predominantly residential street has parkland to the right and will be with you for about 500 metres as you head ever north-westwards and only very slightly upwards. Either follow the main street or, if you've parked at Bankes Park, you can nip through that alongside the tennis courts, ending up eventually on Beacon Road (A).

The houses are predominantly modern, with quite a bungaloid proliferation, although there are some stretches of old sandstone wall here and there. Past Oakley Avenue (right) you go, with a transmitter terminating the vista ahead. Follow the metalled road as it veers right, ignoring the farm-gate and track on the left. Eventually proceed between two garden walls (low brick to the left, red brick and fence to the right) as the track runs in to a wooded area (B).

You carry on in the same direction for the next 150 metres or so (you could break out into the open on the right hand side, however, read on). Either way, keep on going and as you near a small complex of industrial-looking bits and pieces you will soon be at the bottom of the hill proper (C). Already you can sense and see the top of the lump and touching it seems only a formality.

Warning – the following paragraph details the wrong route! This is the way we went – do not go this way!

Given the visual proximity of our target, it would then appear right to take the path off *to* the right for about 100 metres, and then even more tempting to go charging up the hill (as we did), across the open land and past the stone circle (D), defying contours and calves as you do so. However, at the top you are likely to be bitterly disappointed as, with the summit monument almost literally in touching distance (we are talking a matter of a few feet), your progress is checked by a very stubborn, and seemingly interminable, fence which spans the brow of the hill northwest to southeast and then plain north-south for at least half a mile (E). Following this in a northerly, then easterly, direction as we did, we were eventually lucky enough to find that the spirit of freedom has broken out and somebody had broken *in.* That got us there, but clearly this was not the ideal route.

Billinge Hill - a lump on a lump!

For the *correct* route revert to point (C) and take a more westerly path. This time you go all the way to that little industrial apparatus and half circumnavigate it, keeping it on your right. Just a few yards past it is a path off to the right (not to be confused with the one which is right up against it), which then disappears in to the woods. Take this path and be sure to stay low and left (do not stray right, you could find yourself on the path of doom and the wrong side of that blessed fence – keep the fence to your right!) About 150 metres from the industrial stuff you break out in to the open and with the square tower just 100 metres away on your right you make the final (and to be honest, only) ascent of the walk. It's quite steep and it might pay to push on a bit before veering right.

The main landmark is of course the sandstone tower (F), a lump upon a lump, just to the north of the trig. On the day we were there, the views were clear, of the fields in one direction, St. Helens and Merseyside in the other. Our only company was a radio ham with his antenna, making contact with distant strangers.

Billinge Hill, a funny little hill, a lump with a lump upon it and a fence making it more difficult than it needs to be. Still, another one off the list.

Next – the twin peaks of North Yorkshire and Lancashire. Now it's getting serious!

North Yorkshire and Lancashire

North Yorkshire: Whernside 736m (2,414ft)

Lancashire: Green Hill 628m (2,059ft)

Pub: The Old Hill Inn, Chapel-le-Dale, Carnforth LA6 3AR.

(015242) 41256

Parking: Nearby Free

Walk: 10 miles

Map 1

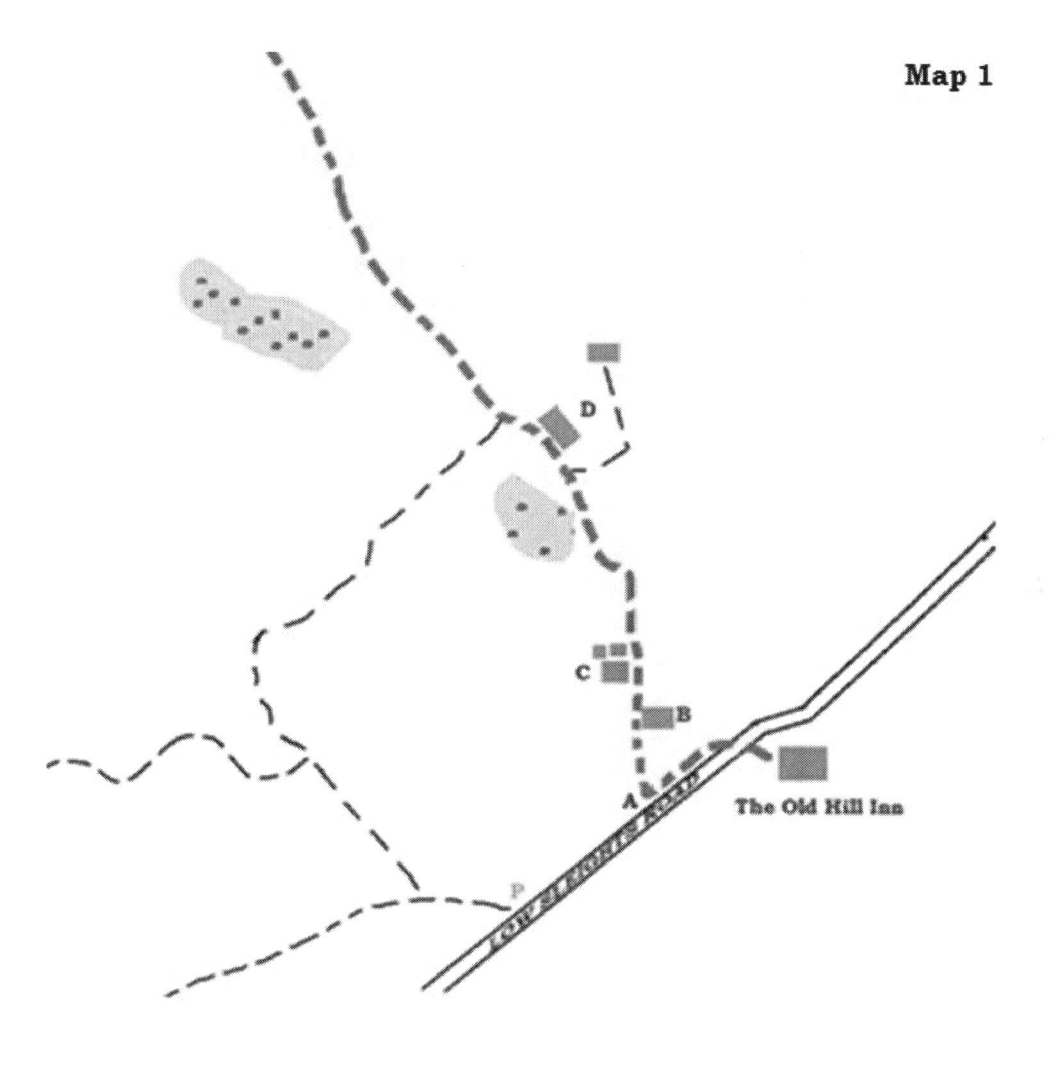

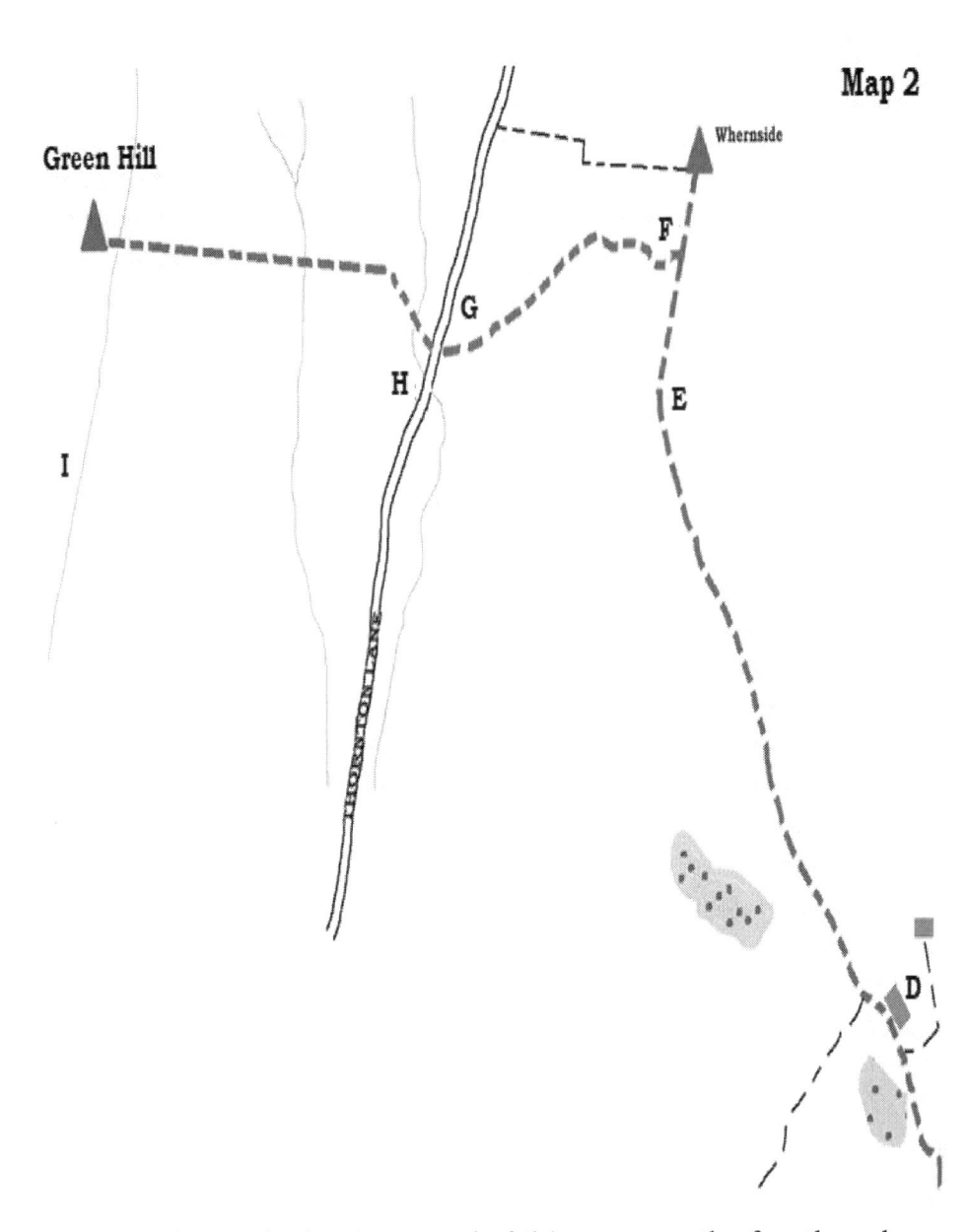

Map 2

Green Hill

Whernside

We are getting to the business end of things now – the fourth and seventh highest county tops, all in one. After this is Currock Hill and then the big three.

The climb up Whernside itself is hard, no doubt about it, and in places is as vertical as you can get without actually needing to use your hands. That said, it is largely on well-trodden, and in places well-made, paths and the climb is not terribly distant from the start point. The summit ridge, if not the peak itself, is also in full view from the get-go, which is very handy for orientation.

As for Green Hill, this is less of a climb, but the trouble is that both peaks are separated by the deep Kingsdale Valley, which means that there is a lot of up and down – worth it though, to slay two beasts in one.

Whernside is North Yorkshire's biggest, in fact the biggest in all the Yorkshires, despite the fact that a different (smaller) mountain bears the name "Great Whernside." There are two alternative pubs to start from – the Station Hotel at Ribblehead, Ingleton or the Old Hill Inn a mile and a half to the west in Chapel-le-Dale. The former is a winding and gentler, if longer, walk, but – sticking to the rules – the latter is nearer by dint of the route taken (if not by how the crow flies, which is roughly a draw) so that gets the nod.

The pub is made of local stone and has a sign which boasts its age – 1615 (unless that's the opening time); it also has *another* sign which quite clearly states that parking is only for pub users and <u>only while they are on the premises</u> adding: "If you leave your car here, a £10.00 parking fee plus a £50.00 clamp removal cost will be made." Right-ho. There is a certain amount of roadside parking still available and, even on what was a busy day, we managed to find a place.

With the inn on your left walk along the road for 100 metres and just across the road is a drystone wall with a sign for Philpin Farm campsite (this sign may not be in place in winter). This wall has a farm gate and next to it a cattle grid (A) which take you down a metalled path called Philpin Lane and past the grey rendered Philpin Farm-house (B). 150 metres on from this, is another farm gate/cattle grid set up and a group of farm buildings, amongst which is a snack bar built in to the wall and selling drinks, sandwiches and all day breakfasts (C).

The road then dips very slightly and a copse heaves in to view on your left. Now the land lifts up very slightly and three quarters of a mile after the last sign of life you pass another final stone farm building on the right (D) and it's on to map 2. Here we part company with Philpin Lane as it makes its way through the gate and we leave behind the building on our right as a finger-post offers us a tantalising promise "Whernside 1 ¾ miles" – together with a "three peaks" plaque and another saying "Pennine Journey" – this is the right way!

1 ¾ miles is not as easy as it sounds, as the path kicks up and up and up, concrete giving way to grass and loose stone. On this day we happened upon those taking the three peaks challenge for worthy causes (Macmillan and the like) and many were *running* down the mount as we huffed and puffed our way up it. For them, Ingleborough and Pen-y-Ghent lay ahead, for us the single summit and a cold drink at the Old Hill Inn.

It's worth pausing once in a while though and looking over right, at the amazing Ribblehead Viaduct, a mile or so to the east. This feat of engineering crosses the very Yorkshire-sounding Batty Moss and the same river which flows in to Preston and then the Irish Sea at Lytham. Reaching 100 feet in height and spanning 400 metres, the building of this bridge required 1,000 workers and led to 100 deaths: some of the victims are buried in Chapel-le-Dale.

One cannot help but marvel at this magnificent structure and ask "should I have walked that way instead?" The answer is "no" and when several people walk past you on their way down saying "oooooh, you've come up the hard way" the answer it still "no" and "sod off".

On this day the path was obvious, it was populated with a generous sprinkling of wayfarers, many walking or running down, others going our way. On a less busy day, whilst the long view ahead may be less packed with dark specks on legs, the step-by-step path is still evident, pitted with the occasional stile or gate. The going is very steep in places and a trial for those whose knees (like mine) have started to ask questions and yearn for those early walks in the soft fields of Essex and the like.

Some way along, a set of granite steps appears, with enough room to pass and if not then a quick skip on to the neighbouring grass, although more than one unfortunate skidded base over apex in so doing.

This is the steepest part of the walk and rivals even the Devil's Bastard for endurance. After another gate the large steps have given way to smaller blocks, still telling us the way, thank the lord. All around are tufts of tousled grass and large shattered rocks on which to sit and take a breather.

A drystone wall over to our left guides us further and here we were surprised to see a Nepalese family with whom we exchanged a "namaste" and joked about the similarities with their homeland. Like mountain goats, their children cashed in on their genetic inheritance and skipped up and down the mountain paths (mind you, ours didn't do too badly).

Looking across the years - from Whernside to Ingelborough

Finally we were at the top of the ridge (E), although a little extra climb did lie ahead. For a short while there was a plateau, on which to gaze over right as we pottered along and regained our breath, and let our hearts sink back to their normal rates. What looked like the final peak was a few hundred metres ahead, still signposted by the drystone wall which some poor souls first assembled so many years before.

Another gate and stile and still not quite there – how many of our ancient hills have never ending tops, rounded by the ages? At this point a path joins us from the left (F) and we gaze along it down into the Kingsdale Valley and then up the great searing range of hills beyond, to Green Hill, where we would be headed soon.

Finally as we pass two men in kit, running down the hill (gits) the largest collection of people yet seen on any of our peaks can be seen sat around the promised land.

The trig point is hidden within a walled area like some sort of turnstile which you have to hoik your butt over in order to get through. For some, whose butts seem only inches from the ground, this seemed a challenge, but I can report no failures. From this point you can see much of neighbouring Cumbria, the Lancashire coast and Morecambe Bay some twenty miles distant.

The deed done and the obligatory photographs taken, it was time for a sandwich and a marvelling at the spectacular scenery that two hours of climbing had earned us.

What glorious views across to the range of mountains which included the Ingleborough that I had climbed as a 15-year-old boy and my 15-year-old son now looked across at, as I had looked across at this place where he now sat, marvelling at all that lay before us both in terms of scenery and what life may offer us as the shadows of low-lying clouds whipped across an ever changing sky, above a never changing landscape, the same today as it was 500 years ago.

Only three county-toppers are greater than this, and they are in the three northernmost counties (historic counties that is, with all respect to Tyne & Wear). After today, these will be the three (plus plucky T&W) which remain, the end of this odyssey can almost be smelled.

Now 180 degrees about turn and to that path on our right, (not the first, which is virtually at the trig, but the second just a few hundred yards away).

The concept was simple – down into the valley, up to the peak, back down in to the valley and back up to where we now were, before the final descent back to the waiting Old Hill Inn. The two peaks are two miles apart, which makes it easier (in principle) than doing a stand-alone from Dent to Greenhill.

The entire Whernside - Green Hill walk (apart from the very beginning and the very end) is in Cumbria – how many more pages of coverage does that county *need*?

The descent, whilst meandering to begin with, takes a roughly western direction towards the valley, before kinking a bit at the bottom as it reaches Long Gill (a tributary stream of Kingsdale). Now it climbs up and reaches a drystone wall which goes along Thornton Lane (G) which links Dent and Deepdale with Westhouse and Ingleton to the south. Here, for reference a gate blocks the narrow road to prevent sheep from wandering, but this can be opened (and then of course closed).

The next trick is to carry on up and west and this will require a bit of gymnastics. Best is to go through said gate, then turn back around and note a slightly lower level of wall on the right – which has no barbed wire on it – then it's up and over.

If you don't fancy that, then stay left of the gate and walk about 100 metres, there is a field gate (H) on the right. After using/vaulting that, try and find your way back to the way you had been walking (including encountering a beck of varying depth).

The peak is now a mile away, although indistinct given that it has Cumbria wrapped around it, parts of which are higher. A branch of Long Gill, then Back Gill are crossed as the path goes north-west, now west. The contours begin to close in, the legs aching on this long trek, but the end is in sight (the end of this part anyway).

There is that Green Hill, not so far away

The peak is indistinct, a small pile of rocks at grid reference SD701820. Nearby (I) is the county stone, marking the historic meeting point of three counties (including the now defunct Westmorland).

With Whernside and co. on your left, stare straight ahead (south-west) along the Green Hill Ridge. There, two miles distant, is Gragareth. This haunting and poetic sounding mount is occasionally referred to as Lancashire's highest. In fact, some measurements actually show it to be a metre higher than Green Hill. It also looks like a proper peak, whilst poor old Green Hill, i.e. this *bit* of Green Hill (the rest of it being in Cumbria) doesn't. Two miles distant, that's *four* miles there and back. Hmm on another day, perhaps. Let's not do our own "three peaks" challenge today. You can if you want to, it's a simple (but long) ridge walk. But not for us, it was a walk too far. The day was done and the main battle won. It isn't higher, it can't be, despite what any subsequent claims might be (best not to check...)

Now the return, the gladness of the down, the energy sap of the up. Now the Whernside summit ridge again and turn right for the final, final, knee aching descent.

Hot choc at the lovely Old Hill Inn, Chapel-le-Dale

But there is a ying to the yang. As is often the way, whilst it may hurt the leg joints more to go down, so also is it easier to fill one's eyes with the landscape when descending as you are coming from the high-point and looking across the sky rather than into a hill, and the sight of those two peaks, plus others is sweet reward as gravity pulls you towards another (reward that is).

And so was drunk a well-deserved pint of the black when we got to the Old Hill Inn in Chapel-le-Dale (whilst others had hot chocolate) together with a hand of old maid (the card game that is).

That, then, was Yorkshire. Another page turned, another bit of the mission done and only the extreme north left. 44 down, four to go. Next, one of the big three – Mickle Fell.

Durham

Mickle Fell 788m (2,585ft)

Pub: The Inn at Brough, Main Street, Kirby Stephen, Cumbria CA17

(017683) 41252

Parking: Nearby, free

Walk: 7 miles* (21 miles from the Inn at Brough)

*or 11 miles if you did what we did)

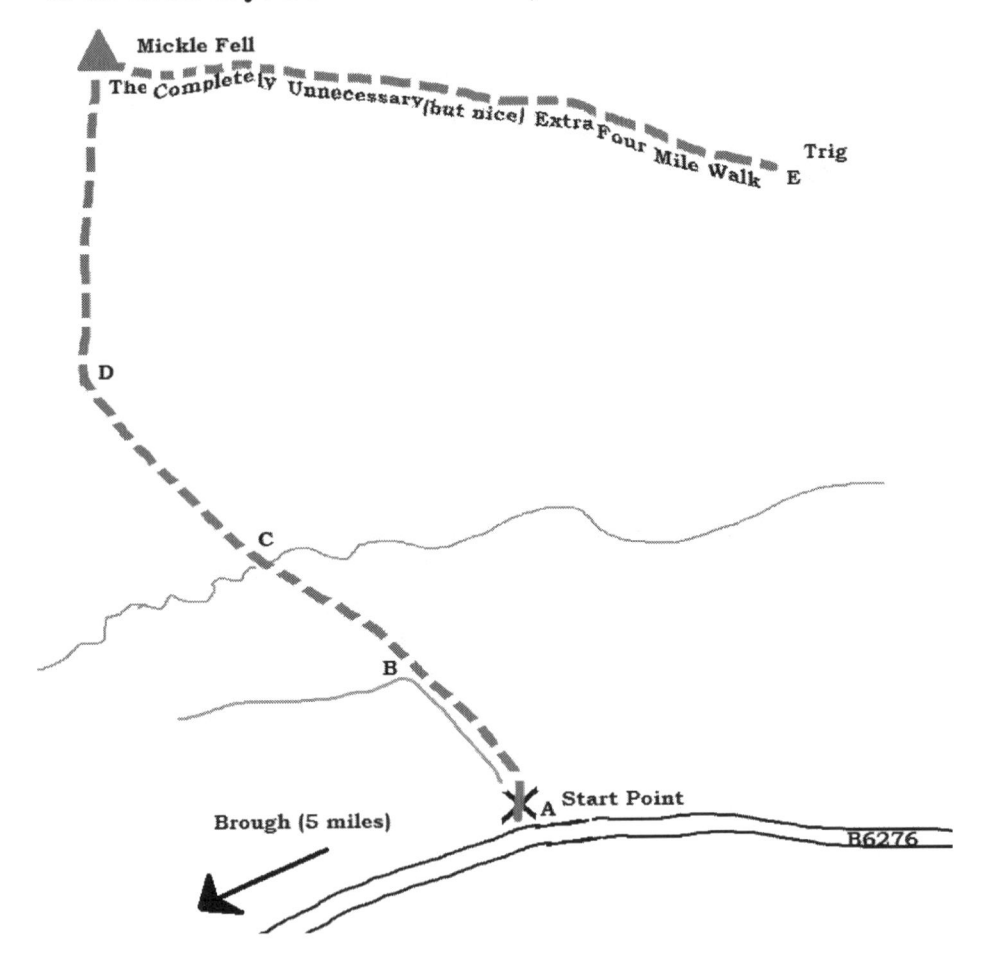

This is one of the beasts of the north, which must be slain ere the quest is done. It is the third highest, came very near the end of our journey and I have to say (for several reasons) was my favourite walk of all.

Some of the challenge is faced even before leaving home – this is the only peak you need a permit to access and that permit comes from the Ministry of Defence! For most days of the year this is part of the Warcop (great name, sounds like a TV thriller) army firing range. It is, however, open to public access for about a dozen days a year (mainly co-inciding with public holidays and associated weekends). What this meant was, because of other commitments during those rare weekends of availability, we had to undertake a specially dedicated 600 + miles round-trip (and take our youngest out of school for the day), just to tick off one peak, but what a majestic beast it is.

It is necessary to apply in advance. To find out which days there is open access, call 0800 783 5181 or go to the www.gov.uk website. There is a form to fill in and send off (and this can also be emailed, at the time of writing the individual was Sarah.Hullock@landmarc.mod.uk)

Permit duly emailed back – and we were good to go. You may think that no-one will check if you have a permit or not, but read on.

We ate at the nearest pub, in the small Cumbrian town of Brough the night before. Brough is pretty in the sunlight, but you must fear for it on days when the weather closes in. The first selected pub was the Golden Fleece on the corner of Main Street and New

Road. We enquired about food: "The chef's nae come in yet, the menu's ovver thee-ah" he pointed to a blackboard with a "list" of two different types of meat pie – and nothing else. Having become vegetarian half way through the odyssey definitely had its draw-backs.

We ventured across Main Street, now becoming High Street and diagonally opposite the Fleece was The Inn at Brough. This had been a candidate, but looked more like a posh restaurant-cum-hotel, which is in fact what it was. They did us proud with food. Tacked on to the Inn (and actually part of it) is the Castle Bar – an unadulterated pub and actually nearer to the peak route than the Fleece. This and a cold pint of Guinness ticked all of the boxes.

We repaired to our youth hostel near Middleton-in-Teesdale ready for the conquest the next day.

Mickle Fell is one of four peaks that we did not walk to from a pub, simply because of the distance involved. If you want to be dogmatic, then march east (right) out of Brough along the B6276, picking up a public footpath on its northern (left) side about a kilometre along and following that until it arches away from the road in a north-easterly direction, then finding again the B6276 near Intake Side Cottage about two kilometres further along and leaving again half a kilometre later and striking north for two kilometres to Woodside, then east for two kilometres to rejoin the same road and follow it first north, then north-east for four of five kilometres, where you arrive at the Cumbria-Durham county boundary and *then* the climb can begin.

OR....

You can cut about ten miles off of the walk (as we did) and avoid a lot of relentless road and moor walking which is rather dull and uninspiring and (apart from the last couple of kilometres) fairly flat. The distances involved are vast and, if you're going to cheat on one, this is probably the place to do it.

So. Park up on a gravelled area on the right, just before the county boundary (which is clearly and proudly marked with a blue sign announcing "County Durham – Land of the Prince Bishops") and then it is time to begin or, if you are very energetic, continue. *If this is full, there is a similar arrangement on the left, about 50 metres or so inside of the land of Prince Bishops.*

Now cross the cattle-grid and enter in to said county and note the array of signage on your left reminding you exactly where you are. Note, also, a dry-stone wall which snakes its way up and up and, unbelievably, this wall and, later, fence, stays with you a great deal of the way (on your left) acting as a handy way-marker should you become lost or the weather close in.

Indeed, navigationally and even without the wall, it is a straightforward job, if physically demanding.

The first task, however, is to breach the southern barrier (A). This is done by skirting around a small stretch of wall and trudging the lower field for ten steps before climbing a wire fence and heading right up that slope where you are imprisoned between dry-stone to the left and post-and-wire to the right.

Passing through the tussocky grass there is a steady climb for about half a mile which is then lost as you dip down towards a beck and say goodbye to the wall (B) as it marches off left (west) and you carry on in the same direction. All along you have been, and remain, *just* inside Durham. After the wall has gone away you could, for some light relief, walk a metre to the left and have one foot in Cumbria and the other in Durham *because you can*. Well, you can't, because a wire fence has replaced the wall. You will have passed through a gate, which will have switched from your right to your left and this will help you on your way.

With a rise and a fall, soon is the Connypot Beck, thankfully with a footbridge (C), which takes you a little bit off of your path which you then have to re-join on the left. There are further becks to ford and leap, with the wire fence always on your left.

Now, as another fence comes in *from* your left, is Hanging Seal (D), a huge massif of rock which is a clear landmark on your way and a good place for our sarnies. From here the walk (and fence) hitch slightly to the right.

The walk takes on a generally reliable theme of fence on the left, general ascent, little becks and boggy peatland. We were fortunate in that there had been *some* rain, but not a great deal. As a general rule, do not stand where the very lush, light-green plant (name unknown) grows, it tends to betoken very soft, wet ground – often tracing a stream.

The last part of the walk is hard, it's almost a vertical climb in places up the bank. I say last part, there is still the technicality of the short walk right (east) to the cairn itself. <u>This is the</u>

summit and I underline this because I had convinced myself that the high point was, in fact the tip of the tongue of land extending away for two miles to our right (south-east). So, we brushed by the cairn and headed along to our false Eldorado (E, fittingly). This was a long walk, if beautiful on a God-given day when the temperature hung around the not-quite-too-hot and our necks were stroked by a just-about-the-right-temperature breeze. Content with our conquest of the "summit" (for there was a trig there) and having luxuriated in the views across Durham, North Yorkshire and Northumberland we made our way back and, half a mile along, met a couple who were also ticking off county top after county top. We exchanged tales of the odd places seen on all of these travels, of the silly little ones in London and Bristol, of the bigger ones. They, also, had two left. "Well, you're not far from the top now, it's just over there" my knowing gaze and sweep of the arm showed them the way and I was happy to help them.

"You do realise that the cairn is the top, don't you? We're just doing this bit of the walk so we can tick off a trig point."

Oh.

We had been within metres of it earlier! So close! Imagine if we had not met them. The way back was going past there anyway (well, it was now) and, half an hour on, we duly stood and photographed ourselves at the *actual* summit.

Mickle Fell - the ridge too far!

And so the long drop down and half way to Hanging Seal my phone rang. "This is the militerry polees, just checkin' that yeez are alreet." Ah, we were past the time I'd said we'd be off the mountain (whatever time that was, I'd done it a few weeks earlier and, obviously, hopelessly underestimated – again). "We'll be another hour" (who was I kidding? We were still not even at Hanging Seal). "Ah well, call uz when yur off the moontain" (he didn't really say "moontain", that's just for effect). "What number?" "The seeyum numba yuz called this mornin' when y'stawted." (I hadn't called in the morning, you're supposed to check in and check oot, I mean out. Oops). "Ok."

The last bit took longer than an hour. It was three miles and boggy and legs were aching. They called again, still we lingered in the forbidden lands. "Sorry."

Eventually, job done and in the car, I tried to call. No signal. Next it was Durham Police who phoned, the matter had escalated. Half conversations were had in patchy network coverage and the message could not be put across that we were fine and off the mountain. There was a very real worry that this would be further escalated and a search party sent out. Eventually though, some miles later and nearer to civilisation, we got the message through. They did call us at home a couple of days later, a security check.

Our apologies to the authorities.

That night we went to sample the delights of Durham. It was miners' welfare night, Jezza Corbyn was in town and had given a rousing speech. It was all kicking off, we were advised to stay in.

Fine by us, we were knackered.

Next – Tyne & Wear

Tyne & Wear

Currock Hill 259 m (850 ft)

**Pub: The Fox & Hounds, Coalburns, Ryton, Tyne and Wear
NE40 4JN**

(0191) 413 2549

Parking: At or next to pub

Walk: 4 miles

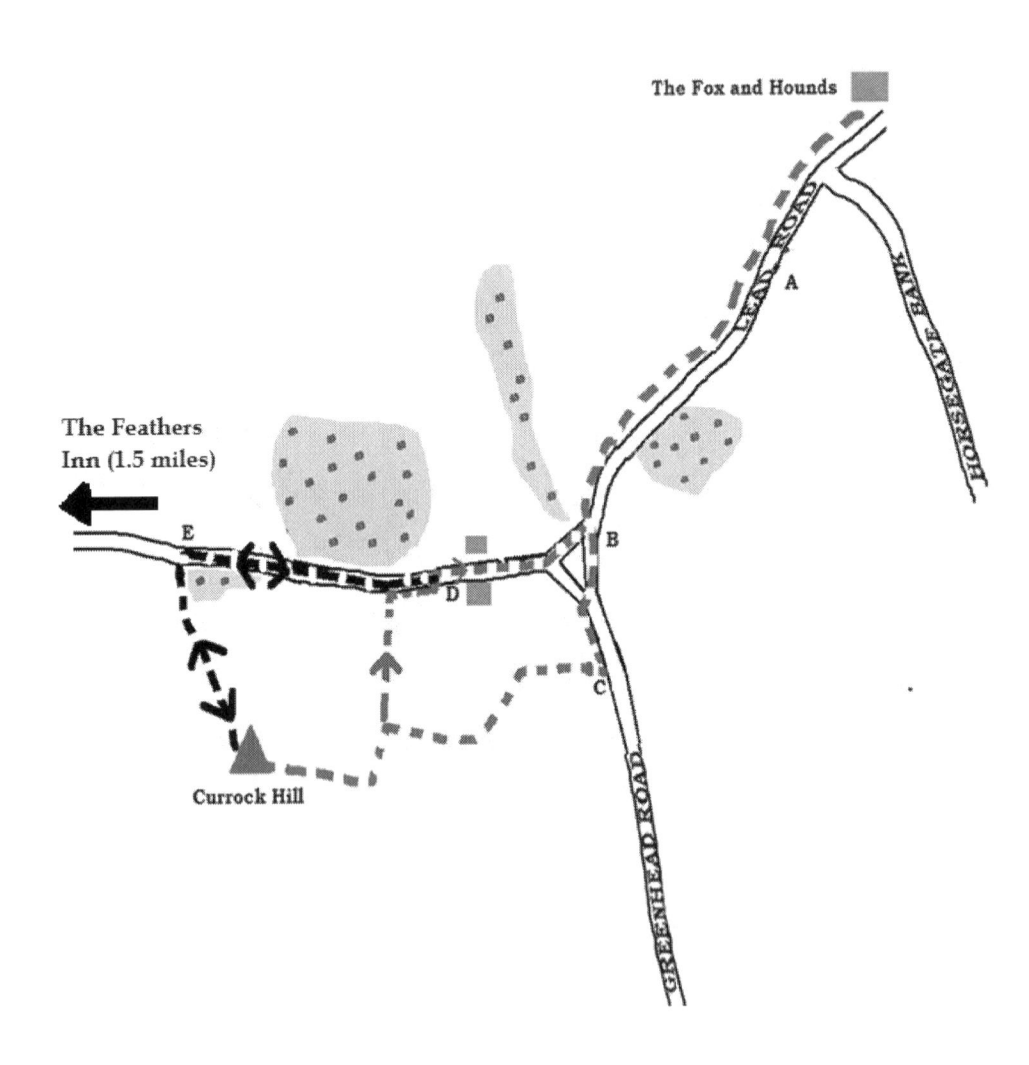

Tyne & Wear, bovine fear. This walk took us closer to nature than we had intended and it was not a friendly encounter. It could all have been so much simpler though on this tiddler amongst giants of a walk if The Bairns had not recently closed down.

As it was, the absence of the former nearest pub to the peak led us to a point two miles further away west in the little village of Coalburn. Just across Kyloe Lane from a little village green, the Fox and Hounds has a reasonable amount of parking which also spills out in front of the neighbouring house. Parking as far away as possible from the pub made it feel like we weren't imposing too much.

So, then, with the pub on your right, proceed along Lead Road (whether relating to a dog or the metal, not sure, probably the latter given the mineral theme to these lands).

Whilst no hardened footway exists, there is a degree of soft verging to separate you from the fast flowing traffic for at least part of the way as the land rises.

The Lead Road is not the most exciting of walks and is followed for about 1.2 miles, past a compound of electricity pylons on the left (A), then sloping downhill slightly before a fork is reached with a triangular grass island housing a signpost for Chopwell (plus directions to "The Feathers" – surely this is not a pub that is nearer? Subsequent measurements showed that, as the crow flies at least, no, phew).   Take the left prong of the fork (B), this is the Greenhead Road which you follow for about 200 metres before (just opposite a farm-gate on the left) turning down a track on the right (C) where you will soon meet another farm gate.

The peak is now about half a mile away and it is a question of snaking your way west-south-west and zig-zagging field edges upwards and leftwards until you reach your goal. We followed the path about 50 metres past the first gate, then arriving at a second, climbed it and turned left along the field edge.

It was as we walked along this field we realised we were being watched. 400 great shining orbs as big as your fist, each eyeing us with no benign intent. Fields of cows normally look at you and show their indifference by failing to move as they chew the grass, not these. Not these Geordie cows "What are yeez lookin' at like?" they seemed to say as they chewed their angry cuds.

They came at us (thank God for the fence and gappy hedge, thank God the gate was shut) not lumberingly, but actually running at us, and then alongside us as they failed to give up their chase. They are normally not to be feared, but, let's face it, they are bloody big and these walls of beef meant business.

We made good our "escape" by turning right (west) into a new field, then left and right into another, all the time going up the hill. It was as we reached the end of this latter tract of land that we encountered the farmer, or rather he us as he raced uphill on his quad.

As you enter this farmland technically you are trespassing. This was the only place in all our walks where we were asked by the landowner what we were doing (and, it has to be said, he was very friendly).

We explained our mission and he replied that we were the second to do this in a short space of time. When asked if it was alright to proceed he told us we were 'alreet.' When we asked about the cows he said they were just inquisitive – yes, inquisitive as to what noise it would make if they crushed me into the muddy ground.

Now the last field, 150 metres and the summit was reached. No crop was growing, so it was alright to walk across the open field, it looked like a fallow year.

The views, as the grass was stroked by a surprisingly warm breeze, were very good indeed. To the east is the North Sea, to the west Cumbria (indeed, the hill is almost on the border with that county), with the Cheviots and Pennines visible on a clear day. Your only company may be the odd glider from the nearby Northumbria Gliding Club.

Ordinarily you should now retrace your steps, down the hill, through the lower fields and back along the boring Lead Road and to a well-deserved pint at the Fox and Hounds. But ah! Someone (presumably the farmer going about his legitimate business) had opened the gate and allowed our bovine foe onto the lower fields that we needed to access. Good for them as they dined on the fresh, sweet meadow grass, good for him as his stock fattened. Bad for us as we faced an enormous detour to avoid Man V Cow II – now it's personal.

As we saw it, the only alternative to walking miles out of our way was to commit a greater act of trespass when, having tracked left down the hill and briefly run the gauntlet of a horse (preferable to the moo cows) we cut through the back yard/garden of a house which, oh sweet bloody irony, was until earlier that year The Bairns public house, with the pub sign still gaily swinging in the breeze.

Luckily the conversion was not complete, so it had an air of "still-looks-like-a-pub-carpark-so-not-really-trespass." Regaining our composure, we asked the man at the neighbouring house (who had an aeroplane in his garden) how far The Feathers was, thinking it close at hand and favouring the idea of a drink there before going to find the car.

Out of the goodness of his heart, he offered us a lift back to the Fox and Hounds and we did, on this occasion, cheat.

The official, proper, non-tresspassing (if more boring) route is the same as the above, up to the grassy island (B); from then you should instead take the *right* fork and continue west for about one kilometre (past The Bairns).

The official (walking) route from here back to the pub takes about 45 minutes, we did it in about five.

This left plenty of time for a cool Guinness in the pub garden with its selection of eccentric wooden furniture.

All in all, an interesting day and a good warm up for the biggie the next day – the second from last peak, Northumberland and The Cheviot.

Northumberland

The Cheviot – 815m (2673ft) Relative Height 556 m (1824ft)

Pub: The Anchor, 2 Cheviot St, Wooler NE71 6LN (01668) 281772

Parking: Near pub (free) or near Langleeford at approx. 951:222 (free)

Walk: 6 miles (or 16 miles from The Anchor)

Map 1

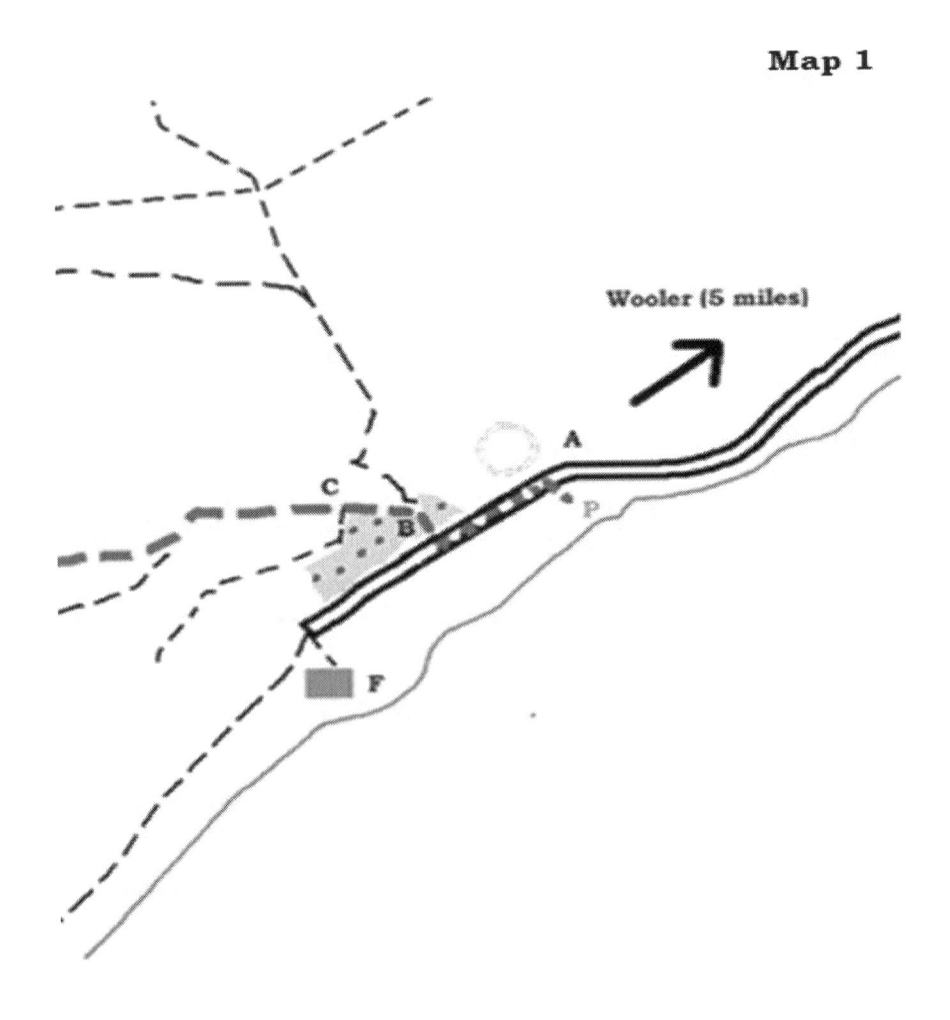

Map 2

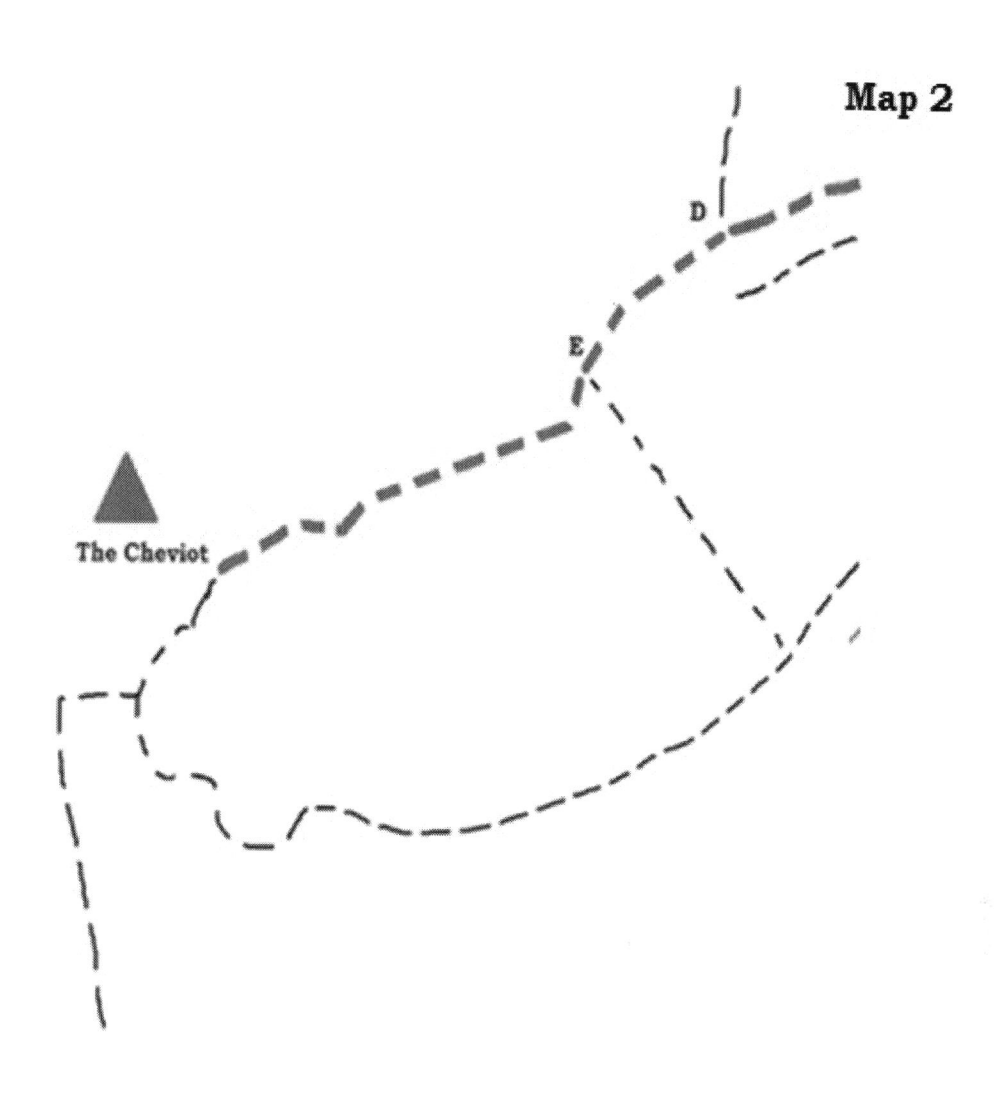

As the end of the mission closes in we are presented with another monster of the Savage North. The Cheviot is second only to Scafell Pike as a county top (historically it would have been third behind the now defunct Westmorland's Helvelyn).

The Cheviot, if caught in the wrong weather, could be troublesome, painful, or worse, but if caught on a clear day is a cinch to navigate as paths, if not well-trodden, then at least established, are followed until a cushy flagstone finish is reached. Beware though, it is still a long, hard walk.

To be true to the pub-to-peak-to-pub ethos you would need to add about ten miles to your journey. Realistically and in common with Mickle Fell, for most people this isn't going to happen. Whilst it's all part of the challenge, it does add somewhat (in fact more than doubles) the distance, albeit that it is reasonably flat as you trace the Harthope valley.

If you are going to add this bit in, then proceed to Route 1 (below), if, like (most) lesser mortals you are content with doing the walk itself and then driving to the pub, then proceed to Route 2.

Route 1: There is ample parking in the charming, if small, market town of Wooler. There is enough in the way of basics to set you up for the trek, including a small Co-op (formerly The Wheatsheaf) from which to buy your water, snacks and bits for sandwiches (or even ready-made if you are of a mind). Parking is here and there in the town, including at the Co-op itself, although they probably wouldn't thank you for an all-day stay.

Wherever you end up parking, clock the pub, it's just opposite the Co-op. Tellingly, it is located on "Cheviot Street." Cross the road towards this lime-cream rendered building and leave it behind on your right and start to climb (a gentle ascent which will be cancelled out by the long, slow descent to the river valley below, before the mission proper begins). Admire the simple buildings of old Wooler, hewn out of the same stone as the rugged locals; the Glendale Hall (previously a Methodist Chapel as the signage still so clearly shows), the tumbledown houses, the United Reformed Church (this is non-conformist hill country, don't forget), then the less inspiring, mundane bungalows in the outlying streets, the Youth Hostel hidden away on the right.

Then, as you crest the hill, Wooler has run out of things to say and it's open country. Follow the road on for about half a mile until a finger post on the left advises you that Middleton Hall is on your right. Take this path and experience a gentle climb and then some undulation as you progress another half mile until a tiny hamlet called Earl comprising very few buildings, but eventually a lawned area that looks like a little village green. This contains a finger post pointing you left a further half mile to

Middleton Hall and yet four miles to Langleeford where the actual climb begins!

Having stepped briefly to the left, follow the wall around as the road straightens out. Moving by pasture land now, do not take the first junction on the left, stay with the same road. A third of a mile after the junction, is a house whose white walls show from some distance. Pass two more white cottages on the right, then the low-walled front garden of "Firwood." Now on a hundred yards or so more is a fingerpost, which rather dispiritingly tells you that Langleeford is still four miles to the right(!) Right you go then, past a small gathering of dwellings and up an, at times, very narrow road. Some time later, pass a disappointing bungalow and an older, but be-dormered, painted stone house and cross a cattle grid. Now you are entering the Northumberland National Park and begin a long, slow drop down towards the Harthope burn, cancelling out any height you have gained, alas. At this point the aspect is more open, huge purple massifs stretching out in front of you. The Cheviot, and its brethren, are over to the right, just out of view for now. Be patient though, you will soon know them well enough.

There is little to report from here, it's about two-and-a-half miles of valley walking with a white railing bridge the only point of note (other than the stark beauty which requires no description). "No Camping" signs vie with cattle fences and the odd farm building to remind you that this is a place that humanity dwells in, if scantly, but the tall walls of land on either side, braided channels of the stream and the rocks it has dumped where it saw fit, are a reminder of who is in charge here.

If it starts to seem like you've gone on forever and have got lost, you have (and haven't). This is the only road and with the stream to your left you are going the right way. Another cattle grid comes and goes, a low fenced bridge and the road winds on. Ignore the fencing and fingerposts over to your left at one point, keep with the proper route. At times the water flows as freely as the sheep wander all over the road. After forever you arrive at a circular stone wall on the right (A) and hereabouts is the place to park up if you have come this far in a car. In fact, you can go no further in your iron steed. Just beyond is a white railed bridge and a little green sign informs you "Limit of Access Land NO PARKING BEYOND THIS POINT." You are now at **Route 2** at roughly 951:222. If you are coming by car set your sat-nav for NE71 6RD (which is the above-mentioned Firwood Country Bed & Breakfast and seems to be the nearest post-code) and then follow the road as described above.

Now, if you're not already done in, it's time for the actual climb to begin!

In dry, or even slightly damp conditions the path you are about to take is usable. If there has been heavy rainfall you might have to rethink. This is the shortest route, but by no means the easiest. If your knees say "no" then now is the time to carry on through to Langleeford and take the Harthope valley route another three and a half miles via Scotsman's Cairn before a shorter climb begins. That, however is about nine miles return. The route below is about six.

Having dumped your motor on any one of several grassy places, at an altitude of about 185 metres, walk towards that circular wall and leave it behind you, taking the valley path just briefly (250 metres) before a woodland appears on your right. Ignore the field gate just before it and take instead the stony path a little further on, with the "Turning Area NO PARKING PLEASE" sign (B). Hereabouts is also a finger sign telling you that this is a permissive path to Scald Hill (the hill next to The Cheviot) whose peak we will reach before the big one. This means that you may pass this way, but there is no expectation that the path will be maintained in the same way as a Public Footpath (as it turned out, we couldn't really tell the difference between one and the other!).

Soon (about 25 metres along) there is a divergence of paths, what looks like the main one goes on. Instead, take the left hand turn which hugs the woods for about 70 metres. Just as this clears the woods, do NOT take the next left hand side path which hugs the northern fringe of the trees, instead carry on in the same direction you were going (C) and now you begin to climb. Over away to your right you may see the rolling contours of the New Burn and beyond that Blackseat at 461 metres in height.

On to Map 2 and if it hadn't struck you already, as you break out into the foothills of this walk you will be blown away by the utter, desolate beauty of the barren heather landscape; bright purples, light greens and yellows turned sombre, brooding dark and black as the clouds mottle and sculpt a different landscape with every minute.

This is the path you will now take for the next mile and a half. As well as a handy fence to the right, it is also defined by the colour and shape of the land where a thousand footsteps have decided that *this* is the way you should go. They can't all be wrong, so follow where they have gone, but tread lightly. This is peat country, a puddle of water could be of indeterminate depth and there's no way of knowing whether your heel, ankle or knee will be the highest up wet place once, and if, you have extricated yourself. Thank God the rain had not been too harsh this week, tales are told of those up to their waists being pulled out by their colleagues. The best advice is to look for grassy upstands and even then to tread carefully. Some bog-hopping is required, and you probably *will* get muddy at some point, just accept it.

Here and there the path may braid, there may be alternatives, but you would do well to stick to the main path in bog country.

You will need to climb a stile on a field boundary, now gently upwards past a stray way-marker which seems to have no relevance to anything.

At an altitude of 500 metres, grid ref: 934:221 is the junction with the footpath "proper" (D) which looks little different, you will note that this has marched in from the north. You have now gained 300 metres in height, with 300 more to go and you may pause to reflect that you have done about half of the outward bound walk.

Now the path nudges on southwest and just 700 metres along and only 50 metres higher, the contours spread out for a while as you reach the top of Scald Hill (E). You are at 549 metres in height and at this point, the top of The Cheviot becomes clear, although that isn't exactly the end of it. Over to the left, though, are the Southern Upland mountains of Scotland, reminding you that this is the northernmost of all of England's county tops (over 500 miles away from its southern-most, Brown Willy, if you're interested).

Embarking on the second leg of the ascent it was interesting to meet at least two sets of people (amongst the very few that we saw) informing us "you've come the hard way" (where have we heard that before?) – not welcome news as legs begin to tire. However, by this time they had already walked about six miles and were still two or three miles from their finish (they having taken a circular route).

The ground here is very soggy, especially due to the relative flatness of the terrain. The latter soon changed, the former not so much. As the weather closed in and the sky threatened to fall onto the land we braced ourselves for a deluge which, thankfully, never came.

Soon odd cairns begin to appear, landmarks with no apparent reason made from rocks tossed in to piles by walkers. By the time you reach 915:208 you've pretty much crested and it's plateau time again at about 808 metres above sea level. There's still half a kilometre to go and, because of the flatness of the land, the bogginess can be quite a trial – but wait!

Those lovely people in the National Park have laid a path more precious than gold – flagstones all the way to the summit! You'll need to cross a last stile at one point, but from here, as is so often the case for climbs preceded by trials and tribulations, the last bit is so simple. A very slight ascent to the climactic height of 815 metres and you're there! Before the last leg, it is worthwhile clocking which direction you have come from, just in case the weather closes in. Relying on the stone path isn't enough as it spins off in more than one direction.

The destination boasts the usual trig point, but this is raised aloft on top of a square brick chimney-like structure six feet high. This has been described by some writers as ugly, for us it was bloody lovely. A tangible reward, a visual depiction of all of the struggles which preceded it.

Photos taken, sandwiches consumed and with the weather still deciding if it was going to dump on us or not it was time to begin the descent – taking care to go back the way we had come. This is the best part of the walk, after just one step you are already more than half way.

As you emerge from the plateau and make towards Scald Hill, you truly feel on top of the world, with the earth floating beneath you. This is the most open aspect you will have, the view here is actually more open than at the round topped Cheviot and these are the best views of the walk.

Over to the right is the impressive Hedgehope Hill at 714 metres; in front of you, roughly in the direction you are going back to, is the North Sea some 17 miles away, a vague blue band on this day, the sky not sharp enough to pick out Berwick, Lindisfarne or the Farne group.

Now the blue disappears into the purple heather and gravity urges you on, having forced you to struggle against it on the way up. It is tempting and easy to build up a head of steam, but remember the bogs – and your knees.

Soon the purple itself yields to green and the harsh undergrowth becomes a little softer, pastureland, meadow, the white walls of Langleeford now visible over right (F).

Through those woods, and at last you are back to base, next to the gurgling stream which you may wish to dip your bottle or feet in to (though the presence of livestock may discourage you from the former).

If you have taken the hero's route, it is now time to walk the Harthope valley with the burn on your right for most of the next five miles. If you are not made of this sternest of stuff then enjoy your comfy seat and easy ride back to Wooler.

The Anchor Inn is a dog and child-friendly, traditional pub offering overnight food and overnight accommodation.

However, before considering the latter you might wish to know that the restless spirit of one William Brown ("Wor Willie") abides there – in the gents' toilets to be specific. He got drunk you see and crashed through a false wall in to the bottle pit beneath.

Enjoy yourself at The Anchor, but be sure that the same fate does not befall you.

Next, the final climb, the majestic Scafell Pike.

Cumbria

Scafell Pike 978m (3,209ft)

Pub: Ritson's Bar, Wasdale Head, Seascale, Cumbria CA20 1EX

(019467) 26229

Parking: Nearby, free

Walk: 7 miles

Map 1

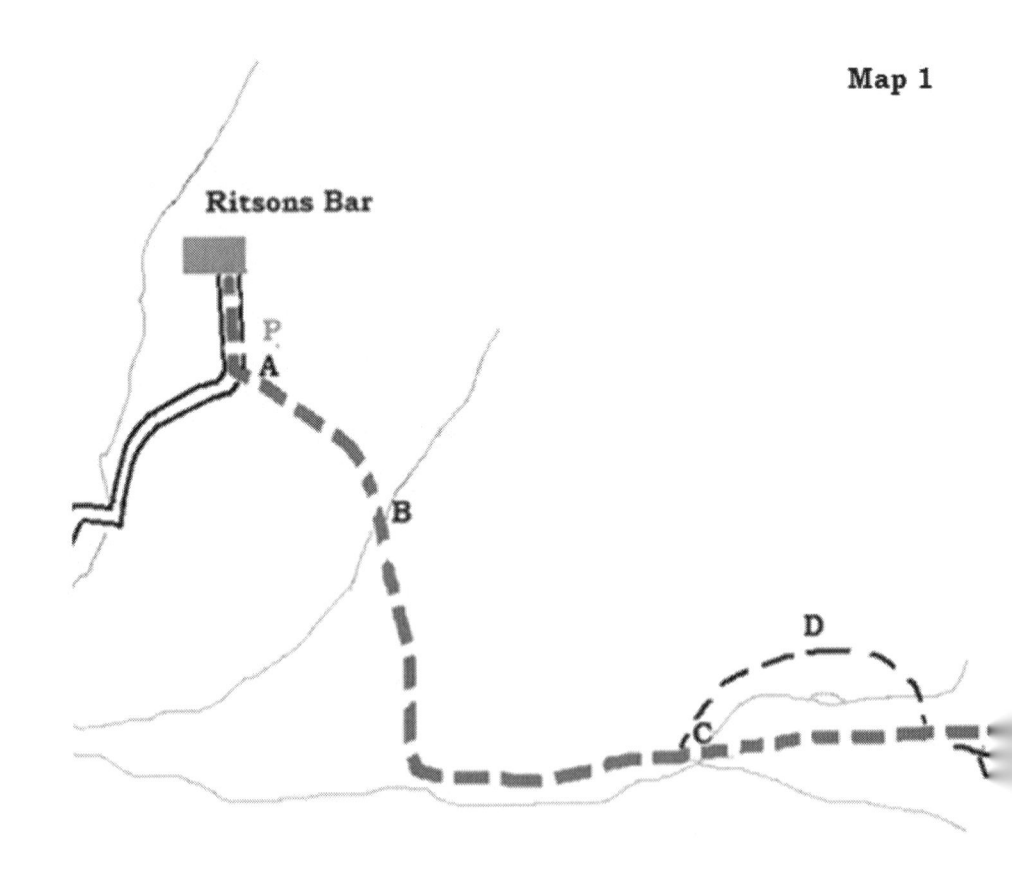

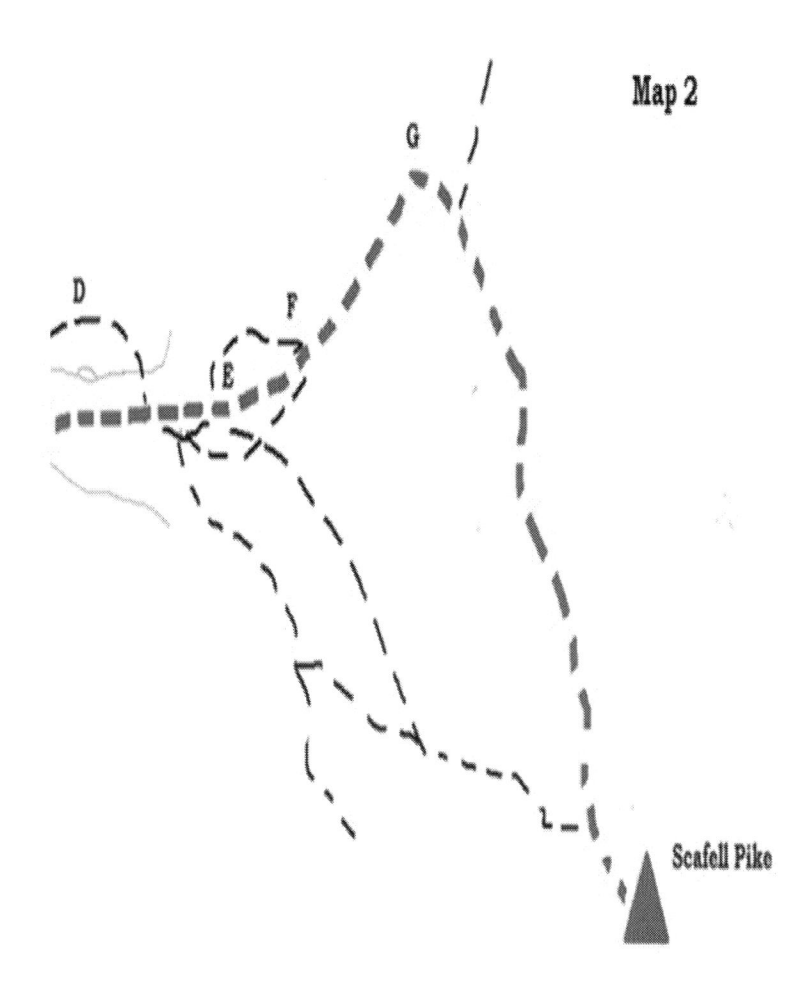

Map 2

Scafell Pike

This was it then, this was the day to end it all, the pinnacle, the very top, the peak to end all peaks. The very roof of England awaited.

We were not lucky with the weather in the week that we chose to top out Albion, rain was forecast all the week. But there was a day, just one day, one hopeful day where it was supposed not to rain. There was, however, a chance of fog.

With much hope, then, we made our way to Wasdale Head. There are, of course, several paths to the peak and this by all accounts is the most straightforward if not necessarily the easiest.

Pleasingly, even at this most rugged of peaks, there is a pub very convenient to the walk, with parking just a couple of hundred yards from it, so bring it on!

As you look towards Ritson's (actually part of the Wasdale Head Inn, a large cream building bearing the word "INN" in huge letters on its flank wall to leave you in no doubt) the car park is just on your right where the wall curls around, leaving a nice, flat field for the hundreds to park up, all free of charge.

Duly parked up and ready to roll, keep the road on your right and where the road bends away *to* the right (A) hang left at a footpath. In summer there may be a toilet portakabin there – handy – use when possible, even if you don't really need to – there aren't any toilets (other than nature's own) on Scafell Pike.

Now follow the path straight on (south-easterly) towards a few trees and over a small bridge over Lingmell Beck (B) which is about 300 metres on from where we left the road and the climb begins.

After the beck, the path arches away to the right a little and should be followed upwards and upwards. You will reach a crossroad of paths at the ridge. Do not take the path hard left, instead carry on with the same path which now sweeps away leftish, and falls with the land. Now it goes hard left and traces the next stream. This one is called Lingmell *Gill* (C) and you will need to cross this – both of its strands. In theory it can be forded, with your path carrying on directly over the other side. I say in theory, but just not today. The heavy rainfall of the preceding days had found its way down the slopes and the little gurgling stream was a raging torrent.

Whilst in principle staying on this side and "not crossing" it might be possible, in practice the chance soon disappears as the path gives way to nothing and a sheer bank is on your left, with the place you need to be about 100 feet away on your right, via a pair of fast-flowing rivers. In addition, you would have a longer, harder walk which would take you near to the top of Lingmell, another fell. All that, just to avoid a river – come on!

Our detour, all-told, was about half a mile and we had gone just about as far as we could before indulging in the inevitable and were able (just) to get across (D). Quite a trial already and only a mile and a half in. It was at this point that the mist began to descend and a mysterious figure appeared beside us. This was Peter the Swede, a man of some tallness; steady, assured quiet like the mountains, (in fact *was* he a mountain? Does not Peter, literally, mean "stone"? Was he figurative? Do we not all yearn for a "Peter" to help us on our way in our hour of need? Was he even *real*? Yes he was real, he shared some sweets with us) and he would stay with us for the rest of our ascent and much of our descent.

Incidentally, the sliver of land between the two strands of the Gill is called Brown Tongue – put that with the rude place names,

Brown Willy and the like. Now on to map 2. About one kilometre from the "official" crossing place – i.e. the ford (and not very far from where we crossed) is a fork of paths. In fact we had not had to double back, so not much extra distance had been required. At this point, there are several smaller paths here and there, but two main ones. Take the left one (E) which is generally in a straight ahead direction. This takes you to Hollow Stones (basically a big pile of stones, well rocks, well boulders really) which are on your left (F).

The climbing really does get steep now, arse-achingly steep as your path veers around to the right near Lingmell Col (G) – Lingmell really has hogged the name-calls on this walk, hasn't it?. This "col" remember from Geography O' Level (or GCSE if you're younger) is a lower area of land between two higher ones – in this case Lingmell (there it is again) a peak in its own right at 2,648 feet and the big daddy himself. The col itself is 2,410 feet, so already higher than Black Mountain and just four feet shy of Whernside.

The landscape is now becoming ever more brutal, lunar, dominated by frost shattered rock. That was as much as we could see. A whisper of wind did occasionally separate the cloud (well, mist, or was it cloud? Is there a difference? Clouds are in the sky aren't they? But weren't *we* in the sky?).

Now, turning right, we were heading mainly south, towards that final peak. Across an area called Dropping Crag. This place seemed familiar, this endless boulder field, it was at about this point that we had got lost last time (20 years ago, before the kids) with the weather closing in, now again the weather closed in, although no rain.

Last time we had turned back, not this bloody time. Onwards.

For the last kilometre or so, there is another gradual climb, easing off a teeny weeny bit just before the end.

And there *is* an end. With the summit paraphernalia in site we wondered who would get there first, touch the trig, be the winner. There had been a longstanding unofficial competition, running the last bit, nabbing the glory.

Eldest had raced to the trig at the halfway peak Bardon Hill when I'd said not to. He half-joked again, not this time though. We had been through all of this together and we would finish it together. Video camera at the ready I commentated the climactic moment "It began four years ago in a Suffolk field and it ends here today" as our hands all touched the final stone at the same time.

Quite a moment. Poor Peter stood there and watched us in silence. He took photographs of us (on our cameras) and we asked if he wanted one taken of him. He declined. Perhaps being the spirit of the mountain he cannot have his photo taken (stop it!).

The trig itself, much like that on other high flung peaks, is made of stone bricks concreted together, topped with that wheel of triumph. Near to this is a walled area, filled with a tonne of hilltop rubble. So, if you want to be the highest person in England, if just for a moment, then stand on this and Blighty will be all beneath you.

The views (it is said) are amazing, dozens of peaks and lakes (sorry, meres) and the sea and beyond the sea – and how!

Southern Scotland across the Solway Firth, Snowdonia, the Isle of Man – even the Mountains of Mourne in Northern bloody Ireland! Woe is me, the thought of being able to see the four nations of the United Kingdom (plus the almost UK Manx) all from the same spot – we could only see a few yards in front of us.

It should have detracted from the moment, but it didn't.

The walk back passed without incident of note. Across Dropping Crag and down to Lingmell Col. Then left and all the way down to Hollow Stones and then that pesky Lingmell Gill.

Mountain Peter had placed a small white rock in a certain place which acted as an aide-memoire as to where to cross the raging stream, Brown Tongue and all (Mountain Peter didn't laugh when I pointed out that was a rude name). Having crossed, as we passed by the official fording point we saw a man with his somewhat older mother who, good for her, had made the peak and was also on her way down. They were seriously looking to do it, but we advised them go back a way and find the safer crossing point that we had. We heard no reports of anyone missing that night, so we presume that all ended well.

The mist continued to toy with us, opening up occasional views of Wast Water and the neighbouring peak of (and not to be confused with today's peak) Sca Fell – two words, same name, different mountain, why? why?

The whole walk had been manageable. I do not recall a single moment of breathlessness or a racing heartbeat – perhaps this lark's good for you. The joints behaved too, nary a twinge until just the last bit of descent where a knee started to ache.

Up and right and away from the Gill and towards the Beck and it was here that we said our goodbyes to our Scandinavian friend who had said that he had been thinking of turning back at the Gill on the way up and that it was only us that had kept him going. How sweet, thank you Mountain Peter. "I must return now to my own world" and with that, he vanished just as he had first appeared all those about four hours earlier.

Oh no, he hadn't disappeared, he just turned left to a different parking area as we turned right. We were overtaken by an accountant (he looked like an accountant) and his family who, having got to the top after us, were determined to get back to the car park first. Which they did. *Well done.*

But it didn't matter, we had done it. Walking boots off, comfy shoes on. Off to the pub. Ritson's is the bar to end all bars, it totally "gets" what it is, the place people go to when they have climbed England's highest mountain.

It's the sort of place where you see sun-blazed, wind-chapped faces, matted with fog wet hair, brightly coloured cagoules slung on the back of chairs, long legs stretched out with metal lace-hooked walking boots. People slunk in their chairs, with the day having taken it out of them, but still so full of the day.

Everyone is talking, everyone is drinking and eating, there is no pizzazz, no noisy music, no tack. There is a feeling of being at one with nature, brothers and sisters in arms (or boots).

Taking a spare table in the covered outside seating area (there were no seats left inside) we spoke of all the climbs we had been on.

Ritson's Bar at the Wasdale Head Inn - the final destination.

The sign says it all - switch off, drop in to your chair, eat and imbibe and remember all of the good things you have done.

Which one was the favourite? We often had this discussion during our little campaign and it is difficult to pick out just one (although I do profess a bias towards Durham's Mickle Fell). It had not felt like 48 (actually, 43) individual experiences anyway, but more like one long ride, one endless day, much like life itself.

As for specific memories, these change from day to day. As I sit here and bring this to an end, I think again of that perfect day on Mickle Fell, of a stolen autumn weekend when we walked forever in Berkshire and Hampshire and it seemed like high summer, of St. Boniface Down just because of its pretty name, I think of the easy triumphs of Dunstable Downs and Worcestershire Beacon and the gritty determination which helped us up Kinder Scout in the freezing fog and of those funny little walks in the West Midlands and Merseyside. On a different day I may think of others.

But most of all, every time I think of it, I think of all those odd places we would never have seen had we not embarked upon this adventure – muddy Northamptonshire, that half destroyed hill in Leicestershire, foggy Shropshire, little Rutland, Shining Tor in stunning Cheshire, the statue of the miner in Notts, places we would not otherwise have seen.

That had been the wonder of it all. There are greater wonders in this world, mountains miles high in eternal snow, coral reefs and enchanting lagoons, but for one small island (and not even the whole island) we don't half have a lot packed in.

Oh England, you are bloody beautiful!

Coming in 2019/20

Walking the Stour – an Essex River

The Ghost Grounds – Discovering what became of England's 100 lost Football stadiums

36325265R00148

Printed in Poland
by Amazon Fulfillment
Poland Sp. z o.o., Wrocław